CHANGING CULTURES

Ambiguous Ethnicity

CHANGING CULTURES

General Editor: Jack Goody

The aim of this series is to show how specific societies and cultures, including sub-groups within more complex societies, have developed and changed in response to conditions in the modern world. Each volume will draw on recent field work to present a comprehensive analysis of a particular group, cast in a dynamic perspective that relates the present both to the past of the group and to the external forces that have impinged upon it. The range of volumes in the series reflects the developing interests and concerns of the social sciences, especially social anthropology and sociology.

Also in this series
The Nayars Today by Christopher J. Fuller
The Skolt Lapps Today by Tim Ingold
The Yoruba Today by J. S. Eades
The Western Isles Today by Judith Ennew
Tázlár: a village in Hungary by C. M. Hann
The Nyamwezi Today by R. G. Abrahams
The Rwala Bedouin Today by William Lancaster

Ambiguous Ethnicity

Interracial Families in London

SUSAN BENSON

Assistant Lecturer in Social Anthropology, University of Cambridge and Fellow of New Hall, Cambridge

CAMBRIDGE UNIVERSITY PRESS

CAMBRIDGE

LONDON   NEW YORK   NEW ROCHELLE

MELBOURNE   SYDNEY

Published by the Press Syndicate of the University of Cambridge
The Pitt Building, Trumpington Street, Cambridge CB2 1RP
32 East 57th Street, New York, NY 10022, USA
296 Beaconsfield Parade, Middle Park, Melbourne 3206, Australia

First published 1981

Printed in Great Britain at the University Press, Cambridge

Library of Congress catalogue card number: 81-6172

British Library Cataloguing in Publication Data

Benson, Susan
Ambiguous ethnicity. – (Changing cultures)
1. Miscegenation
I. Title   II. Series
306.8′09421′65   GN237

ISBN 0 521 23017 9 hard covers
ISBN 0 521 29769 9 paperback

Contents

List of maps and diagrams		*page*	vi
Preface			vii
1	Racial intermarriage in England		1
2	The pattern of interracial unions in England today		14
3	Introducing Brixton and the borough of Lambeth		23
4	The social world of Brixton		39
5	The dynamics of interracial marriage choice		51
6	Coping with opposition: the reactions of family and friends		70
7	The construction of a domestic world		78
8	The construction of a social universe		95
9	Living in a divided community		116
10	Parents and children		134
11	Concluding remarks		145
	Appendix 1 The research project: development and methodology		151
	Appendix 2 The calculation of births by parental ethnic origin		155
	References		158
	Index		169

3.10.83

8.96

Bailey

Maps and diagrams

Maps

1 The London Borough of Lambeth   *page* 26

2 The London Borough of Lambeth; distribution of
households lacking three basic amenities, 1971   27

3 The London Borough of Lambeth: distribution of
population born in the countries of the 'New
Commonwealth', or with both parents born in the
'New Commonwealth', 1971, by enumeration
district   32

4 Distribution of 'immigrant' children in Lambeth
primary schools, September 1970   33

Diagrams

9.1 Household with black-oriented social network:
the Riches   119

9.2 Household with white-oriented social network
(1): the Ojos   120

9.3 Household with white-oriented social network
(2): the Hendersons   121

9.4 Household with Janus network: the Kaliphas   123

9.5 Household with interstitial network: Mr Lowe
and Mrs Simmons   126

9.6 Household with racially composite network: the
Rowlandses   129

Preface

This is a study of a small number of interracial couples and their children, twenty households in all, living in and around Brixton, in south London. It is concerned with four main areas of enquiry: the establishment of the interracial households; the character of these couples' domestic lives and how these were organised; their social world; and the problems faced by their children. On one level, it is an account of the practical difficulties of accommodation and adjustment that must arise when individuals from different cultural backgrounds decide to construct a life together. On a second level, however, it is an exploration of the precise meaning of ethnic identity in contemporary Britain, and of the ways in which this, and other, social identities may be negotiated by the individual.

The fieldwork upon which this study is based was carried out between February 1970 and September 1971, in the course of more extensive research in the Brixton area.[1] It had originally been my intention to carry out a small-scale statistical study of the interracially married in Brixton, concentrating in particular upon Anglo-Caribbean and Anglo-African couples. Difficulties in the field, and an increasing awareness of the inappropriate nature of impersonal survey techniques for work in Brixton and on this subject, led me instead to focus upon an intensive study of a small number of couples. Many of these were recruited through personal introduction; information on the everyday lives and personal histories of each couple was collected through lengthy conversations, formal interviews, and informal participation in household activities. A more detailed discussion of methodology and of the recruitment of the research set may be found in Appendix 1, below.

This is not, then, a study which claims to present a methodologically rigorous account of 'interracial marriage in London'. It is an account of a handful of interracial families, and of the impact of racial divisions upon their lives. It is, inevitably, a study of individuals and of individual attitudes, of individual problems and the way in which individuals regard those problems. Both I, and, I believe, the families whose everyday lives are the subject of this book, would reject any analysis which sought to reduce the complexity of human experience to the cruder categories of social science. Nevertheless, it is possible to detect,

[1] Research for a Ph.D. degree in the Department of Social Anthropology, University of Cambridge (Benson, 1975).

in the ways in which each of these households sought to organise their lives and confront their problems, the close interrelationship between individual choices and wider social forces, and to explore, through an analysis of personal attitudes and strategies, the character of the system of race relations in which these households are located.

Much has changed in Brixton in the years since this study was completed. The casual visitor, walking around central Brixton in 1981, will find many immediate and striking differences between the physical landscape described in this book and Brixton today: here, much new building, there, signs of accelerating decay. Streets, pubs and cafés once important as the centres of social life have vanished and been replaced; sections of what used to be the focus of black Brixton street life, Railton and Mayall Roads, were destroyed in the April riots. The social landscape too has altered over the past decade. In 1971, the black world of Brixton was still dominated by the 'first generation' of migrants, mostly from the Caribbean. Economically disadvantaged and politically inarticulate, their attitudes towards the white world that encompassed and excluded them were inevitably shaped by their divided experience; they were prepared, on the whole, to live in uneasy co-existence with that white world, sustained by the growth of a local West Indian community which had learned to look inwards, to fellow-members, for friendship, solidarity and support. Today, it is the children of those first-generation migrants, many of them Brixton born and bred, who form the core of a very different black Brixton world, facing increasing levels of economic hardship and less willing to compromise in the face of discrimination and racism. In many senses, then, the 'Brixton' that provided the framework for this study no longer exists, and the social landscape I describe is a part of historical, not contemporary, reality.

In another sense, however, nothing very much has changed in the decade since this study was begun. Brixton remains an area of poverty, poor resources and high unemployment. The social forces that found expression in the problems of the early 1970s – the first skinhead craze, a significant increase in the number of racist assaults, the firebombing of black shops and houses, a rise in the level of street crime in the area, complaints of 'harassment' made against the police – have only been accentuated by the serious economic recession of 1979–81. To anyone who had spent any time in Brixton previously, the events of April 1981 were entirely predictable.

My research in Brixton was funded by a Social Science Research Council studentship; further financial support was provided by my parents, who were, as always, both generous and understanding. My debts to them are considerable. I profited greatly, at all stages of fieldwork and of writing up, from the advice and comments of my doctoral supervisor, Professor Meyer Fortes, as well as from the unfailing interest and support of Dr Esther Goody. It is thanks to her, as well as to Professor Jack Goody, that this research has finally reached the point of publication. I am also indebted to Dr Nicky Hart, for her stimulating criticisms of some of my material on marriage and conjugal roles; to Ms Lynn Garrett, for sharing with me her knowledge of sources relating to the history of West Africans in England; to Robert Buckler and Ms Linda Hunt who, at different times, gave considerable help in the compiling and processing of statistical material; and to Robert Kessler, Principal Planning Officer for the London Borough of Lambeth, for making available to me unpublished material from the 1971 census. I owe special thanks to Dr Thomas McCaskie, without whose practical and intellectual support, generously given in often trying circumstances, this manuscript would never have been completed.

My greatest debt, however, is to the people of Brixton themselves; to the staff of the local community organisations, churches, and youth clubs who patiently answered my questions and allowed me to share in their activities, as well as to many private individuals, some of whose views and comments on the area in which they live are reproduced below. Many were generous both with their time and hospitality. In particular, I remember with gratitude the kindness of Betty and Adedotun Adeseye, Marjorie and Charles Buckler, Charles Howe, Birdie Howe, Rosie and Rudolph Ricketts and A. K. Tejumola. Above all, I owe thanks to the twenty families whose everyday lives form the basis for this study, and who must, of course, remain anonymous. They spent many hours in what must, at times, have seemed like a never-ending and intrusive study. This book would not have been possible without their tolerance, patience and generosity, and I dedicate it to them.

1 Racial intermarriage in England

In 1957, an observer could assert with confidence that 'the "racially" mixed family is an essential feature of race relations in Britain' (Collins, 1957, p. 23). Newspapers and magazines ran features on the problems of 'mixed' marriages, while miscegenation occupied a prominent place in popular consciousness, regarded by racists as a serious threat to the future of Britain and by liberals as the key to racial harmony. Today, interracial families and their problems receive much less attention from the news media and no longer figure significantly in publicly expressed anxieties and hopes concerning Britain's multiracial future. Indeed, statistical evidence suggests that, since 1957, the proportion of interracial families within the black population of England and Wales has steadily declined, as more West Indian, Asian and African women have come to Britain to join the predominantly male black population already settled here.

The interest of any study of interracial families does not, then, derive from the demographic significance of interracial unions, nor from their 'typicality'. Indeed, it is precisely the opposite quality that gives the study of such families its importance. Interracial unions are, above all else, the exceptions that prove the rule of ethnic differentiation, the outcome of deviations from a statistical and cultural norm. Interracial marriages are, in popular English parlance, 'mixed' marriages, between 'white' and 'coloured', while the children of such unions are referred to as 'half-castes'. These commonly used terms indicate, quite clearly, the social significance of this boundary in everyday perceptions. But beyond that, a terminology of this nature reflects the ambiguous position of such families in our society, where ethnicity is a significant component of social identity and an important principle of association and dissociation in social life. To study the everyday lives of interracial families, then, is to study the nature of British race relations as it impinges on the lives of individuals. Through a consideration of the ways in which interracial families handle their ambiguous ethnicity, we can learn a great deal about the tensions and constraints of the ethnically divided society in which they, and we, live.

1

The historical context of interracial unions in England, 1555–1945

The pattern and structure of interracial unions in contemporary Britain inevitably reflect the character of the specific system of race relations of which they form a part. But British attitudes and practice respecting interracial sexual relations have also been shaped by a long history of contact between black and white. This began with the first voyages made by English adventurers to the West African coast in the 1550s, the involvement of the English in the trade in slaves to the New World and the development of the plantation societies of the Americas, and the importation of the first black slaves into England in 1555 (Hakluyt, 1589, p. 97). A consideration of this long and troubled history reveals several significant transformations in the nature of interracial sexual relations over time, together with the gradual evolution of a cluster of attitudes towards miscegenation which continues to have considerable impact today.

It is clear from the earliest published accounts that a strong sense of physical and cultural difference informed the reactions of those Englishmen who, from the sixteenth century onwards, voyaged to the West coast of Africa.[1] Nevertheless, as one would expect, sexual relations between white men and local women followed upon the establishment of trading posts along the coast; such relations ranged from simple commercial transactions to durable concubinage.[2] Indeed, by the eighteenth century, relationships of this nature were accepted as being a customary aspect of life on the coast, albeit one which occasioned the disapproval of some visitors from Europe. In the English colonies of the Americas, a more brutal sexual exploitation of female slaves by their white masters developed in the context of slave societies. In the Caribbean, such relationships were openly condoned, while on the North American mainland attitudes were markedly more ambivalent (Jordan, 1968, pp. 136–78). Although legal marriage between black and

---

[1] For general accounts of European ventures on the West African coast, see Blake (1937, 1942); Rodney (1975, pp. 223–325); Fage (1978, pp. 215–88); Curtin *et al.* (1978, pp. 213–48). Excellent analyses of European attitudes towards Africa and Africans in the era of the slave trade may be found in D. B. Davis (1966), and Jordan (1968), while literary images of the negro in sixteenth- and seventeenth-century England are discussed by Jones (1965).

[2] Jobson (1623, pp. 35–41) speaks of a well-established population of mixed Portuguese and African descent, living among the westernmost segment of the Mande peoples in the area of the River Gambia. Other references to concubinage, casual sexual encounters and miscegenation on the coast may be found in Barbot (1732, pp. 34, 36, 238); Atkins (1735, pp. 40, 94); Moore (1738, p. 121); W. Smith (1744, p. 213); and Durand (1806; reprinted in Hargreaves, 1969, pp. 65–73). Children of interracial unions played an important role as mediators between Europeans and local society, and, together with the children of prominent indigenous traders, were sometimes sent to Europe for training and education (see, *inter alia*, Brown, 1929, Vol. 1, p. 130 and Vol. 2, pp. 112–15; Tenkorang, 1964, p. 251; Walvin, 1973, pp. 7, 21; Shyllon, 1977, pp. 46–65).

white was rare in the Americas, it should be pointed out that institutionalised concubinage was common, and led, as on the West African coast, to the emergence of a relatively privileged stratum of 'Mulattos', or people of mixed blood, from whose ranks, in turn, further concubines were recruited.[3] Thus, interracial sexual relations in the racially stratified slave societies of the Americas – and, to a lesser extent, in the trading enclaves of the West African coast – took, for the most part, the form of hypergamous concubinage. This, unlike marriage, implied no equality of status between the partners, and the woman and her offspring were not incorporated into the dominant racial 'caste' (K. Davis, 1941; Van Den Berghe, 1960). Such a pattern was an inevitable reflection of a system of social relations in which colour – socially defined – and socio-economic status were clearly associated.

In England, the context of interracial sexual relations has always been very different. Black slaves and domestic servants were sufficiently evident in the London of the late sixteenth century for Queen Elizabeth I to order their deportation in a period of famine and unemployment (Walvin, 1973, p. 8). But her ordinances did little to halt the long-term growth of a sizeable black population in the metropolis and other large cities. Among these were free Africans, the sons of prominent traders on the West African coast sent to Europe for education or training (see n. 2, p. 2). However, most, it seems, were imported as domestic servants, although from the sixteenth century onwards we have evidence of free blacks working in a variety of occupations. Black pages enjoyed a considerable popularity with fashionable ladies until the middle of the eighteenth century, and some black household servants, like Francis Barber who worked for Samuel Johnson, held respected and secure posts (Reade, 1912). However, contemporary accounts suggest that most were less fortunate: a predominantly male population, they came as slaves or indentured servants with their masters from the West Indies. Many, once brought to England, ran away or were abandoned to fend for themselves (George, 1925, pp. 134–8; Hecht, 1954, pp. 43–4; Walvin, 1973, pp. 56–9; Shyllon, 1977, pp. 75–83); eighteenth-century sources mention black apprentices, beggars and criminals, as well as a black maritime community (George, 1925, pp. 134, 137).

In 1772, during the Somerset case – which resulted in the ending of legally enforceable slavery in England – the black population of the country was estimated to be between 14,000 and 15,000; other estimates made in the latter half of the eighteenth century ranged from 3,000 to 30,000 (Walvin, 1973, p. 46). Most of these black Britons were resident in the capital where, unlike other immigrant groups, they did not form

[3] The scope and nature of sexual relations between white men and black women in the slave societies of the Americas has been the subject of much debate; see, *inter alia*, Frazier (1937); Freyre (1946); Boxer (1963, pp. 13–16, 27–39); O. Patterson (1967, pp. 159–62); Johnston (1970); Martinez-Alier (1974); Gutman (1975, pp. 158–60 and 1976, pp. 388–404); Genovese (1976, pp. 413–31).

a geographically discrete community. Evidence suggests, however, that they did form a close-knit social world, united by their common oppression in slavery and the adversities of their position once free (Dover, 1943, p. 159; Hecht, 1954, pp. 48–9). While there is no evidence for any consistently expressed hostility towards blacks on the part of the ordinary populace of London – indeed, rather the opposite seems to have been the case (Hecht, 1954, p. 46) – the uncertainties of their legal position and their limited range of skills made it difficult for servants out of place to find employment.

From the 1770s onwards, the activities of Granville Sharp and other anti-slavery campaigners, together with the vigorous response of their opponents, directed public attention to the problem of the 'black poor' (Walvin, 1973, p. 48; Shyllon, 1974; D. B. Davis, 1975, pp. 343–468; Anstey, 1975 and 1976; Drescher, 1976). The arrival of numbers of black seamen, disbanded at the end of the American War of Independence, as well as of black Loyalists, made matters worse. A small proportion of this population was lost through re-emigration, to the Caribbean and to the newly formed colony of Sierra Leone (Fyfe, 1962, pp. 13–37; West, 1970; Norton, 1973); most, however, were simply absorbed, socially and biologically, into the mass of London's white poor. In the first decades of the nineteenth century, the number of new black residents declined sharply; in 1814, the plight of destitute Negroes was drawn to the attention of Parliament, but some fifty years later Mayhew, in his surveys of London life and labour, found few black servants and only a very few black mendicants (George, 1925, p. 138; Walvin, 1973, pp. 189–99). Blacks were still to be found, however, as seamen in the dockland districts of London, Cardiff, Liverpool and elsewhere; and it was these districts that formed the nuclei of the 'coloured quarters' of the twentieth century, to which a new wave of black migrants, drawn to England to serve in her army and navy and to supplement her attenuated labour force in two world wars, made their way (Little, 1947, pp. 52–102; Walvin, 1973, pp. 202–15).

The history of black settlement in England, up to the middle of the twentieth century, is therefore the history of a racial minority, predominantly male, who for obvious demographic reasons have always drawn their sexual partners from the host population. In 1578, George Best, in a discussion of the origin of skin pigmentation among 'blacke Mores', had remarked that 'I my selfe have seene an Ethiopian as blacke as a cole broughte into Englande, who taking a fair Englishe woman to wife, begatte a sonne in all respectes as blacke as the father was...' Two centuries later, the white Jamaican writer Edward Long, after accusing the black population of London of idleness and dissolute living, went on to assert that

The lower class of women in England, are remarkably fond of the blacks, for reasons too brutal to mention...By these ladies they generally have a numerous brood. Thus in the course of a few generations more, the English blood will be so contaminated by the mixture and from the chances, the ups and downs of life, this alloy may spread so extensively, as even to reach the middle, and then the higher orders of the people, till the whole nation resembles the *Portuguese* and *Moriscos* in complexion of skin and baseness of mind. (Long, 1772)

Other eighteenth- and early nineteenth-century accounts, by observers less racist than Long – a notable campaigner for the continuance of slavery and the African and West Indian trade – remark upon the willingness of women of the 'lower orders' of English society to enter into unions with black men (Walvin, 1973, pp. 52–5). Perhaps the attraction of the exotic, and the relatively favourable position enjoyed by some black servants at the time, had something to do with this. Many blacks were, however, poor, and it is to be expected that their partners would be drawn from the same depressed stratum of society; it seems that at least some of the white women who made the ill-fated journey to Sierra Leone in 1787 were prostitutes (Fyfe, 1962, p. 17; Norton, 1973).

It is impossible to determine, now, what were the prevailing attitudes towards interracial unions in the eighteenth century. It seems that many of the upper classes viewed such liaisons, the amours of servants and the lower orders, with a certain amount of tolerant condescension. Others, like Long, translated the ideology of black inferiority which had been fashioned in the slave societies of the Americas into the language of a new scientific racism, and opposed miscegenation on eugenic and moral grounds. The evolution of English racial thought is a complex subject that can only be adumbrated here. By the last quarter of the eighteenth century, European awareness of differences in physical appearance and in culture had crystallised into a number of conflicting patterns of thought, which, despite their differences, all drew upon a widely accepted classification of humanity into different varieties, or 'races', to which were attributed not simply differentiated physical characteristics, but also differing mental and moral capabilities (see, for example, Linnaeus, 1758; Burnet, 1773; Long, 1774, Vol. 2; Home, 1788; Blumenbach, 1865; Hunter, 1865; Hume, 1898, cited in Curtin, 1964, Vol. 1, p. 42). Stereotypes concerning Negro amorality, sexuality and lustfulness, together with others which assert the stupidity, brutality, and savagery of the African, may be traced back to the earliest English interpretations of African society and culture. Such stereotypes were to be given new impetus in the course of the nineteenth century by the ideology of an expansive imperialism, by proselytising Christianity, and by the cruder theories of social Darwinism and evolutionism (Count, 1946; Curtin, 1964; Burrow, 1966; Banton, 1967 and 1977; Stocking, 1968; Kiernan, 1969; Bolt, 1971; Haller, 1971; Poliakov, 1974; Street, 1975; Biddiss, 1976 and 1979; Barker, 1978; Lorimer, 1978). And with the development of scientific racism came the notion that not only were those of African descent of inferior racial stock, but also that miscegenation was a physically harmful and socially dangerous process.

It is one of the ironies of history that the nineteenth century, which witnessed the full flowering of that scientific racism which was to play a crucial role in shaping the racist attitudes of today, was an epoch in which the issue of race relations was one of little domestic importance in England (Lorimer, 1978). Miscegenation was a subject of debate in the context of learned societies, or in discussion of the affairs of the colonies or of America, but one cannot infer from such discussions very much concerning popular attitudes in England itself. However, it is, perhaps, significant that the offence taken by the local white population at the development of sexual relationships between black men and white women was cited by contemporary accounts as one of the principal causes of the race riots that occurred in Liverpool, Cardiff, London and elsewhere in the summer of 1919 (Little, 1947, pp. 57–60; Walvin, 1973, pp. 203–10; Henriques, 1974, pp. 140–3). Economic tensions, and especially competition for employment in the unfavourable conditions of 1919, were clearly responsible for much of the hostility directed towards the visible, and therefore vulnerable, black dockland communities. The selection of interracial sexual relationships as a significant issue reflects, however, not simply local social tensions, but also the focusing of concern upon one aspect of race relations in the English context: the dangers and problems of miscegenation.

The situation after 1945

As in the First World War, the years 1939–45 saw the arrival in Britain of large numbers of West Indians and Africans, as soldiers, sailors and industrial workers. Many of these returned home in 1945, but others stayed to swell the population of the well-established 'coloured quarters' in which most of England's black population then lived. Between 1947 and 1957, a number of social scientists, their interest stimulated by the growth in black immigration in the post-war years, published a series of studies of such districts (Little, 1947; Richmond, 1954; Banton, 1955; Collins, 1957) which, for the first time, offer information about interracial relationships at the local level. Here, as in earlier settlements, the black population was predominantly male, and interracial liaisons were the norm. There was much deeply-felt prejudice amongst the local white population against black people, who were perceived as savages, as criminals, and as physically frightening and repulsive. There was also much hostility towards those prepared to enter into an interracial relationship. It is hardly surprising that such women tended to be socially disadvantaged themselves, in some respect or other: prostitutes and ex-prostitutes, girls rejected by their families after bearing an illegitimate child, migrants with poor social resources from other areas of England, the mentally subnormal or unstable. Consensual unions were frequent, as were casual, short-term associations. The hostility of white society, coupled with the depressed social and economic position of the black community on the margins of English society, ensured that interracial couples moved largely in a black social world, as did their children. Women, once associated with black men, found it difficult to find white partners at a later date; they thus tended to be incorporated into the social universe of the 'coloured quarter', and to identify with its interests (Collins, 1951; Richmond, 1954, pp. 18, 77, 83; Banton, 1955, pp. 150–81; Little, 1972, pp. 138–40).

At the same time, it appears that there were local variations. Collins, writing of the stable, well-established community of Africans and Asians in South Shields, suggested that the identification of white spouses with this predominantly Muslim community was strong. The more able of such women acted as mediators between the black population and the wider white society, and were often instrumental in obtaining jobs for their menfolk; as a result, they could earn a respected place in the black community (Collins, 1951 and 1957, p. 24). In a less well-ordered district such as Stepney, however, white consorts played no such role. Indeed, Banton (1955, pp. 150–81) suggests that the attitudes of such women towards their black partners were often ambivalent, and that the opportunism often implicit in such relationships – on both sides – led to a mutual distrust and contempt.

A similar sense of distrust emerges from accounts of life in England given by those colonial students who found themselves in England in the 1950s and the early 1960s. Speaking of relations with English women, one West Indian student recalled that 'It seemed rare to find a close...relationship which was simply a friendship, not a love-affair or a bed-arrangement' (Tajfel & Dawson, 1965, p. 20). A more general complaint was that those women prepared to enter into some kind of relationship with them were generally of a lower social class and educational level than themselves (Carey, 1956; Banton, 1959, pp. 140–4).

The nature of post-war black immigration into Britain radically altered the demographic structure of the black population, and with it the demographic imperatives for interracial unions. The 1961, 1966 and 1971 censuses show a gradual reduction in the proportion of men to women in all categories of the British population born in the 'New Commonwealth' – the Commonwealth countries of Africa, Asia, the Mediterranean and the Caribbean. This was especially significant in the case of the Caribbean-born population, among whom, by 1971, women outnumbered men (see Tables 1.1 and 1.2). This tendency was evident by the late 1950s, but the assimilationist perspective of most researchers writing at that time led them to overlook its implications; instead, they argued that racial intermarriage would play an important role in assimilation and integration. Collins (1957, p. 23) regarded the interracial family as an 'essential feature' of British race relations; Banton (1955,

7

Racial intermarriage in England

Table 1.1. *Ratio, males per 100 females, by date of entry into the United Kingdom and place of birth: Great Britain, 1971*

Place of birth	Date of entry				
	Before 1954	1955– 1961	1962– 1966	After 1967	All years
Africa	174	224	163	127	147
West Indies	167	120	65	65	98
India	122	190	147	82	127
Pakistan and Bangladesh	238	235	424	135	286
British Isles	—	—	—	—	94

From Lomas (1973), p. 79, table 3.5.

Table 1.2. *Ratio, males per 100 females, by place of birth: England and Wales, 1961, 1966, 1971*

Place of birth	1961	1966	1971
Africa*	(195)	(161)	(122)
West Indies	125	105	99
India	157	148	124
Pakistan and Bangladesh	538	354	295

* Figures in brackets refer to West African Commonwealth countries only.

All categories save those in brackets amended to exclude those not of New Commonwealth ethnic origin.

From Lomas (1973), tables 3.6, C.5; Rose *et al.* (1969), table 11.1.

p. 151) suggested that the arrival of large numbers of women from the Caribbean, Africa and Asia would lead to many marriages between themselves and the males of the host population; Sheila Patterson (1963, p. 359), in her study of Brixton, guessed that, over time, the 'adaptation and advancement' she predicted for the West Indian population of the area would 'lead to closer social relationships with the local population, and probably to increased intermarriage and to an at least partial biological absorption of the West Indians in the local population...'

Patterson's optimism was belied by her own evidence: in the Brixton of the late 1950s, she could find 'only about a dozen' interracial families, about half of which involved 'old-timers' resident in England from the inter-war years. Then, as in Stepney, there were numerous relationships between West Indian men and those Patterson termed the 'casuals', some of whom she described as 'low-class, professional prostitutes. Most, however, seem to be young girls, usually from the rural areas of England and Ireland.' White spouses played no prominent role within the black community, and such relationships were not favourably regarded by the local white population, whose reactions ranged from indifference to intense hostility (Patterson, 1963, p. 280).

Evidence from other, more recent, community studies suggests that Brixton was not untypical in this respect. Hill (1965, p. 222) reports that in the year ending in March 1963, the 1000 parish priests questioned in areas of immigrant settlement solemnised only 84 marriages between 'white' and 'coloured'; Rex and Moore (1967, p. 68) recorded only thirteen interracial households among the 232 interviewed in the area they term 'Sparkbrook 1' in Birmingham, and none in the other two Sparkbrook zones; Richmond (1973, p. 74) found 'very few interracial marriages and little cohabitation' in his 1965 survey of the St Paul's area of Bristol.

If the question of racial intermarriage played an important role in the analysis of social scientists concerning the future of Britain's new black population, it played an equally important role in popular consciousness of the nature of this new, and, to many, threatening immigration. Banton's survey (1959, pp. 203–7) of English attitudes in six areas outside London led him to conclude that the proportion disapproving of racial intermarriage 'definitely lies over 45 per cent'. Gallup polls in 1958 and 1961, quoted by Patterson (1963, p. 278), report 71% and 68% as hostile, while Hill (1965) found that 91% of his sample disapproved of racial intermarriage. A 1970 Gallup poll, of teenagers only, recorded that 41% of those interviewed would not consider dating a partner 'of a different colour', while 50% would not consider marriage (*Daily Telegraph* 30 July 1970). A small study of adult English males in a provincial town (Wells, 1970) recorded 68% of respondents as hostile to the idea of their daughter marrying a West Indian, although even higher percentages – 75% and 77% – objected to Indians and Pakistanis respectively. Much of the variation in these results is attributable to differences in survey location, the composition of the sample, and to variation in the phrasing of the question itself. The general conclusion is, however, clear: despite some tendency towards greater tolerance over time, interracial marriage remains the object of considerable disapproval on the part of the white, adult, English population.

Hostility towards miscegenation, however, is more than a simple reflection of changing English perceptions of 'social distance', to be assessed in conjunction with other data on attitudes towards black neighbours, or black workmates. Between the arrival of the first significant numbers of post-war black immigrants in 1948, and the crystallisation of xenophobic anxieties around the twin issues of rates of 'coloured' immigration and the increasing black population of Britain's inner cities, which occurred between 1964 and 1968, miscegenation acted as the focus of much broader anxieties. The question of interracial sexual unions was perceived as an important issue, and one to which newspapers and magazines were prepared to give publicity.

Interracial unions and the press

The marriages of well-known black men and women to white spouses have always been seen as 'news' by the British press, but have usually been reported in a neutral manner. However, in the late 1950s and early 1960s, newspapers, especially the 'popular' press and those with local or parochial readerships, were prepared to give prominence to the opinions of those for whom miscegenation represented a threat to English society and culture. In 1963, for example, the *Morning Advertiser* (6 August 1963) reported the plea for 'chastity' made by Dr Ernest Caxton, Assistant Secretary to the British Medical Association, to remove 'the fears of mixed marriages resulting in children of mixed blood that are becoming an increasing problem'. Wider coverage was given to the pronouncements of Dr J. W. Hall, Medical Officer for the Borough of Barrow-on-Soar, Leicestershire, when, in May 1965, he asserted that racial intermarriage threatened the 'national characteristics' of the British, and to those of the various politicians who, between 1964 and 1968, deployed a fear of miscegenation in their argument for tighter immigration controls.

Newspapers were also prepared to publish gloomy letters from the public on the same theme. Such epistles, often combining popular interpretations of the doctrines of scientific racism with a crude and unreflective chauvinism, make fascinating, if distasteful, reading. One example of the genre is indicative: a letter from a lady in Kingston-upon-Thames, complaining that 'immigrants' – in other words, black people – were responsible for Britain's housing shortage.

...with their extremely high birth-rate it has been estimated that by the end of the century through intermarrying with us they will completely have mongrelised the British race... it is idle to imagine that character will remain unchanged. The irresponsibility of the negro and the fatalism of the Asian will have passed into our make-up and we shall never be the same again.

Do we really want to see our island peopled with either Mullattoes or Eurasians? The Marxists do, as a hybrid race – with its diminished patriotism – is much easier to manipulate than a thoroughbred with its roots in its country's age old traditions... The Devil would like to see us, the race which has done most to Christianise the world, disappear. (*English Churchman*, 10 April 1964)

Journalists themselves recognised that cases combining interracial sex with crime and 'depravity' were 'good copy'; as one told Sheila Patterson during her research in Brixton, 'Sex and colour are always news. When they come together the effect is more than doubled.'

Patterson herself cites several examples of local reporting which could only serve to reinforce stereotypes of the unfortunate consequences of interracial liaisons (Patterson, 1963, p. 284, Appendix VII).

In other contexts, the subject of interracial marriage was treated directly. Straw polls were conducted by newspapers on this 'burning issue'; advice was given in the 'Agony' columns of women's magazines. In general, such unions were presented as a 'problem', as is still the case, although the perception of the 'problem' involved has changed significantly over time.

... many coloured men are fine people, but they do come from a different race, with a very different background and upbringing. Besides, scientists do not yet know if it is wise for two such very different races as white and blacks to intermarry, for sometimes the children of mixed marriages seem to inherit the worst characteristics of each race. (*Glamour*, 20 November 1951, quoted in Banton, 1955, p. 152)

Only if you are so much in love and can't be bothered with the odd cold shoulder can differences in race, background and skin colour be overcome. (*Honey*, January 1969)

This perception of interracial marriage as a 'problem' marriage, which, because of its social implications, is a subject for popular concern, also forms the basis of what might be termed the 'Love Against the Odds' genre of feature, in which a number of interracial couples are interviewed with varying degrees of sensitivity or sensationalism. Many such features evidence considerable ambiguity in their handling of their subject matter. On the one hand, the popular ideology which Goode (1959, pp. 38–47) has termed the 'romantic complex' leads writers to see the interracial couple as two courageous individuals, battling against society for the sake of 'love'. In the 1960s, such a perspective dominated, for example, in 'human interest' features that dealt with the consequences of the South African Immorality Laws, which prohibit interracial sexual relations. The *Sunday People* (10 May 1962), for example, spoke with righteous indignation of people being 'hounded to death' under these 'vile laws'. But the same newspaper, some four months earlier (7 January 1962), had adopted a very different tone when discussing interracial unions in Britain. Under a headline which read, 'Is This Hope or Horror?', the feature began, 'A secret fear will gnaw at the hearts of thousands of British mothers in 1962... they dread the thought of their daughters marrying a coloured man.' Such marriages were, according to the authors, increasing 'rapidly'. Later (1 February 1964), the same newspaper was to pioneeer a fruitful line in sensational journalism for the popular press, the unhappy histories of women married to Pakistanis. Under the headline, 'Five Years of Hell in a Native Hut, Trapped by a Husband Who Betrayed Her', appeared a lurid article which concluded, 'What happened to Mrs. Alam during 19 years of marriage to a Pakistani may serve as a warning to others.'

It is only fair to add that since the 1965 Race Relations Act, and the emergence of liberal and radical pressure groups against racism in the 1960s, newspapers have shown more sensitivity in their treatment of such themes. This cannot, however, be attributed entirely to an increasing awareness of the destructive effects of prejudice. The anxieties of the white community continue to be reflected in the output of the communications media, but these are now focused upon a different cluster of 'folk devils' (S. Cohen, 1972): not upon the sexually predatory black male and his 'mongrel' offspring, but upon the undilutedly black mugger, the illegal immigrant, and the social security scrounger.[4]

The attitudes of black people towards interracial unions have attracted a good deal less attention. Most writers, both journalists and academics, have assumed in the past that they were bound to be favourable, sometimes citing the comments of social scientists on the importance of 'raising the colour' of one's offspring in Caribbean societies (Eggington, 1957, p. 114; Tajfel & Dawson, 1965, p. 12). It is clear, however, that from the 1950s onwards an awareness of the forces at work in shaping the decision to enter into an interracial relationship led many black people to regard such relationships with considerable ambivalence. Indeed, the stigmatisation of 'black men's women' is not the monopoly of whites, as was demonstrated by a heated dialogue which took place in the correspondence columns of the weekly *West Indian World* in the spring of 1974, initiated by a female correspondent who had criticised black men for associating with white women. A second female correspondent chose to blame the white bias of West Indian culture:

There is no point in our exhorting ourselves to think Black when three hundred years have conditioned us into thinking white. Nor should we kick up a fuss because Black men are marrying...white women, in preference to Black. Rather I would advise young Black girls to be honest and admit that they do not want the Black man anyway, because their own ideals of beauty are white...

This produced a lively response from indignant black men and women. One 'disgusted' male correspondent emphasised the inadequacy of white women who chose to associate with black men:

It is positive to think she is ignorant to the fact that the white woman parading the streets locked to a black arm is a reject, in that formerly she had failed to hit it off with white men, then had to settle for what is in her belief second best...

Another, a woman, contrasted the attitudes of black men and women, when she wrote,

I agree that the black men who marry white women have an inferiority complex, but that we should not be. Let us as Black women demand respect from our

---

[4] The shift in white anxieties may, perhaps, be attributed to the considerable publicity given to the statistics respecting birth rates for various 'immigrant' populations, to the activities of various politicians, especially those of Enoch Powell, opposed to black immigration at the end of the 1960s, and to the impact of events in America upon English consciousness (see Hall *et al.*, 1978). The dangers inherent in the 'tainting' of English blood remains a popular theme, however, in the newspapers produced by the parties of the racist Right (see, for example, *Spearhead*, July 1975).

men...Let us as a Black race be proud of our beauty, be proud to produce black children.

In response, came a letter from a man which asserted,

What this woman fails to appreciate, is that...Attitudes which she quotes are antiquated and obsolete...The modern black man has a new and contemporary approach both to his race and women. We are predominantly proud of our black women and that feeling is reciprocated. (*West Indian World*, 22–8 February, 15–21 March, 22–8 March 1974).

That some black women, at least, did not see much evidence for this 'new and contemporary approach' was apparent from correspondence later in the year, when women members of the West Indian Students' Centre called for the banning of white female guests: 'Ban all white girls from the centre, let their so-called Black men take them somewhere else' (*West Indian World*, 21–7 June 1974).

As in the treatment of this theme in the white British press of the 1950s and 1960s, the overall impression to be gained is that interracial sexual relations are perceived in terms of a deviation from a morally and socially desirable norm. Here, however, the emphasis is on the psycho-sexual implications of wanting a white partner, rather than on the undesirable social consequences of such a relationship – a natural reflection of the evolution, in the 1960s, of the ideology of black consciousness and pride.[5]

Interracial unions as a 'social problem'

Contemporary popular ideology tells us that marriage is a matter of individual decision and private significance. In the context of a racially divided society, however, the decision to enter into an interracial union is, inevitably, a political act. As I have indicated above, at various times in the history of black settlement in England, perhaps most notably in the 1950s, racial intermarriage has occupied an important place in popular consciousness. This is no longer the case. Nevertheless, it should not be assumed that the stigma attached to such unions has diminished into insignificance: evidence suggests that, even today, those who take the decision to enter into an interracial union are regarded with suspicion and disapproval by a significant proportion of both the black and the white populations. Interracial marriage itself is regarded as a 'social problem' which brings difficulties, not only for those who enter into it, but also for those around them. Attitudes towards this issue continue to reflect the central obsessions of European – and, more specifically, English – racial thought. It remains, however, to discover how these attitudes affect the pattern and structure of interracial marriage choice in England today.

[5] Such an interpretation of black–white sexual relationships, is, of course, nothing new: see, for example, Fanon (1968); Bastide (1961); Hernton (1969).

2 The pattern of interracial unions in England today

Problems in the statistical evidence

There are no reliable statistics at present available regarding the pattern and incidence of interracial marriage in England today. The General Household Survey, a continuous social survey conducted by the Office of Population Censuses and Surveys from 1971 onwards, gives some indication of the likely proportion of interracial households within the population at large: of the 399 couples interviewed between 1973 and 1975 where at least one partner was 'coloured', one in five involved an interracial union[1] (Office of Population Censuses and Surveys (Immigrant Statistics Unit), 1978, p. 5). Two other sources give some indication of probable trends, for, unlike the General Household Survey, they permit the analysis of data over time; firstly, the vital statistics collected by the Registrar General, which since 1969 have recorded parental birthplace for all live births in England and Wales;[2] and, secondly, the 1971 census which for the first time included questions on parental birthplace.

There are serious problems, however, in using either of these two sources to make inferences about the pattern and incidence of interracial unions. Both sources provide information, not on interracial unions *per se*, but on individuals categorised by the birthplace of their parents. One difficulty, then, in extrapolating from births to unions is that childless unions are excluded from these data; moreover, variation in the cultural norms that influence family size and the spacing of children throughout the female reproductive cycle may well distort the relationship between one category and another at any single point in time.

More importantly, however, there is the question of the degree of correlation between country of birth and ethnic origin. From a survey of names carried out by the Office of Population Censuses and Surveys, it is evident that apparently interracial pairings in fact include a

[1] The General Household Survey was concerned only with couples where the husband was under forty-five years of age. Whether or not an individual was 'coloured' was assessed by the interviewer.
[2] For the years 1969 to 1975 these figures may be found in the Registrar General's *Quarterly Returns* for June or September in each year, and in the Registrar General's annual *Statistical Review*, where they are given as an appendix in the volume concerned with population tables. From 1975 onwards, they have been published as one of the *OPCS Monitor* series.

Problems in the statistical evidence

considerable number of ethnically endogamous unions – where, for example, one parent is English or Irish but born overseas. Using these survey data, it is possible to amend the Registrar General's published figures for births, involving Asian, African or Mediterranean Commonwealth parents – but not, of course, to amend those involving West Indians, whose names are indistinguishable from those of the English.[3] Nor is it possible to amend the published figures in order to exclude cases where the British-born parent is in fact of Asian, African, or West Indian ethnic origin. Until the early 1970s – given the age structure of the British-born black population – this was not an important consideration. Today, however, it must be assumed that in a significant proportion of apparently interracial pairings, especially those involving parents born in the West Indies and in England, both parents will be of 'New Commonwealth' ethnic origin.[4]

In the analysis that follows I have based my argument on data for 1971. No firm conclusions, however, may be drawn from such ambiguous information, and it is my intention to give only a broad indication of the probable structure of interracial pairings in Britain.

The impact of cultural attitudes

From the 1971 census data – which cannot, of course, be amended to reflect probable ethnic origin of parents – it seems that, while the actual numbers of children born to interracial couples rose between 1956 and 1971, the proportion of such children to those born of ethnically endogamous pairings within the Asian, African and Caribbean populations had steadily declined (see Table 2.1). The Registrar General's statistics for the same year point to the same conclusion, as do – more tentatively – those most recently published (See Table 2.2). By the early 1970s, no longer could the interracial household be regarded as 'an essential feature' of English race relations.

The decline in the significance of interracial unions which may be inferred from these data is clearly attributable, in part, to the arrival in this country of increasing numbers of women from the New

---

[3] Personal communication, Office of Population Censuses and Surveys. For the basis upon which amendments to the published figures have been made, see Appendix 2.

[4] It is impossible, given the way in which United Kingdom official statistics are compiled, to avoid the use of terms such as 'New Commonwealth', 'Old Commonwealth' and 'Mediterranean Commonwealth'. It must be emphasised, however, that these are categories derived from census classifications, and have little autonomous social or cultural meaning. Australia, New Zealand and Canada comprise the 'Old Commonwealth', while the Commonwealth countries of Africa, Asia, the Caribbean, the Pacific and the Mediterranean comprise the 'New'. In 1971, at the time of the last census, Pakistan – then comprising East Pakistan and West Pakistan – was a member of the Commonwealth, and individuals born there were thus included in the 'New Commonwealth' category. In 1973, East Pakistan became Bangladesh, and West Pakistan became Pakistan and left the Commonwealth. Throughout this chapter, however, 'New Commonwealth' should be taken to include Pakistan.

Table 2.1. *Children born in the UK to parents from selected areas of the New Commonwealth as at 1971: percentage involving one parent born in the UK*

| Parental birthplace | Children | | | | | |
| | 0–4 years | | 5–9 years | | 10–14 years | |
	Total (000)	% with 1 UK parent	Total (000)	% with 1 UK parent	Total (000)	% with 1 UK parent
India	75.0	27	41.2	47	26.2	69
Pakistan and Bangladesh	23.1	19	6.7	51	3.7	59
Africa	21.6	36	10.7	37	3.9	64
West Indies	123.1	12	90.9	15	37.3	21

Not amended for ethnic origin.

From Lomas (1973), table A.7 (a).

Commonwealth, and to the establishment – or, in many cases, the re-establishment – of conjugal households among the British New Commonwealth-born population (see Tables 1.1 and 1.2). A consideration of the evidence, however, suggests that demographic factors do not provide a sufficient explanation of the pattern of interracial unions in contemporary Britain: indeed, the impact of the generally hostile attitudes towards miscegenation, discussed above, and of differential attitudes towards 'white' and 'coloured' migrants amongst the host population is clearly apparent.

It may be seen from Table 2.3 that 88% of all births in 1971, where one UK-born parent was involved in an ethnically exogamous pairing, involved a partner from another 'white' category – those born in Ireland, in the Mediterranean Commonwealth, the Old Commonwealth countries of Australia, New Zealand and Canada, or outside the Commonwealth altogether. That this distribution was not simply a reflection of the relative sizes of the populations concerned may be seen from Table 2.4. While the Irish-born, for example, comprised 23% of the non-UK-born population in the sexually active age groups between 15 and 55, Anglo-Irish births comprised 40.9% of the total. Anglo-Caribbean births, on the other hand, comprised only 6%, less than one-sixth the Irish share, although the Caribbean-born population was approximately half the size of the Irish population. The discrepancy between population size and share of births was even greater for Africans, Indians and Pakistanis, and especially significant if we accept the suggestion of American research (Adams, 1937; Barron, 1946; Heer,

Table 2.2. *Live births for England and Wales, 1971 and 1978; percentage distribution by probable ethnic origin of parents*

Ethnic origin of at least one parent		Total no. of births	Endogamous births %	One parent of different 'New Commonwealth' origin %	One parent of UK or Irish ethnic origin %	One parent of foreign or 'Old Commonwealth' ethnic origin %	Origin of one parent not stated %
Indian, Pakistani, Bangladeshi	1971	22,463	84	8	5	2	[163]
	1978	27,296	81	14	3	1	[74]
African Commonwealth	1971	5,996	58	29	8	3	2
	1978	10,322	49	37	9	3	2
West Indian*	1971	15,155	63	3	19	2	14
	1978	9,868	43	4	34	2	16

* West Indian categories not amended to reflect probable ethnic origin. The 1971 figure for the percentage of interracial pairings involving West Indians is probably a slight overestimate; the 1978 figure is inflated by an unknown but significant proportion of cases where the UK-born parent is in fact of West Indian ethnic origin. The 1978 figures in general must be treated with some scepticism.

Percentages rounded to nearest whole number; numbers too small to be thus expressed given in brackets.

From Registrar General's *Statistical Review*, 1971 (OPCS, 1973c); *OPCS Monitor*, Births by birthplace of parents 1978 (OPCS, 1980). Amended as in Appendix 2.

Table 2.3. *Live births for England and Wales, 1971: percentage distribution of 'exogamous' births for each ethnic category, by ethnic origin of other parent*

Ethnic category	Other parent								
	UK	Rep. Ireland	Med. Commonwealth	Old Commonwealth	Foreign	India, Pakistan, Bangladesh	Africa	West Indies	Other New Commonwealth
United Kingdom origin		41	3	5	39	2	1	6	2
Ireland	94		1	—	4	1	—	1	1
Mediterranean Commonwealth	77	5		—	13	1	1	1	—
Old Commonwealth	87	2	—		9	1	—	1	—
Foreign	88	3	1	1		2	1	—	2
India, Pakistan and Bangladesh	31	3	1	1	11		43	2	8
Africa	19	2	1	—	7	62		8	1
West Indies	75	6	1	1	8	2	6		2

— Indicates percentage share of less than 0.5%.

Percentages rounded to nearest whole number.

From Registrar General's *Statistical Review*, 1971 (OPCS, 1973c). Amended from data on birthplace to reflect probable ethnic origin for all 'New Commonwealth' categories apart from West Indians.

Table 2.4. *Selected birthplace categories: percentage share of non-UK-born population in sexually active age groups (15–55 years), compared with percentage share of births involving one UK-born parent, England and Wales, 1971*

	Share of non-UK population %	Share of births with 1 UK parent %
Republic of Ireland	23.0	40.9
Old Commonwealth	3.8	5.6
West Indies	11.8	6.0
Africa*	5.2	1.0
India, Pakistan and Bangladesh	15.6	2.3
Other	40.6	44.2
Total	100.0	100.0

* Amended for ethnic origin.

From Registrar General's *Statistical Review*, 1971 (OPCS, 1973c); 1971 Census, Advance Analysis and Summary Tables.

1962; Christensen & Barber, 1967) that rates of intermarriage tend to vary inversely with group size.

Cultural factors are clearly of importance in facilitating or inhibiting exogamous unions. It is only by taking into account the strong commitment of Britain's Pakistani and Bangladeshi populations to their own culture and country of origin that we can explain why, in these two populations where demographic imperatives are at their strongest, the incidence of ethnically exogamous pairings should be so low (Rose *et al.*, 1969, pp. 440–72; Thompson, 1970; Dahya, 1974; Saifullah Khan, 1976; Ballard & Ballard, 1977; Ballard, 1978; Brah, 1978). But, as with demographic factors, these cultural variables cannot be regarded as a sufficient explanation of the existing pattern. In several respects, the Irish and the Caribbean-born populations of the United Kingdom could be described as similar in terms of their social structure and degrees of linguistic and cultural 'differentness' from the English; yet in 1971 64% of births involving a parent born in Ireland were ethnically exogamous, compared to 27% of those involving West Indians. And West Indians did significantly worse in this respect than those from the Mediterranean Commonwealth countries of Gibraltar, Malta and Cyprus, where linguistic boundaries, as well as cultural differences, might have been expected to inhibit interaction with the host population. The criterion of cultural distance, however that might be computed, cannot be

Table 2.5. *Children born in the United Kingdom, with one parent born in the United Kingdom, the other born in selected areas of the New Commonwealth, as at 1971; percentage with UK-born mothers, by age and parental birthplace*

	Children								
	0–4 years			5–9 years			10–14 years		
Parental birthplaces	Total (000)	With UK mother (000)	(%)	Total (000)	With UK mother (000)	(%)	Total (000)	With UK mother (000)	(%)
UK/India	20.5	12.2	59.5	19.2	12.2	63.5	18.0	9.9	55.0
UK/Pakistan or Bangladesh	4.3	3.8	88.4	3.4	3.1	91.2	2.2	2.1	95.5
UK/Africa	7.7	4.1	53.2	4.0	2.4	60.0	2.5	1.8	72.0
UK/West Indies	15.2	12.5	82.2	13.4	11.8	88.1	7.7	6.7	87.0

White Indians, Pakistanis, etc. *not* excluded.

From Lomas (1973), table A.7 (a).

adduced as the sole explanation of the striking difference between 'coloured' and 'white' migrant categories with respect to the incidence of exogamous pairings with the host population.

Male and female rates of intermarriage

The distinction that may be observed between the structuring of exogamous pairings for 'white' and 'coloured' migrant groups is paralleled by another, which is apparent if we consider the relative frequencies of pairings involving men and women from each area of origin. From both the 1971 census data and from those provided by the Registrar General, it may be inferred that the dominant pattern in interracial pairings remains, as in the 1950s, that of black men and white women (see Table 2.5). The General Household Survey also supports this conclusion (Office of Population Censuses and Surveys (Immigrant Statistics Unit), 1978, p. 5). Since in each case these sources are concerned with unions of varying duration, it is unsurprising that the data for the 1970s reflect the demographic imperatives of the past. Indeed, as male dominance has declined amongst migrant populations, so has the incidence of male dominance in ethnically exogamous pairings. Yet, again, there are other factors at work. In all migrant populations, with the exception of those from the Old Commonwealth, there was a tendency for men, rather than women, to make exogamous unions; this tendency, however, was much stronger in the Asian, African and Caribbean-born populations, and cannot be explained entirely in terms of differential sex ratios for each population. Thus, in 1971, there were 94 males to every 100 females within the Irish-born population aged between 15 and 55, as compared to 100 among the Caribbean-born population, and 162 among the African-born population. Yet the percentage of births involving a British-born mother and an 'immigrant' father for these three categories was 53%, 80% and 81% respectively.

This tendency for the males of stigmatised ethnic minorities to be disproportionately involved in unions with the dominant population is not unique to Britain; it has been reported for Arabs and Jews in Israel (E. Cohen, 1969), Berbers and Arabs in Morocco (Rosen, 1973), and, most significantly, for Afro-Americans and whites in the northern and eastern areas of the United States (Wirth & Goldhamer, 1944; Drake & Cayton, 1945, pp. 129–73; Burma, 1952; Golden, 1954; Barnett, 1963; Heer, 1965; Carter, 1968; Monahan, 1970). This pattern, of racial or ethnic hypogamy, is one which stands in sharp distinction to that of racial hypergamy, which obtained in the slave societies of the Americas and which persisted in modified form in the 'colour-class' systems of these areas in the twentieth century (Lowrie, 1939; Gordon, 1949; Carter, 1968).

How may this pattern be understood? 'The fact that males have been traditionally freer to explore new territory and new social relationships than women' (Bagley, 1972, p. 320) is hardly a convincing explanation. More plausible is the argument advanced by Merton (1941) in his discussion of interracial marriage in the United States. Marriage, in the United States, as in Britain, is conventionally a union of social equals; where, as in the case of interracial unions, there are marked inequalities on one axis of social differentiation, that of ethnic status, one may expect to find compensations on another. Thus, the combination that would occur 'most frequently', he suggested, would be 'reciprocal compensatory' pairings between 'upper-class' black men and 'lower-class' white women, in which the latter exchange high ethnic status for high socio-economic status. Comparable pairings between 'upper-class' black women and 'lower-class' white men are less likely, given the primacy of male status ranking in determining socio-economic status for the family as a whole in American society. Other pairings would be found amongst those whom Merton termed 'the pariahs of the society, among those...who have become, as it were, "cultural aliens" denying the legitimacy of much of the social structure in which they occupy disadvantaged positions', as well as among the 'emancipated' or 'rebellious'.

The manifest shortcomings of this type of functionalist analysis of stratification and marriage choice need not detain us here. What is of interest, however, is the implication that interracial unions may be viewed, not simply as deviations from a statistical and cultural norm, but also as a reflection of the system of race relations of which they form a part. Racial hypergamy reflects, very clearly, the inequalities of power and status in a system where colour is coterminous with class; racial or ethnic hypogamy reflects the complexities of a system of race relations in which ethnicity is only one of a series of different axes of social differentiation, and in which status upon one axis may be traded against status on another. This, precisely, is the situation which obtains in Britain; more specifically, it is the situation which obtains in Brixton, the area that forms the geographical focus of this study.

3 Introducing Brixton and the borough of Lambeth

The borough of Lambeth lies adjacent to the south bank of the River Thames. From its riverside frontage between Waterloo and Vauxhall Bridge, it spreads south, through Stockwell and Kennington, as far as the suburban slopes of Norwood and the Crystal Palace. At the heart of the borough, at the intersection of several major routes, lies Brixton, a watershed between the congested districts of urban south London and the great sprawl of the suburbs. Cars, buses and lorries, heading for outer south London or for the City and the West End, pack Brixton Road; overhead, two dirty green metal railway bridges carry trains to and from Victoria and London Bridge. More bridges span Atlantic Road, where a network of railway lines converges on Brixton station. The trajectory of these railway lines is a defining feature of the urban landscape; along them runs a thriving street market, and their arches furnish space for a multitude of small businesses. The goods and services available in these crowded streets reflect the diversity of those who shop here: Brussels sprouts and carrots, yams and pigs' tails, okra and palm oil, olives and feta cheese. There are Indian snack bars, West Indian barbers, and travel agents specialising in flights to the Caribbean, to West Africa, and to Cyprus. And, over all the other noise, of traffic, trains and market hucksters, drifts the sound of reggae, harsh and strident from the competing loudspeakers of the various West Indian record bars: 'Martin's Records', 'Nat Cole – Joy, Health and Beauty', 'Desmond's Hip City'.

Away from the push and bustle of the market, however, another aspect of Brixton asserts itself. There are streets of half-demolished houses, their front gardens littered with rotting chairs, discarded bottles and wind-blown paper; other streets look as though they are about to demolish themselves, with windows broken and boarded, dustbins overflowing, paint and plaster peeling from the walls, all the outward signs of an oppressive poverty. Yet Brixon is not a uniformly depressing place. There are yet other streets with carefully tended houses as well as neglected ones, and new council estates and renovated houses are to be found among the decaying terraces. And in the rest of the borough of Lambeth, while some parts of it are as shabby and as poor as Brixton itself, other districts offer to Brixton residents the chance of a better life – for those able to move.[1]

---

[1] It must be emphasised that all this refers to Brixton as it was in the early 1970s. Since then, the social geography of the area has inevitably changed: the focus of black street

Brixton was not always a name synonymous with poverty and its attendant social problems. Indeed, its history is one common to many depressed inner-city areas – it was first a beneficiary and then a victim of those powerful tendencies towards centrifugal movement which have characterised the development of London since the early nineteenth century. It was the building of new bridges and roads, followed by the expansion of the railway network in the 1860s, that first encouraged wealthy Londoners to move to the green and peaceful districts south of the river Thames. As transport became less costly, other, less prosperous, families followed, and speculative builders erected streets of terraced and semi-detached houses to meet the demands of a growing population. By the 1880s, Brixton, at the intersection of several important routes, had become the focus of a new southward extension of the metropolis, with a lively market, well-stocked shops, and the first electric street lighting in London. Booth's survey of the area (1891, Vol. 2, Appendix, pp. 39–41) found a mixed population of 'comfortably off' skilled workers and members of the petty bourgeoisie in Kennington; well-to-do and even wealthy households in Brixton proper, with pockets of artisans and working-class housing in the Railton Road area; and, to the south, the large detached mansions of the affluent bourgeoisie. The only areas of poverty in what is now the borough of Lambeth lay to the north and north-west, in Clapham and in the old riverside district of Lambeth itself.

Brixton's heyday was, however, short-lived, for the area carried within its very prosperity the seeds of its own decline. Booth noted the beginning of decay in the 1890s: 'Southwark is moving to Walworth, Walworth to North Brixton and Streatham, while the servant-keepers of outer South London go to Croydon and other places' (1903, Vol. 4, p. 166; quoted in S. Patterson, 1963, p. 49). As the city and its less select inhabitants moved southwards, Brixton was abandoned by its original residents. Its large houses were beyond the purses of its new population, and the area deteriorated over time into a depressing district of cheap flats, theatrical boarding houses, and rented rooms. By the 1940s, accommodation in the area was relatively cheap and landlords complaisant; the attractions for migrants newly arrived in London were obvious. The years immediately after the Second World War saw the arrival of significant numbers of Irish, Poles, Cypriots and Maltese; then, from the late 1940s, came a steadily increasing number of West Indians and West Africans. In 1971, at the time of this study, Lambeth had not only one of the largest populations of any London borough, but also the highest population density south of the Thames.

life, for example, has moved away from Brixton market, several blocks down Railton Road towards Herne Hill; massive new housing estates have replaced many streets of crumbling terraces; old cafés and clubs have closed and new ones appeared. The nature of sub-cultural style discussed in Chapter 4 below has been subject to equally important changes.

Table 3.1. *Borough of Lambeth: population by birthplace, 1966 and 1971*

	1966		1971	
Birthplace	Number	(%)	Number	(%)
United Kingdom	266,110	83.0	241,655	78.6
Irish Republic/Ireland, part not stated	12,730	4.0	12,700	4.1
Old Commonwealth	1,300	0.4	1,280	0.4
New Commonwealth, total	27,180	8.5	33,475	11.0
Africa	3,440	1.1	6,075	2.0
Caribbean America	16,620	5.2	18,320	6.0
Asia/Oceania	4,560	1.4	5,740	1.9
Europe	2,560	0.8	3,345	1.1
Other countries/at sea	11,590	3.6	12,335	4.0
Visitors	550	0.2	760	0.2
Not stated	1,320	0.4	5,310	1.7
Total population	320,780		307,515	

From Sample Census, 1966, County Report: Greater London (General Register Office, 1967); 1971 Census, County Report: Greater London (Office of Population Censuses and Surveys, 1973b).

Some 21% of this population were born outside the United Kingdom, 11% in the 'New Commonwealth' countries of Asia, Africa, the Mediterranean and, most importantly, the Caribbean (see Table 3.1).

The period of black settlement in the borough, from 1948 onwards, was also a period of considerable housing stress. The Milner Holland Report (Holland, 1965, pp. 73–8) placed Lambeth seventh in the list of London boroughs where housing had become increasingly subject to multi-occupation between 1951 and 1961; between 1961 and 1966, the percentage of households in shared dwellings reached 38%, an increase of nearly 10% in five years (Greve, Page & Greve, 1971, pp. 12, 14, 22). Between 1966 and 1971, this percentage fell slightly, but for those remaining in the shrinking privately rented sector (just over 40% of the borough's population) there were indications of increasing overcrowding.[2] The property boom of the early 1970s exacerbated these problems. In 1970, one in eight families in the borough was on Lambeth's housing waiting list, while the borough was admitting seven families a week to its temporary accommodation for the homeless. The

[2] Between 1961 and 1971, the percentage of Lambeth households in rented accommodation fell by 7.4%, to 50.1%; but the percentage of the housing stock, defined in terms of rooms, occupied by these households fell even faster, by 10.2% to 40.2%. Overcrowding was especially bad in the furnished sector, where 11.2% of the population occupied 8.5% of the housing stock.

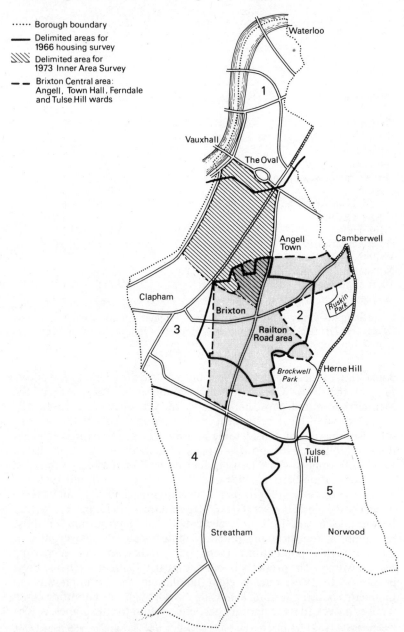

Map 1. The London Borough of Lambeth. (From Research Services Ltd, 1966; London Borough of Lambeth, 1975.)

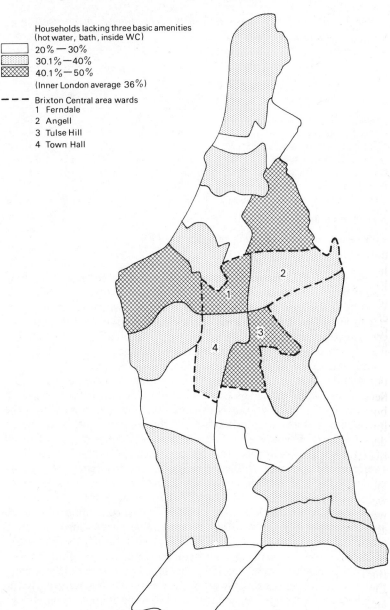

Households lacking three basic amenities
(hot water, bath, inside WC)
20% — 30%
30.1% — 40%
40.1% — 50%
(Inner London average 36%)

━ ━ ━ Brixton Central area wards
1 Ferndale
2 Angell
3 Tulse Hill
4 Town Hall

Map 2. The London Borough of Lambeth: distribution of households lacking three basic amenities, 1971. (From London Borough of Lambeth, 1971, based upon 1971 Census data.)

Table 3.2. *Percentage distribution of household heads in Lambeth, by occupation and area, 1966*

Occupations	% All borough	% Survey areas				
		1	2	3	4	5
Managerial/professional	10	2	6	9	19	8
Other non-manual	22	13	18	22	28	26
Foreman/skilled manual	24	25	23	22	24	34
Semi/unskilled manual	25	39	38	26	12	21
Own account/other	5	5	3	5	4	2
Not employed	14	16	12	16	13	9

For distribution of survey areas, see Map 1.

From Lambeth Housing Occupancy Survey, 1966.

development of Lambeth's central districts into a congested lodging-house zone, the impact of extensive demolition and redevelopment of housing stock, and the beginnings of middle-class colonisation in the northern and western segments of the borough all played their part in creating this unhappy situation, in which Lambeth's black families found themselves especially disadvantaged (Burney, 1967, pp. 110–146; Shankland Cox & the Institute of Community Studies, 1974c).

From the 1971 census data, and from an earlier survey of household occupancy commissioned by Lambeth Borough Council itself (Research Services Ltd, 1966, 1967), it is evident that housing stress within the borough was at its worst in Brixton and the districts which surrounded it (see Map 2). This was also the case for other manifestations of social deprivation. It was in this area, for example, that schools were most overcrowded and understaffed. Levels of unemployment were high; in 1971 over 6% of the 'economically active' population of Ferndale Ward and over 7% in Tulse Hill and Town Hall wards were seeking work (London Borough of Lambeth, 1975). The percentage of manual workers, especially those in less remunerative occupations, was well above the borough average (see Tables 3.2 and 3.3). In Tulse Hill ward, in the overcrowded centre of Lambeth, the percentage of children who received free school meals in 1972 was more than three times greater than in the prosperous south-west of the borough, while referrals to the Lambeth social services department were running at approximately two and a half times the borough average (Shelter, 1972). There was a high level of petty crime. To live in Brixton, then, was to live in an area where opportunities were few and problems pressing; and for this, the people of Brixton tended to blame each other.

Table 3.3. *Economically active household heads, Lambeth, 1971: percentage distribution by socio-economic group, country of birth, and area of residence, 1971*

	Household heads born in				
	Asian Common-wealth/ Pakistan %	African Common-wealth %	American Common-wealth* %	Household heads, all Lambeth %	Household heads, central area %
Professional and managerial	20	9	3	12	7
Own account non-professional	5	1	2	4	4
Other non-manual	47	36	12	27	23
Skilled manual	7	21	34	20	21
Personal service/ semi-skilled	13	16	25	15	18
Unskilled	5	13	20	10	12
Armed services	—	—	—	[15]	[2]
Occupation not properly described	4	3	6	12	14
Total	101	99	102	100	99

* American Commonwealth comprises Commonwealth countries of the Caribbean and of Central and South America.

Socio-economic groups derived from the classification of occupations to be found in Office of Population Censuses and Surveys, 1970.

Percentages rounded to nearest whole number; numbers too small to be thus expressed given in brackets.

For the boundaries of the central area, see Map 1.

From Census 1971, Small Area Statistics (10% sample census, economic activity tables), unpublished; Census 1971, Table DT 1553 (10% sample census, economic activity tables), unpublished.

The people of Brixton

The history of West Indian settlement in Brixton has been described in some detail by Sheila Patterson (1963, pp. 52–9) and need not detain us here. Initially, settlement was concentrated in the Coldharbour Lane area, to the east of Brixton market, where there were a handful of lodging-houses owned by long-established black residents. Enterprising migrants soon began to buy property there themselves. By 1966, over 50% of the families living in the streets between Coldharbour Lane and

Loughborough Park were black (Burney, 1967, p. 141), and there was also significant black settlement across the railway lines around Railton Road, in Angell Town, between Brixton and Stockwell and Brixton and Clapham, in Tulse Hill and along the line of the railway between Brixton and Camberwell. Brixton, in short, had become the geographical focus of an expanding and diversifying black community.

Yet – and this is an important point – Brixton in the early 1970s was not a black ghetto, despite the overwhelmingly Caribbean ambience of the market and the streets which surround it. Of the hundreds of enumeration districts that comprise the borough, only six had a 'New Commonwealth' population of over 50 % in 1971 (see Map 3). Rather, it was a 'residual area' in the true sense of the term, an area whose heterogeneous population reflected the changing nature of inner south London. In 1966, the Lambeth Housing Occupancy Survey (Research Services Ltd, 1966 and 1967) had found that 21% of household heads polled in Brixton had been born in the borough, while 22% of households had been living at their 1966 address prior to 1945. While this proportion was certainly lower than in the districts to the north of Brixton proper, it nevertheless represented a considerable degree of continuity with the Brixton past.[3] Among this long-established local population could be found some elderly English residents who could remember Brixton as a prosperous suburb, including artisans and white-collar workers who had lived in the area before the Second World War, and even a few 'theatrical' residents who had stayed on after the music halls had closed. A significant proportion of the English population could be described as proletarian in occupational terms. Yet Brixton was not, and never had been, a 'working-class community', in the sense of having the strong ties of horizontal solidarity that are said to have characterised the neighbourhoods of nearby Southwark, of Lambeth itself, or of Bethnal Green in the 1950s (Firth, 1956; Young & Willmott, 1957). There were, of course, many families whose idiosyncratic social worlds resembled those described in such literature; but there were also many others, new arrivals often, who had been attracted to Brixton for the same reason as the area's black population: cheap housing, complaisant landlords, and anonymity. Thus, the 'English' of Brixton and the districts which surrounded it were far from being members of one homogeneous community. On the one hand, there were the obvious divisions of taste, orientation and interest that arose from broad differences in what might be described, very crudely, as 'class'. But there were also more subtle distinctions, drawn by the residents themselves, which could not so easily be reduced to observable economic differences:

[3] Seven years later, these findings were confirmed by the geographically more restricted *Lambeth Inner Area Survey* (Shankland Cox & the Institute of Community Studies, 1974c). Within the survey area (see Map 1), while 28% of households had lived in the area for less than five years, a much greater proportion, 40% in all, had lived in the area for twenty years or more in 1973.

between different life-styles and life goals; between those who were 'rough' and those who 'kept their families decent'; between those who seemed 'common' and those who were judged to be 'nice people'; between those who were 'stuck up' and those who were 'good sorts'; between 'flash Harrys and wide boys' and 'good family men'. Such evaluations implied no shared moral universe, no all-embracing system of social control; rather, they provided the basis for idiosyncratic patterns of association and dissociation in an often confused and fluid social universe.

In 1971, more than one fifth of the population of Lambeth was born outside the United Kingdom, and one in three births in the borough were to mothers born abroad. Of the various European migrant groups, the most significant were the Irish, who, with a population of 12,700, comprised just over 4% of the borough's population. This proportion was, however, only 0.9% greater than the Greater London average, and considerably lower than in west or north London boroughs such as Hammersmith or Islington. Similarly, although there were significant numbers of Cypriots, both Greek and Turkish, and Maltese in the borough, the geographical foci for these populations lay over the river, in the boroughs of north London. Lambeth, and more especially Brixton, was above everything else an area of West Indian settlement, and, more specifically, of Jamaican settlement.

In 1966, the 'coloured' population of Lambeth, African, Asian and West Indian, including the children of migrants born in the United Kingdom, was something of the order of 10%. By 1971, this proportion had risen to approximately 12%.[4] The geographical distribution of Lambeth's black population, and its concentration in the central districts of the borough, may be seen from Maps 3 and 4, which give the distribution of 'immigrant' children in Lambeth schools[5] and the distribution of Lambeth's 'New Commonwealth' population by enumeration district, in 1970 and 1971 respectively.[6] Within this

---

[4] Amended population figures for 1966 are based upon the calculations of E. J. B. Rose and his colleagues (1969, Appendix III.3). These figures, in fact, correspond very closely to those which may be derived from the *Lambeth Housing Occupancy Survey* data (see Benson, 1975, p. 85). Figures for 1971 are based upon unpublished census material tabulating individuals by birthplace and parental birthplace.

[5] The ILEA define an 'immigrant' child as one either born overseas, or one whose parents had settled in the United Kingdom less than ten years previously. This definition includes, of course, Irish, Maltese, Cypriot and other white migrant categories as well as black children. On the other hand, many black children in 1970 were not 'immigrants' by this definition; 94% of black children less than five years old in 1966 and 54% of five to eleven year olds (i.e., the school population of 1970) were born in the United Kingdom, many to parents resident before 1960. It seemed from a random inspection of a number of Brixton secondary schools that these two ambiguities roughly cancelled each other out, and that the ILEA figures offered an approximate guide to the numbers of black children in each school.

[6] No data are available, in published or unpublished form, concerning the distribution of different segments of Lambeth's black population across the borough in 1971. I have chosen to use data on the distribution of the population of 'New Commonwealth' origin

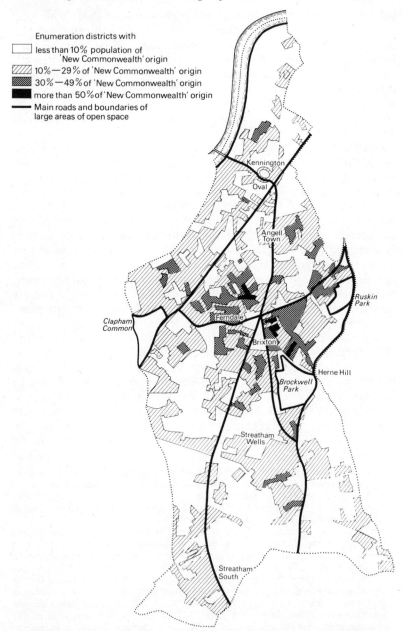

Enumeration districts with

less than 10% population of 'New Commonwealth' origin

10%—29% of 'New Commonwealth' origin

30%—49% of 'New Commonwealth' origin

more than 50% of 'New Commonwealth' origin

Main roads and boundaries of large areas of open space

Kennington

Oval

Angell Town

Ruskin Park

Clapham Common

Ferndale

Brixton

Herne Hill

Brockwell Park

Streatham Wells

Streatham South

Map 3. The London Borough of Lambeth: distribution of population born in the countries of the 'New Commonwealth', or with both parents born in the 'New Commonwealth', 1971, by enumeration district. (From unpublished material from 1971 census: Enumeration district tabulations, Tate Central Library, Lambeth.)

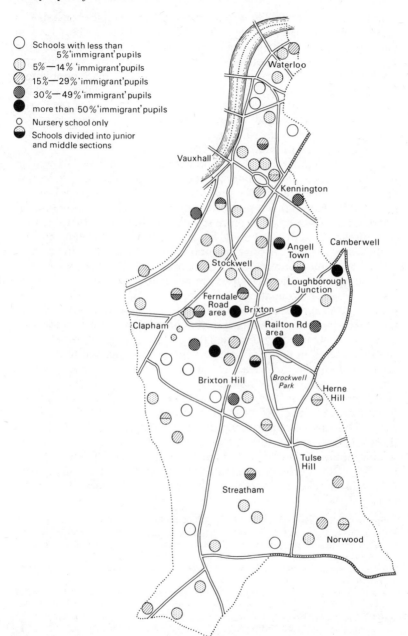

Map 4. Distribution of 'immigrant' children in Lambeth primary schools, September 1970.

population there were, of course, variations. For example, Africans – in the case of Lambeth, mainly West Africans – were to be found in especially large numbers in Ferndale ward, between Brixton and Clapham, but on the whole tended to live together with West Indians in roughly similar proportions in each ward with a high black population. It was in these wards too that the borough's Irish population, whose socio-economic characteristics were very similar to those of the Caribbean population – tended to be concentrated.[7] Enumerated Asian residents, however, were distributed very differently, being concentrated in wards to the south and west of the borough.

Demographically, the black population of Lambeth differed in several respects from the white; it contained a much higher proportion of men to women, a smaller proportion of those ages sixty-five and above, and a much greater proportion of those of school age and under. There were, however, other more significant differences. In 1971, 79% of economically active household heads born in the Caribbean and 50% of those born in the African Commonwealth were engaged in personal service or manual occupations, compared to 51% for the borough as a whole; and both these groups were under-represented in managerial and professional occupations (see Table 3.3).[8] In the 1960s, a detailed study of housing allocation in the borough (Burney, 1967) indicated how black families, as relatively recent arrivals in south London who were also confronted by discriminatory housing policies, were significantly worse off in terms of access to council housing and to desirable accommodation in the private sector than their white peers. The 1971 census data and the 1973 Lambeth Inner Area Study gave little sign of any improvement in this respect (Shankland Cox & the Institute of Community Studies, 1974c). And, perhaps most important of all, the early 1970s saw no improvement in the life chances of the children of those migrants settled in the area. While 17% of Lambeth's secondary school population in 1970 were 'immigrant' pupils, such pupils occupied only 4% of the borough's grammar school places, and unemployment among black school-leavers was running at several times the national average.[9]

(that is, all those residents of Lambeth both of whose parents were born in the 'New Commonwealth') rather than data tabulating individuals by birthplace alone, since by 1971, a significant proportion of Lambeth's black population were in fact born in England.

[7] A pattern similar to that reported for London as a whole by Doherty (1969) and by Lee (1977).

[8] Again, these findings are supported by the *Inner Area Survey* of 1973; 29% of the coloured men in the survey area had non-manual jobs, compared to 39% of whites, and 38% compared to 24% had unskilled manual jobs (Shankland Cox & the Institute of Community Studies 1974b, p. 14).

[9] It is depressing, but hardly surprising, to note that these patterns have been perpetuated throughout the 1970s. In 1977–8 black people in Lambeth – then comprising almost 25% of the borough's population – remained significantly over-represented in unskilled and semi-skilled manual work and under-represented in professional occupations (Department of the Environment, 1978).

Residents and outsiders

If blacks were the most disadvantaged of Brixton's residents, all shared, to differing degrees, in the problems attendant upon life in a poor district of the inner city. To many outsiders, especially those living in the more affluent neighbourhoods to the south and west of the borough, these problems stemmed from the residents themselves, who were widely regarded as 'rough' people unwilling to conform to the standards of mainstream English society. Indeed, Brixton itself was sometimes presented as a 'blight', whose vigorous growth was undermining the security and well-being of other districts. Outsiders frequently contrasted the ordered, well-kept streets of Streatham or Herne Hill with the dirt and disorder of Brixton, and these attitudes were both reflected and reinforced by the way in which Brixton, and the people who lived there, were reported in the press.

It was the press, for example, which, from 1970 onwards, focused public attention upon the problem of street robberies – soon to be labelled 'muggings' – in the area. It was during the 1970 election campaign that Enoch Powell delivered his now notorious 'Rivers of Blood' speech, predicting violent racial confrontation in Britain and demanding the repatriation of black immigrants. The Tory candidate for Brixton, James Harkness, was quick to align himself with Mr Powell. Thus, in a meeting at Lambeth Town Hall, he called for the voluntary repatriation of 'immigrants' and drew attention to the 'scandalous' housing conditions and high rate of unemployment in Brixton which, by implication, were associated with Lambeth's expanded black population. He then went on to announce his support for 'law and order' issues.

While campaigning in Brixton, I have been appalled at the number of old people who locked themselves behind shuttered doors in the burning sun for fear of being attacked. It is not safe for them to walk in Brixton streets at night. (*Brixton Advertiser*, 12 June 1970)

The facts were less dramatic than Mr Harkness's rather confused account would imply; the level of street violence in the area, running, as far as could be ascertained, at between two and five incidents a week at the time, could hardly be described as an epidemic of lawlessness. 'Mugging', however, acted as the focus for a much wider range of fears and anxieties concerning the development of Brixton, and channelled these anxieties towards one particular section of the local community, the young and the black. Feelings in this respect ran especially high in the summer of 1971, when an elderly white woman died of the injuries that she had received in such an attack; her assailant had reportedly been black.

Brixton residents were aware of the unfavourable attitudes held by outsiders towards the area and its population, and were often understandably reluctant to identify themselves with it in any way. Those living on the boundaries of Brixton proper often preferred to say that they lived in 'Angell Town', for example, or in 'Loughborough Junction' – names which meant little in social terms – rather than admit to living in Brixton. Similarly, an English woman who had been moved to a flat off Brixton Hill told friends and relations she was living in 'Streatham': 'I was ashamed to say I lived in Brixton.' For her, as for a significant section of the white population living locally, and for outsiders, 'Brixton' was firmly identified with its black population, and its black population with its problems. Indeed, for those who remembered the area from the war, its respectable past was often contrasted with present conditions, and blame for the area's decline allocated to the impact of West Indian settlement. The comments of one elderly Englishman, a retired plumber living in Tulse Hill, may be taken as typical of many:

> 'Brixton used to be all right before the immigrants came. They spoiled the area. They haven't got our ways, what's dirty to us isn't dirty to them... I know there's some English people as bad as them, but they never used to live around here. They come here after the darkies moved in.'

Black residents too perceived Brixton as a hostile and difficult environment. Their attitudes were, however, markedly more ambivalent. Mrs Davis, for example was a Jamaican woman in her late twenties who, together with her husband and three children, had been living in two rooms in her brother's overcrowded house off Railton Road for four years. To her, Brixton was 'one of the worst places I ever did see', despite the convenience of the market and the shops. She worried particularly about her children; there was nowhere for them to play safely outside and two of them had already been knocked down by traffic in the busy street only a few yards from her front door. Two were at school but making little progress, and for this she blamed the lack of attention they received there. She would have preferred them to go to a school 'where there is not so many coloured, I think they learn better'. And, as they grew older, her sons were likely to fall in with 'the bad Brixton boys without work' and take to a life of petty crime, as, indeed, one of her nephews had done. Or they would end up like her other nephew, in his family's opinion a 'good boy', who had been convicted of an offence they were sure he did not commit, but who emerged from prison 'just like his brother'. Moreover, like many white women in the area, Mrs Davis was nervous about walking through Brixton streets at night:

> 'A woman walking alone... gets stop by all kinds of funny people. You walking along the road late and some man sure to slow his car down alongside you and ask, "You doing business?" They think all coloured women prostitutes anyhow.'

Yet when Mrs Davis was given the chance of a new council house in Greater Peterborough, and the assurance of a job for her husband there, she turned it down. There were sound economic reasons for her decision. The rent and rates would be expensive, and the family would be dependent upon her husband's income alone. In Brixton, she could pay a fellow tenant 50p a week to keep an eye on her small daughter while she was at work; in Peterborough, she would be housebound. But, as Mrs Davis was the first to admit, she also disliked the idea of moving away from an area of Jamaican settlement. Living in and around Brixton, she had a brother, a sister, an aunt and several cousins, all with their families, as well as numerous friends from 'back home'; in Peterborough, she would have English neighbours, and, 'You know how most of English people don't get along a-us.' What Mrs Davis wanted, like many West Indians in Brixton, was improved accommodation in a 'better' area – but near enough to stay in touch with the Brixton social universe.

Indeed, some sections of the area's black population, the hustlers and 'rude boys' to be found 'hanging out' in the West Indian-run record bars and basement drinking clubs, had a wry affection for the area, which stemmed precisely from this comfortable feeling that in Brixton could be found Jamaica in microcosm. In the reggae songs immortalising this black Brixton world, just as in the views of politicised black people for whom Brixton was 'the Ghetto', to be both reformed and cherished, 'Brixton' was much more than a mere aggregation of buildings, a collection of problems; it was a state of mind, an orientation. To be part of 'Brixton' was to be a brother; to reject it was to reject one's roots, to reject the black experience.

There were, of course, many West Indians who did precisely this. Mr Holder, for example, was a Jamaican entrepreneur living in Norwood. For years he had lived in Brixton, which he described as a 'jungle', but he had little sympathy for West Indians who, unlike himself, lacked the resources to get out; these, he saw as

> 'low-class people who come stink up the country for the rest of us – how white people is expect to think when they see those bad Brixton boys carrying on like they do?'

Like Mr Holder, some West Indians chose to distinguish themselves from the black residents of Brixton on the basis of class; others chose to emphasise differences in ethnic or national origin. Thus, 'small islanders' often chose to blame the predominance of Jamaicans in the black Brixton population for the area's problems. Similarly, West Africans frequently drew a distinction between themselves, educated people here in Britain to study, and 'ignorant' West Indians who made life difficult for them. In this manner, the black residents of Brixton, like the white, often sought to dissociate themselves from the 'problem' of Brixton, as perceived by themselves and by others.

It may thus be said that although the black residents of Brixton did share a certain sense of solidarity, born of the many common facets of black experience in this country, they, like the local white population, were a 'community' only in the broadest sense of the term. Although class differences were less strongly marked than among the English population, they did exist, as did noticeable differences in outlook, orientation and style of life; in addition to which there were those differences rooted in national origin and a diversity of ethnic identities. Such divisions formed the basis of a complex and fluid social order.

4   The social world of Brixton

The meaning of ethnic identities: cognition and action

'I don't like white people. They're nasty, they don't like coloured people.' (Jamaican girl, aged 7 years)

'The trouble with Indians, they think them white.' (Jamaican unskilled worker, aged 45 years)

'The way she carries on, you'd think she's got coloured blood.' (English housewife, of an untidy English neighbour)

'We don't count Jimmy as coloured.' (English statistician, of a Nigerian colleague)

The terms 'white' and 'coloured', or their synonyms, were in frequent use by Brixton residents of all ethnicities. In practical descriptive terms this dichotomous classification was not as clearcut as it might first appear, for individuals were sometimes described as 'not very coloured', or as looking 'white' but having 'coloured blood'. Yet as conceptual categories, 'white' and 'coloured' remained sharply distinct in most people's minds, and, as the statements quoted above indicate, this distinction implied far more than a difference in physical appearance.

To most, if not all whites, the visible differences between 'white' and 'coloured' were the external signs of important differences in habits, tastes and abilities, in which, typically, 'coloured' people compared unfavourably with 'whites'. Underpinning such comparisons was a range of implicit assumptions shared by a large section of the white Brixton population concerning the close connection between 'colour', as it was socially defined in the Brixton context, culture, and social identity. To be 'coloured' then, in Brixton as elsewhere in Britain, was to be assigned a stigmatised identity. Yet, as Wallman (1978) has pointed out, the boundary denoted by 'colour', for all its practical importance in the lives of immigrants from the New Commonwealth and their children, may not indicate the most important ethnic identities as perceived by blacks themselves. West Indians and West Africans, for example, indistinguishable from each other to many English eyes, and often to be found living in the same houses and shopping in the same shops, nevertheless felt themselves to be very different people, with very little in common, as the following extract from field notes indicates.

Tuesday afternoon was not very busy, and several [West Indian] men killing time in the community centre office began discussing the problems of having tenants in the house. Mr Phillips happened to remark that his tenants were Nigerians. They paid the rent regularly and even went out of their way to be helpful – by cleaning windows, for example – but, 'somehow me and them have never got along'. For this he felt their liking for 'secrecy' was responsible: 'Nigerians are funny people.'

Mr Hunt agreed with him: 'You can't never tell what they are doing behind closed doors.' But, he added, Ghanaians were 'not so bad'. Mr Phillips disagreed with this; he thought Ghanaians were 'much worse'. Mr Scott, on the other hand, had nothing good to say about any Africans: 'They dirty, they lazy, they never clean the room.' He went on to recount a couple of unfortunate experiences with West African tenants... 'if you let a room to a man one day, next day he is moving his whole family in'.

The others agreed, and another man present chipped in that Africans were unpleasant to live with anyway: their food 'smell terrible from that pepper they put in it' and they left their meat to go off before they cooked it. Mr Scott concluded: 'And I say to you that I am not prejudiced, I just will not have them in the house. I will go for a drink with them, lend them a quid, but as tenants, never again.'

From the West African point of view there was a similar emphasis on the inherent untrustworthiness of West Indians as tenants and landlords, but here the complaints tended to centre around noise and immoral living rather than around 'secrecy'.

In the context of Brixton, perceptions of ethnic difference were the product of a set of segmentary oppositions in which differences which were important in some social situations were submerged in others. Take, for example, the individual case of Mr Jimmy Brown, born in the parish of Clarendon, Jamaica. Within his intimate circle of kin and friends, most of them also from Clarendon, ethnic identity was not a significant factor. As a customer in the local 'Caribbean' bakery, however, he was a Negro Jamaican buying bread from a 'babu man', an Asian Jamaican. In the West Indian-run drinking club where he spent a good deal of his leisure time he was a Jamaican amongst a circle of Guyanese, Trinidadians and Barbadians, engaging in friendly competition over which island produces the best rum, women or cricketers, and occasionally less friendly backbiting about island character ('Man, Jamaica got nothing! Big island, big mouth!'). At his workplace, a paper factory in outer south London, he was a West Indian in a workforce of Africans, English, Asians and Irish. Yet in speaking of the difficulties he faced in finding a house, he chose to define himself differently again: 'It hard for a coloured man to find somewhere to live in this country.'

At all levels, perceptions of ethnic difference were related to an awareness of physical and cultural difference: skin colour, physical appearance, distinctive styles of dress, linguistic usage and social presentation, all served to differentiate one segment of the Brixton population from another. The extent to which individuals took cognisance of such diacritical signs was determined, to a considerable degree, by their own position within the Brixton social universe. Many English residents, for example, could distinguish English regional accents with considerable precision, and could frequently list a series of 'signs' – accent, style of dress, hair-style, non-verbal communicative devices – which, they believed, enabled them to distinguish the Irish from themselves. Yet they could hear no difference in the speech patterns of West Indians and West Africans, nor discern any differences in physical appearance, hair-styles, or ways of wearing European dress between these two segments of the 'coloured' population. Even those who could make such broad distinctions could not, in general, make the more subtle distinctions that permitted West Indians and West Africans to identify individuals from different islands or from different African cultural and linguistic groups. Awareness of such distinctions was determined, in the final instance, by interaction across ethnic boundaries; and, as we shall see below, in Brixton this interaction was limited by the pattern of informal avoidance that drew black and white into separate social worlds, as well as by the segregation of different ethnic groupings – English, Irish, Greek Cypriot, Turkish Cypriot, Yorubas, Igbos, Jamaicans, Barbadians and so on – within different primary communities.

The diacritical signs of group differences were not, however, merely inert signifiers of a socially significant boundary. Observable cultural differences could play a considerable part in maintaining category boundaries, as well as defining them. This was especially the case where differences in social behaviour meshed with the unfavourable stereotypes that Brixton residents tended to hold about each other. Thus, differences in conversational convention, linguistic usage, and non-verbal communication devices such as gesture, movement and eye contact, were often much more than just uncomfortable for the speakers concerned: they also contributed to breakdowns in communication which reinforced suspicion and hostility between strangers. For example, one reason given by English boys for their reluctance to share club premises with West Indians was their fear of violence; English boys found it difficult to distinguish between West Indian teasing and testing behaviour and intimations of real trouble. Similarly, adult English people tended to interpet the much higher levels of interpersonal aggression, both verbal and physical, tolerated in interaction by West Indian males as evidence of the 'excitability' and propensity to violence that their stereotyped view of the 'uncontrolled savage' led them to expect.

Many other ethno-specific cultural traits were similarly open to misinterpretation, and were seized upon by individuals to justify their conjectural beliefs about members of other categories – as we have seen in the case of West Indians and West Africans obliged to share common accommodation. Nevertheless, these cultural misunderstandings cannot be considered as the 'cause' of the numerous stereotyped beliefs that many Brixton residents held about each other. While these beliefs did, to some extent, derive their character and force from the structuring of interaction in Brixton, their roots must be sought elsewhere, in historical processes which have determined the nature of the economic and political relationship between English and Irish, Africa and the Caribbean, black and white, and shaped the way in which these peoples have come to regard each other.

Ethno-specific traits did more than indicate ethnic affiliation to outsiders; they also acted as the means of focusing and maintaining solidarity between sharers of the same cultural orientation. The use of patois within the West Indian population was a case in point. Most West Indians in Brixton who had come to England as adults habitually spoke to fellow islanders in the dialect of their respective islands, and modified their speech in the direction of some variant of 'London English' when speaking to English people. Their children learned 'Standard English' at school, cockney dialect from their white peers, and often continued to speak patois at home. For both immigrants from the Caribbean and their children, then, language choices were strongly associated with demarcated domains (Fishman, 1972). Yet the individual's choice of dialect was not necessarily defined situationally. Take, for example, the case of two brothers, well known in Brixton, who had come to England separately and followed very different paths in life, one becoming a successful local businessman and marrying an English wife, the other developing a strong commitment to Garveyism and radical black politics. The first habitually spoke London English with a Jamaican accent; the second, Jamaican patois. Similarly, West Indian adolescents often chose to express their alienation from the wider white world that encapsulated them through the adoption of patois as their habitual mode of speech.

It is thus necessary to qualify the observation that ethnic identities in Brixton were situationally defined, by pointing out that individuals often sought to define, for themselves as well as for others, their social allegiances in a manner which transcended the exigencies of particular circumstances. However, such attempts successfully to negotiate a social identity consonant with the personal orientations of the individual were in no sense free choices, for in Brixton social identities were assigned by others as much as constructed by the individuals concerned. Thus, black people in Brixton could attempt to neutralise a stigmatised ethnic identity by claims to high status on other axes of social differentiation, such as class; they might anchor themselves within a narrower, black social world in which the fact of colour was not significant; or they might seek to reject and to transform the basis upon which social identity was assigned. But they could not deny the importance of colour within the Brixton social universe, and its implications might be neutralised, but not ignored. Moreover, these implications were rooted in the social ecology of the area.

Ethnic dimensions of the social order

A survey carried out in Lambeth in 1966 (Rose *et al.*, 1969, p. 573) reported that half of the English interviewed had, at some time, worked alongside black workmates. In 1970, there were only three schools in the entire borough – and these all church primary schools – with no 'migrant' children on their roll. All sections of the Brixton population could be found living side by side in the same streets, often, indeed, in the same houses. Yet, on closer inspection, these manifestations of an apparent social integration dissolve; instead, we see a series of segregated social worlds, geographically overlapping but structurally distinct, which were linked by a series of neutral arenas – work, school, the public areas of streets, parks and shops – in which Brixton residents expected to encounter members of other ethnic groups. In informal areas of interaction, however, a pattern of reasonably tolerant avoidance was the norm. Thus, Mr Holding, a Jamaican who had worked for London Transport for fifteen years, was careful to distinguish between the quality of relations between black and white 'on the job' – which, he felt, had improved 'tremendously' – and the quality of relations 'off the job':

> 'I get on all right with the English at work but there is no friendship there really. We are mates on the job and joke together but when we get to the canteen it is each to his own colour. I don't mind that – they don't bother us and we don't bother them.'

Similarly, a Eurafrican woman working as a domestic supervisor in a local hospital commented on the divisions evident in her work milieu:

> 'We get English, Irish, West Indian and Spanish, only a few African...African women never get along with the West Indians, their temperaments are entirely different...They will not make friends outside their own set. A few West Indians will have tea with the Irish girls, they are more open than the Londoners, I think.'

In schools, as at work, ethnic divisions were readily apparent. In primary schools, ethnically mixed play groups were a common enough sight, and individual friendships persisted right through secondary school and sometimes beyond. The level of interethnic hostility increased, however, as children became more and more conscious of the role played by race and colour in society around them. In some schools, violence was a problem, as one male teacher reported:

> 'If there's a fight in the playground they join in along colour lines, black on one side, whites on the other. They expect this of you as well.'

Culturally, many of the black children growing up in Brixton in the early 1970s were virtually indistinguishable from their white peers. They admired the same popular heroes, watched the same television programmes, supported the same football teams, and followed the same fashions. It was a common complaint among West Indian mothers that their children often demanded baked beans and chips to eat rather than saltfish or rice and peas. Yet black adolescents, as the time to leave school drew nearer, were increasingly aware that they were about to enter a world in which their life chances were very different from those of their white peers, and of which even their white friends had very little understanding. 'You might go around with a white spar', said one such boy, 'but the time come you start to think how much you can depend on him.' There was a strong sense, among black school-leavers, that whatever inter-ethnic friendships had been made in school had little to do with real life; as another young Jamaican put it, 'After school days everything done, man – outside life is sort of different, ennit?' And in 'outside life', for West Indian youngsters as for their parents, the assumption was that colour would be an important principle of association and dissociation.

For obvious reasons, English, Irish, Greek Cypriot, Turkish Cypriot, West African or West Indian residents of Brixton tended to move in segregated primary communities, drawing upon their personal networks of kin and friends to supply significant social relationships. With such people, an individual could be assured of at least a minimum level of shared understandings and could avoid the dangers and possible humiliations of interaction with strangers. Such tendencies towards compartmentalisation were further reinforced by the social ecology of Brixton itself – an ecology predicated on the fact of ethnic segregation.

Every section of the local community, for example, could be found in the shops and chain stores along Brixton Road, or shopping side by side in Brixton market. But within the single square mile of central Brixton there were also to be found many smaller concerns which catered specifically for the needs of one segment of the local population and where the clientele reflected that fact. Such locations often served as nodes in a parochial communication network and as informal meeting places where people could spend varying amounts of leisure time in the company of their ethnic peers. In the Greek Cypriot delicatessen in the market area, for example, business was habitually conducted in Greek, and favoured customers often spent as much as half an hour chatting over their purchases; gossip was also an important aspect of a visit to the Jewish delicatessen which sold Jewish, Greek and Polish foodstuffs, as it was in the Yoruba-owned grocery which specialised in West African products. Local West Indian entrepreneurs used the West Indian beauty salon, the West Indian barber shops, and the various record bars specialising in reggae and soul music to sell tickets for West Indian 'functions' and to advertise coming events; the record bars acted as 'hangouts' for the younger generation, where they could meet their friends and listen to the latest sounds, while older men could be found in one of the three West Indian drinking clubs that survived in central Brixton, or in one of the cafés specialising in jerk pork, rice and peas, or other Caribbean dishes.

These parochial establishments did not encourage the patronage of outsiders. Indeed, many outsiders felt ill at ease even walking past their doors, let alone venturing inside. Then there were other establishments – cafés, betting shops or pubs – which, although they offered general services, had come to be recognised with varying degrees of permanence and importance as gathering places for one segment of the local population and were likewise avoided by outsiders. Several public houses, for example, had sizeable West Indian clienteles, and two in the market area could be described as West Indian-dominated locations; nearby, another served as a meeting place for local Irish residents. Elsewhere, West Indian and Irish customers could be found sharing the public bars, while the English drank in the saloons.

Undoubtedly, divergent tastes and interests took different sections of the local community into different leisure and commercial locations. This tendency was, however, reinforced by the reluctance of Brixton residents to risk interaction with strangers that I have discussed above. In the same way, those formal institutions – political parties, social clubs, the major Protestant denominational churches – which aimed to recruit their membership from all sections of the local community had little success in this respect. In any case, in general such institutions played little part in the lives of Brixton residents. As one Anglican vicar remarked:

> 'I have three coloured families who are regular churchgoers and a few more who come occasionally. Of course they come to the church for baptisms and weddings...rather like the English nowadays, I'm afraid.'

In contrast, the various Roman Catholic churches in the borough and the parochial schools attached to them acted as focal points for the local Irish, Maltese and black Catholic population, while there flourished a number of pentecostal churches which catered specifically for the religious preferences of West Indians and West Africans.

Several community projects operating in the area attempted, explicitly or implicitly, to bring together large numbers of Brixton residents. In Brixton itself there were two multi-purpose community organisations, one sponsored by the Methodist church and the other a West-Indian-dominated association which had grown out of a group formed in 1965 to protect the interests of tenants living in what was then the centre of black settlement in the area, Somerleyton and Geneva Roads. Another community centre was located on a new council estate in Stockwell. There were also several projects – one at the Oval, another operating out of YMCA premises at Stockwell, two which opened in central Brixton in 1971, and an adventure playground complex in Angell Town – with a strong commitment to youth work, as well as numerous smaller ventures – mother and baby clubs, pre-school play groups, church clubs for old age pensioners or for teenagers – aimed at providing more specific services.

The character of the clientele attracted to these projects varied considerably. Projects for small children, pre-school play groups or children's summer projects, were popular with all sections of the local population. However, most of the smaller social clubs – the mother and baby clubs, for example – had great difficulty in attracting non-white members. Indeed, the only community organisation that had succeeded in involving large numbers of West Indians in its projects for adults was the former tenants' association, where most of the staff, as well as the clientele, were black.

In complete contrast was the situation in projects aimed at the younger members of the local population. Facilities for adolescents in the area were on the whole so poor that any project, even a church-run youth club offering dominoes and football in a dingy church hall, was attractive in comparison to the cramped and bleak conditions faced by many children at home. There was no difficulty in attracting youngsters, both black and white: the problem facing the organisers was rather to maintain a racially mixed membership. Indeed, at the time of this research, only one such project, the Angell Town adventure playground, had succeeded in doing so, perhaps because of the nature of its catchment area, perhaps because of the uniquely attractive nature of this facility which encouraged youngsters to share the site rather than to withdraw.

Competition and conflict, however, was a more typical response. St Peter's, for example, was a church youth club located in an ethnically mixed neighbourhood off Brixton Hill, offering music and limited sports facilities. Until the autumn of 1968, its membership had been predominantly white; then, after the closure of the Ram Jam, a commercial dance club in central Brixton, increasing numbers of West Indians began to attend. According to a report produced by the club organiser:

'There was little mixing between the new arrivals and the white members. A number of the white members were resentful of the newcomers and some tense situations developed over which records were to be played. The West Indians wanted blue beat while the white members wanted pop music. Eventually the white members gave up the room where the records were played...' (Community Development Project Working Paper 4, Section 2, Part C)

When I visited this club in the summer of 1971, the membership was overwhelmingly West Indian, and there were no white boys there at all. The same process was typical of many youth clubs in the area. The Denbigh Road Community Centre, for example, was a purpose-built complex which opened in 1970. Before starting up a youth club to replace one which had been forced to close for lack of premises, the Youth Leader sent out circulars to members of the former club and to households in the neighbourhood, asking young people to come along and decide what kind of club they wanted. Those who came were almost all English and Irish, although as the date fixed for opening approached, more West Indians began to attend. It was decided that the club should open with a meeting in the afternoon, followed by a dance in the evening. Attendance at the meeting was approximately 50% black and 50% white. Many of the West Indians, however, turned up wearing the then fashionable attire of Black Panthers – black berets, shades, clenched fist badges – and many white youngsters did not come back for the dance. None stayed to the end. Two months after opening, the club was, in the words of the Youth Leaders, '75% black and going blacker'.

Various factors contributed to this tendency for whites to withdraw from such youth clubs. One was the white boys' perception of black people as social inferiors, so that voluntarily to share premises with them reflected badly on a boy's self image and status in the eyes of others. 'When *they* [West Indians] come in here', said one English thirteen year old, 'I packed it in. Fucking rubbish, that's what they are.' Another was the greater success enjoyed by black youths in the minor confrontations within the clubs. One youth worker, for example, felt that the black boys who visited his club were 'more aggressive in demanding their rights...they back each other up'. Undoubtedly, they also made white youths anxious over the possibility of violence; certainly, the more astute among them capitalised on the unease generated by white inability to 'read the signs' of West Indian interaction ritual. Indeed, the development of what might be termed 'Rude Boy' culture among West Indian youth must be seen, not simply as an attempt to construct a viable social identity among those who could no longer retreat into the parochial securities of island culture, but also as a strategy for dealing with, and excluding, an essentially hostile white world (Hebdige,

1976; Pryce, 1979). For rather different reasons, then, but with the same result, among young people, as among the older generation, ethnic segregation was the norm – not only in youth clubs, but in dance halls, cafés, and in informal areas of interaction.

Guests, hosts and marginals

Given the strongly marked segregation of social worlds, it is hardly surprising that relationships between individuals of different ethnicities in Brixton were, typically, relations between strangers, albeit strangers who might well live in the same street or work in the same factory. Most relationships across the boundary of colour developed in what we have termed 'neutral' arenas and involved only limited social relationships. Yet it would be misleading to suggest that the social universe of Brixton was composed of a set of self-contained ethnic groups interacting only in the impersonal arena of the market place. Even in Brixton, ethnic boundaries were not entirely impermeable.

'Guests and hosts' is, perhaps, an apt way of characterising the nature of much interaction that did develop across such ethnic boundaries. This could be limited in scope, as when Englishmen visited a West Indian-run café to buy 'ganja' (cannabis), or could involve more durable relationships between individuals – as when a Jamaican electrician invited his English workmate to attend his family weddings and christenings. Such interaction did not negate the boundary in question: indeed, in the way in which individuals involved in such relationships spoke of them the importance of such boundaries was given tacit recognition.

> 'I've got a good friend at work, a coloured girl, she's from Jamaica. When she had a little girl last year, she invited me to the christening – I was a bit nervous at going, but I really enjoyed it, it was quite an experience. I was the only white face there.' (White woman, 26 years)

Such 'guest–host' relationships, then, acknowledged the distinctive ethnic identities of those concerned, and the temporary and situational nature of their shared social activities. Such relationships were unproblematic between individuals of the same sex; relations between men and women of different ethnicities were, however, regarded rather differently. For an English boy to go to a football match with a West Indian friend was one thing; for an English girl to visit West Indian clubs had very different implications.

Even a cursory survey of the pubs, clubs and discotheques in the Brixton area revealed that, while ethnic segregation might be the general rule, there could be found white women who, far from withdrawing when black people began to use a location in significant numbers, actively sought out contact with black men. In West Indian drinking clubs, for example, apart from the occasional white 'guest', there were usually a number of English, Scottish or Irish women, sometimes casual girl-friends or wives of the clientele, sometimes prostitutes in search of custom. Such 'black men's women', as they were termed disparagingly by local English residents, moved almost entirely in a black social field; unlike white 'guests' in black locations, their sexual involvement with black partners had, in the eyes of the wider white community, committed them irrevocably to the black Brixton world.

Other, younger, women merely flirted with this world. In the early 1970s, few West Indian parents would permit their adolescent daughters to visit discotheques and youth clubs, and the only girls to be seen at locations which catered for younger teenagers were, in fact, white. Such girls often lived at home with their parents and concealed their activities from them; as one club manager put it, 'This...lot come for kicks and then slide off home to Mum.' Precisely why involvement with black boys should appear, as it certainly did to many of these girls, as daring and exciting is hard to define. While some girls vehemently rejected the idea that they were especially interested in black boys, others freely expressed their preferences; white boys were 'all beer and football'; they 'only want you for one thing'; 'they just want to go around with their mates'; while West Indian boys were 'more considerate'; 'more interested in girls really'; 'they dress well and make you feel noticed, chat you up better...more sexy really.'

There were, however, serious risks for girls who drifted into too close an involvement with West Indian life. As one thoughtful sixteen year old put it:

> 'I like coloured boys, they're more fun to go out with...there's no future in it, though, is there, know what I mean? *Your* parents don't like it, *his* parents don't like it, think you're a bloody tart, know what I mean? I wouldn't go out with any of them regular, too many bloody problems. But I'll go to the clubs.'

Because of the compartmentalised nature of the Brixton social universe those girls who did commit themselves to a black social field found themselves in a position of marginality *vis-à-vis* the white community. Such detached individuals were not, however, necessarily whites. Examples could also be found of black individuals, marginal to their own communities, who had chosen to align themselves with another ethnic category. There were, for example, West Indian boys to be found in some of the skinhead gangs of Stockwell, as virulent in their hatred of 'Pakis' as their white peers. And there were West Indians or West Africans who because of their 'respectability' on other axes of social differentiation and their involvement in a predominantly white social field through work or vocational interests were regarded by their white acquaintances as 'not really very coloured', and accepted as exceptions to the rules that governed local patterns of interaction. The cognitive dissonance which was created for others by the ambiguous position of both black and white marginals was handled by assigning to them other social characteristics which 'explained' their deviation from the norms of segregation. Thus, for the English, 'black men's women' were stigmatised as deviants in more respects than in their choice of sexual partners, while those who were 'not really coloured' were distinguished, implicitly or explicitly, from the generality of the black population in terms of their personal characters and social attributes. Such attitudes defined the range within which those who ignored ethnic boundaries in their choice of friends and sexual partners were able to negotiate their own identity.

To enter into an interracial union in the context of Brixton was thus directly to confront the problems and paradoxes inherent in an ethnically compartmentalised social universe. In their domestic choices, as in the construction of a viable and satisfactory social network, the interracial couple is faced with the problem of integrating two discrete social worlds, and of working out a *modus vivendi* within a framework of race relations where ethnicity, if not always the sole determinant of patterns of everyday interaction and perception, remains an important axis of social differentiation and an important determinant of social identity.

5   The dynamics of interracial marriage choice

To enter into an interracial union was, even in the Brixton of the 1970s, to enter into a union likely to arouse considerable public disapproval, as well as the hostility of family and friends. Such couples faced even greater difficulties in the past. What factors, then, led the twenty couples who form the focus of this study to ignore the social forces which maintained the pattern of tolerant avoidance so characteristic of Brixton life?

It is tempting, when reviewing one's personal history, to reconstruct the events of the past in the light of the present; it is even more tempting for the social scientist, anxious to elicit regularities from the confusion of experience, to impose an order upon events which may, in fact, best be seen as a series of accidents. In any analysis of the past histories of those individuals who, at some point in their lives, took the decision to enter into a relationship which, in the eyes of the wider society, was bound to meet with disapproval, it is dangerous to look too hard for simple causes; like all couples, such people found themselves together for a variety of reasons, many of them highly idiosyncratic.

Indeed, it would be hard to find a more diverse set of couples than those with whom this study is concerned. There were fourteen Anglo-Caribbean couples, including two cases where West Indian women had married British men; one Irish-Yoruba and three Anglo-Yoruba couples; and two cases of Rhodesian Coloured women married to British men[1] (see Table 5.1). There was considerable diversity of occupation and income, from eight households with men in semi-skilled or unskilled manual occupations to four households with men engaged in professional, semi-professional, or executive work (see Table 5.2). Couples also varied widely in terms of their age, the duration of their respective relationships, and stage of family development (see Tables 5.3 and 5.4).

The relationships of longest standing were those which concerned two black men, Mr Horace and Mr Clough, who had come to England at the time of the Second World War, stayed on, and found wives among

---

[1] 'Rhodesian Coloured' is here employed as a general term to refer to two respondents who were, in Rhodesian ethnic terminology, 'Eurafrican' and 'Cape Coloured' respectively. In referring to what is now the Republic of Zimbabwe, I have used the term 'Rhodesia' throughout, as did these respondents, rather than attempt to distinguish, by point of reference in time, between Southern Rhodesia, Rhodesia, Rhodesia-Zimbabwe, and Zimbabwe.

Table 5.1. *Research couples: country of origin*

	Male partner	Female partner
Naylor	England	Rhodesia
Henderson	Scotland	Rhodesia
Handbury	England	Trinidad
Sidey	England	Jamaica (Chinese/Indian)
Abbott–Pound	Barbados	England
Jay	Barbados	England
Birchall	Guyana	England
Kalipha	Guyana (E. Indian)	England
Lowe–Simmons	Guyana	England
Clough	Jamaica	England
Curtis	Jamaica	England
Gomez–Mackie	Jamaica	Scotland
Homer–Brettle	Jamaica	England
Rich	Jamaica	England
Rowlands	Jamaica	England
Collet	St Lucia	England
Ademola	Nigeria	Ireland
Horace	Nigeria	England
Oluwole	Nigeria	England
Ojo	Nigeria	England

Unless otherwise stated, all partners born outside Great Britain and Ireland are of African or Afro-Caucasian descent.

Where couples were living in consensual unions, the surnames of both partners have been given, that the male partner being given first.

the local population. Not all men who came at this time, however, settled down in this way. Mr Lowe had arrived from Guyana in 1942, to serve in the British armed forces; on demobilisation, he tried work 'in the engineering line' and drifted into an unsettled life as a part-time musician, passing through several careers and two unhappy marriages before meeting his present partner. Mr Abbott (WI)[2] arriving somewhat later, had a similar history.

Among those of the black respondents who came later still, during the main wave of immigration from the New Commonwealth between 1955 and 1962, three patterns may be distinguished. Firstly, there were those, Mr Ademola, Mr Ojo and Mr Oluwole, all Yorubas, who came

[2] The following abbreviations have been used throughout the text to indicate ethnic identity: WI: West Indian; RC: Rhodesian Coloured; Y: Yoruba; GB; English and Scottish; I: Irish. All personal names, occupational details, and the particulars of residence and everyday life have of course been changed in order to ensure the anonymity of all members of the research set.

Table 5.2. *Research couples: occupations at time of interview*

	Male partner	Female partner
Sidey	Partner in public relations firm	
Birchall	Social worker	
Handbury	Careers Officer, local government	Librarian
Horace	Statistician, mail order firm	
Curtis	Draughtsman, mechanical engineering firm	Typist (part-time)
Henderson	Telephonist, GPO	SRN (ward sister)
Lowe–Simmons	Owner/manager car hire firm	Waitress (part-time)
Ojo	Clerical worker, GPO	
Oluwole	Clerical worker, local government	Drama teacher, ILEA
Clough	Electrician, electrical engineering firm	
Kalipha	TV repairman	Community worker/ cinema usherette (both part-time)
Abbott–Pound	Van driver, catering firm	
Jay	Scaffold construction worker	
Rich	Tyre fitter/driver, local tyre firm	
Rowlands	Plasterer	
Collet	Hospital porter	Office cleaner
Gomez–Mackie	Unemployed	
Homer–Brettle	Labourer	
Naylor	Office messenger	Supervisor, catering section, local firm

as students but never completed their courses of study; these men were in relatively humble occupations, but educational aspirations continued to play an important part in their lives. Then there were those, Mr Curtis and Mr Birchall, from well-to-do Caribbean families, who had come already possessing some education, but who hoped to improve their position in England. Mrs Handbury (WI) might also be included in this second category; she had come to England as a child when her father, awarded a training scholarship by the Government of Trinidad, had decided to stay on in Britain. In contrast to these middle-class, or aspiring middle-class, migrants were those – Mr Collet, Mr Homer, Mr Jay, Mr Kalipha, Mr Rich and Mr Rowlands, all from the Caribbean,

Table 5.3. *Research couples: duration of relationship and stage of family development*

Stage in developmental cycle	Duration of relationship from date of cohabitation		
	3 years and under	4–9 years	10 years and over
No children	(Handbury)* Lowe–Simmons		
Youngest child under 5 years	Gomez–Mackie Homer–Brettle Rich	Abbott–Pound Birchall Collet (Jay)* Ojo Oluwole Sidey	
Youngest child 5–9 years		Ademola Kalipha Rowlands	Curtis
Youngest child 10–15 years			Clough Henderson Horace Naylor

* Relationships terminated by date of interview.

all artisans, peasants or unskilled workers – who had arrived with few industrial skills and little or no education. Finally, there were the three black women who had come to this country not as independent migrants, but because their British husbands had brought them here: Janis Sidey, who had met her husband during a period when he was living in Jamaica, and Mrs Henderson and Mrs Naylor, both Rhodesian Coloured women who had left Rhodesia with their families when government policies began to make things difficult for racially mixed households.

In charting the past histories of each of these couples, and in examining what factors brought them together, we are concerned, then, with a considerable diversity of social context. Far from reflecting one single pattern, these relationships were the product of very different circumstances; reflecting, as one might expect, the very different characters of the systems of race relations of which they formed a part.

The context of first meeting

Two relationships were the product of a racially stratified colonial social order. Mr Henderson (GB) and Mr Naylor (GB), both uneducated men, had gone out to Rhodesia in the decade after the Second World War

Table 5.4. *Research couples: marital status and age at inception of cohabitation*

	Male partner		Female partner	
	Age	Marital status	Age	Marital status
Abbott–Pound	37	S	17	S
Ademola	23	S	28	S
Birchall	34	S	22	S
Clough	22	S	21	S
Curtis	39	S	31	S
Handbury	20	S	19	S
Horace	36	S	27	S
Kalipha	23	S	16	S
Naylor	29	S	19	S
Oluwole	27	S	26	S
Rich	23	S	17	S
Rowlands	29	S	24	S
Sidey	25	S	22	S
Collet	34	S	24	S/C
Gomez–Mackie	36	S	27	S/C
Henderson	25	S	26	D/C
Homer–Brettle	34	S	23	D/C
Jay	27	S/C	21	S
Lowe–Simmons	47	D	33	D
Ojo	32	S	32	D/C

S: Single; D: Divorced or separated; C: dependent child or children.

to work on the railways. As whites, they found themselves in a relatively privileged position. To Mr Naylor, who, as his wife freely admitted, was 'a very prejudiced person', this seemed 'only right', but Mr Henderson disapproved of the economic inequalities he found in the colony. These 'strong social views' led his white colleagues to brand him a Communist; yet even he more or less accepted the *status quo*:

> 'In Rhodesia you were brainwashed, you mustn't mix with black people...we were just navvies really, but the way they spoke you were on a higher level...I'd been led to believe there weren't any professional coloured people.'

The attitudes of Rhodesian Coloureds towards whites were characterised by considerable ambivalence. On the one hand, Coloureds were proud of their white ancestry and distinguished themselves from the African population on the basis of their education and their adherence to English cultural mores. In the words of Mrs Naylor,

'We saw mixture as a good thing. To the Cape Coloureds, the African was just a servant, a nothing. The Eurafricans also gradually acquired these attitudes...We had few African friends – there were some, but there was always a barrier. If you have too many you become like them.'

Nevertheless, between white and Coloured, 'there was always friction'. Even Mrs Henderson, who came from the 'professional' stratum of the Coloured community, where interaction with whites was the norm 'in certain social fields', was all too keenly aware of being 'a second-class citizen in most respects'.

Personal relationships between white and Coloured were not uncommon – both the Naylors and the Hendersons first met through mutual friends – but it is not surprising that, in these circumstances, relations between white men and Coloured women tended to possess some element of mutual exploitation. According to Mrs Naylor, for a Coloured girl to marry a European was

'a means of getting out of the rut and into a better standard of living...a white man could give you a better home...if we were honest, money was a very important factor'.

White men in Rhodesia, however, were unlikely to marry Coloured girls; they 'gave illegitimate babies' instead. And if, like Mr Naylor and Mr Henderson, they did decide to marry, the conventions of racial hierarchy continued to operate: such men continued to move in a white social field, from which, of course, their wives were excluded.

The decision to enter into an interracial union had very different implications, for both partners, in the British context. Like Mr Naylor and Mr Henderson, a number of the black male respondents had migrated as single men, obliged, because of the dearth of women within the black population in the early years of post-war immigration, to seek their sexual partners within the host population. But, unlike white male migrants to Rhodesia, such men did not find themselves in a privileged position. As Mr Clough (WI) recalled of his time in the RAF,

'It became clear that in England it was almost impossible for a black man to find a woman who was his equal in mentality, in education...Some girls were quite frank and said to us it would "finish" them with a white man if they were seen with us...whenever we moved camp we used to find out whether there was a remand home nearby...because they were shut off from society they seemed to have more sympathy with us.'

Nevertheless, because there were so few black people resident in England at that time, outside the boundaries of the 'coloured quarters', Mr Clough, like other men in his position, did spend much of his time with white acquaintances; indeed, it was through one such friendship that he encountered his future wife.

At that time, before the arrival of substantial numbers of black migrants, West Indians and West Africans were exotic figures, inspiring considerable fear, hostility and curiosity. Mrs Horace, for example, born in outer south London in 1919, recalled growing up in 'a totally white world'; she could not 'remember seeing more than a glimpse of a coloured person before the War. People had very strange ideas about them – touching for luck and so on.' Mrs Curtis, also born in south London but some ten years younger, first encountered significant numbers of black people when she and her widowed mother moved to Streatham in 1956. There was a West Indian family in their street, but 'I had ideas about coloured people that made me hold back a little. Of course you only saw the worst side of things in Brixton.'

None of the English respondents who reached their fifteenth birthday before 1955 could recall any black children in their classes at school: of those whose fifteenth birthday fell between 1955 and 1964, three were brought up in areas with no significant black population and one, David Handbury, grew up in Brixton but was educated privately elsewhere. The three remaining all recalled one or two black children in school, but stated that they had been treated 'the same as everyone else'. 'But then there weren't so many of them then', as Mrs Rowlands remarked. Mrs Kalipha, brought up in Battersea, made the point more fully:

> 'You didn't see so many coloured people around then, it hadn't become a "problem", in inverted commas. We had just one Jamaican girl in our class...no one ever thought to abuse her like you see white children doing in the street today. Her parents came to speech days and everything, just like the rest.'

Compare this with the descriptions given by the two girls who left school in the late 1960s:

> 'Yeah, there were a lot of them but you never had nothing to do with them. We used to call them names – if anyone went around with them, we'd call them names too.'

> 'When I was smaller, I didn't really notice so much...but when I started going to [secondary school] my Mum told me to stay away from the coloured boys – she said they'd get me into trouble.'

Blacks were no longer exotic, if despised, individuals, but members of a local community which was the focus of considerable hostility. Yet to encounter black people, in school, at work, or casually in the streets and parks of the area was, by the 1960s, a normal and unexceptional part of life, and this is reflected in the range of situations in which these younger couples first encountered each other.

Some of these encounters appear, at least at first sight, to be entirely fortuitous. Mrs Oluwole, for example, first met her future husband when they got talking on the Underground; Mrs Brettle, like Mrs Ademola, met her present partner in a casual encounter in the street. The Jays first met in a large commercial dance hall, the Riches in a West End club, and Mr Gomez and Miss Mackie in a Brixton pub. Other encounters, in contrast, developed from the routines of everyday life. Four couples, the Horaces, the Birchalls, the Rowlandses, and Mr Lowe and Mrs Simmons first met at work. The Handburys met through their families' common involvement in a local church, while the Curtises met at evening class. The remaining eight couples met because they had friends or acquaintances in common.

In a minority of cases, the white partner was already moving in a black social field at the time of this first meeting. When Christine Kalipha, for example, met her future husband, in 1961, she was still at school. Her previous boy-friends had also been West Indians, some years older than herself. West Indian boys seemed 'a lot more grown up, treated you better...they had better manners and girls like that...they were nice to have as friends because they would talk to you, they weren't just after one thing'. Carole Rich, too, preferred West Indian boys; she had met her husband in a club specialising in reggae and Blue Beat music. Susan Pound and Janet Mackie were even further involved in this aspect of black life. Both had left home at an early age and survived by a mixture of petty crime, prostitution, and short-term relationships with men prepared to support them. Both were regular visitors to pubs and clubs that catered for a black clientele, and it was in such locations that they had met several of their previous partners. Mrs Birchall and Mrs Oluwole had also both had previous black boy-friends.

Not all the white respondents, however, could be said to have favourable or even neutral attitudes towards black people at the time of their meeting with their present partners. Mrs Jay, for example, described herself as 'prejudiced'; before meeting her husband, she had avoided all contacts with black people: 'I really hated them.' Others, like Mrs Curtis, shared in many of the negative attitudes towards black people commonly held by English people of her age and social background. However, all the white partners, with the exception of Mr Sidey, realised that to enter into this relationship was to confront hostility and the stigma of society; many also knew it would bring them more direct difficulties in the form of the disapproval of parents and kin. Similarly, the black partners involved also were aware of the social costs of an interracial relationship. What factors led them, then, to take this decision? Despite the diversity of circumstance which brought these couples together, certain recurring themes are apparent.

Demographic imperatives

A number of the older black respondents, like the two British emigrants to Rhodesia, had been obliged, for obvious demographic reasons, to find their sexual partners within the host population. Such relationships were often unsatisfactory; when stable relationships did develop, therefore, they exercised a powerful attraction for the isolated migrant. Mr Henderson (GB), for example, recalled that he met his future wife when, after he had complained that 'all the girls in Bulawayo were easy', some friends had introduced him to a 'nice Coloured girl'. Despite being the 'restless type', he was won over. Similarly, Mr Clough (WI) made it clear what had attracted him to his wife: '...she was not apologetic, not patronising...I liked how she kept herself.' However, 'I was not prepared for embarking on a permanent relationship at that time [1946]. My finances were not good enough...also I was enjoying my life with male companions.' Nevertheless, he was drawn back to his future wife: 'I was lonely, and that was a pretty big factor.'

Marginality: structural and cultural

Even more recent migrants, however, could find themselves unable to meet eligible partners from their own ethnic group, if they lacked access to the social fields in which unattached West Indian or West African women moved. It was noticeable, for example, that, in contrast to many endogamously married West Indian men in Brixton, these men had come to England as single migrants rather than as part of a compound, 'family' migration; they tended to have few kin in England, especially few immediate kin. Mr Collet, for example, came to England from St Lucia in 1961; his brother had paid his passage for him as Mr Collet was bringing over his brother's wife's young son. Between Mr Collet and his brother there was, however, no strong relationship. Their parents had died when Mr Collet was very young, and he had an unsettled childhood, being cared for by one relative after another. He never attended school with any regularity, and could neither read nor write. Both his brother, and a cousin and his family also resident in London, fared somewhat better. It was clear that in his first few months in England, Mr Collet was very lonely; speaking only broken English and with few kin to visit, he spent most of his time in the multi-occupied house in which his brother had found him a room. It was here that he met his future wife.

Many of the black respondents, like Mr Collet, were the products of what would, in English terms, be called disrupted childhoods, marked by the death or desertion of one or both parents. Nine had spent significant portions of their childhoods as 'outside children' in the homes of kin or friends. While such arrangements could be happy – and were certainly not uncommon in the cultures from which these individuals came – they were often insecure. Mrs Henderson (RC) and Mr Oluwole (Y) both had, on their own account, difficult relationships with the step-parents responsible for their welfare; Mr Jay (WI), like Mr Collet (WI) had been orphaned in early childhood and brought up by a succession of relatives, none of whom particularly wanted him; Mr Horace (Y) and Mr Clough (WI), both of whom lost their fathers in childhood, had spent significant portions of their childhood in the care of absolute strangers.

The impact of such experiences was twofold. Firstly, and most obviously, even where such experiences were not regarded as especially unhappy, they served to detach the individual concerned from his family of origin and from his kin. For such individuals, migration was not entirely fortuitous; the decision to leave home often reflected an already weakened bond between the individual and his primary community.

Mr Lowe, for example, born in Guyana in 1924, left in 1942 and joined the British armed forces. He had never returned and had no intention of doing so in the future. His mother died at his birth and he was raised by a paternal aunt and her husband as their only child; they taught him to be self-sufficient and to manage for himself. Although his father remarried and there were eleven other children, Mr Lowe did not see much of them during his childhood. By 1971, at the time of interview, they were scattered across the world, some in Guyana, some in the United States, one brother in England. In several respects, Mr Lowe was the 'odd man out' in his family: he was very dark, for example, and all but two of his siblings were very fair, and married fair people. Although he was the first of his family to migrate, he had been less successful than the rest; one brother had qualified as a doctor, another as an accountant, another was proprietor of a chain of laundries in America, while his sisters worked as secretaries and nurses. He certainly kept in touch with his extensive family, largely through the good offices of his accountant brother who lived in Streatham, but contact was limited to Christmas visiting and big family reunions. Kin played no very large part in Mr Lowe's life.

For the more reflective individuals among these respondents, such experiences also served to alienate them from the values and orientations of their natal culture, especially those which concerned family and domestic life. Mr Oluwole, for example, left Nigeria for England in 1962. He came without any qualifications, intending to study, although he had little idea of what this entailed; but he also wanted 'to get away from my family. Things were getting very sour.' He described his childhood as an 'unhappy time'. His mother had been the second – and hence junior – wife of an important man. After continuous marital discord, his parents had separated when he was three, and his mother, who kept her two children with her, was then obliged to rely on what help her kin would give her. When he was ten, Mr Oluwole went to live with his father, still married to his senior wife, and their children. His position as 'outside child' was made worse by his physical inferiority and mental superiority to his half-brothers and sisters, and by the quarrels over his father's successive junior wives that continued to dominate the household. 'My background was not full of love. I can't trust people...in my father's household I learnt to keep my thoughts to myself.' These experiences left him with a strong dislike of polygyny, as of several other aspects of Yoruba culture, including the outlook of Yoruba women. This sense of detachment, Mr Oluwole was at pains to point out, was not the result of his marriage:

> 'I had detached myself from my background for some time before we met, I did not come with my background intact...I am not a typical Yoruba man, I am not a typical anything. At home I was always being accused, "you're too European!"'

For such individuals, the choice of a partner from outside their own ethnic group could be seen as a reflection of their personal situation of marginality, a choice which reinforced, but did not produce, their sense of detachment.

A natural decision

For others among the black respondents, however, the choice of a partner from outside their own ethnic group was not so much an aspect of personal alienation, or even a question of necessity, but a reflection of the values of their segment of society. Within Rhodesian Coloured society, as we have indicated above, racial mixture was viewed as 'a good thing'; similarly, several of the West Indian members of the research set – including both the women – came from ethnically mixed families, and from a segment of Caribbean society where a strong positive orientation towards English culture and mores was widespread.

Lorraine Handbury, for example, the oldest of seven children, arrived in England when she was fourteen. Her father, an electrical engineer, had been sent abroad for further training on a Trinidad Government scholarship, brought his family over to England, and decided to stay on. In 1971 he was working as a qualified electrical engineer, while his wife worked as a librarian. Both parents had always been anxious to get on in the world; the rest of their family in Trinidad, according to Lorraine, 'couldn't keep up'. Contacts with relatives were strictly limited, and the children carefully brought up: 'at home we were never allowed to speak badly or use patois at all'. And, 'although colour was never mentioned, you noticed that the children you were told not to play with were usually black'. Lorraine herself, like the rest of her family, was light-skinned. In England, her parents 'had a lot of white friends, more white than coloured. They were forward-looking people...not like most West Indians who just pull each other down. They didn't want to associate with them.' Lorraine's friends too were usually white. It is hardly surprising that she, like her only other married sibling, should have chosen a white spouse; as she herself remarked, 'Mixed marriages are nothing new in our family; we've been mixing for generations.'

Janis Sidey, too, had been encouraged by her parents to develop friendships with whites. Her Chinese businessman father had sent her to an expensive Jamaican boarding school where 'we all mixed in'. Her father wanted her to marry and settle down in Jamaica, which Mrs Sidey described disparagingly as 'a narrow-minded society', in which 'everyone moved in his own little circle'. She, however, 'could never see myself married to a Chinese boy. But I always had a soft spot for the English.'

Status and security

For women such as Mrs Sidey, to marry an Englishman was undoubtedly to marry well. Nevertheless, this was not a straightforward matter, determined entirely by ethnicity. Mrs Henderson, for example, recalled that, in Rhodesian Coloured society, men in semi-skilled occupations, like her husband, 'were not classed as eligible for the better class of Coloured person... people were very hostile... with time they realised – well, that he wasn't illiterate'. Social life did, however, present its difficulties. Mr Henderson felt awkward with his wife's well-educated acquaintances, while with *his* friends, who tended to be 'patronising' on the grounds of his wife's colour, there were further difficulties because the wives 'were not her social level'.

With few exceptions, both black and white respondents made it clear that they recognised that, in the eyes of the white Brixton population and of English society at large, theirs was not a union of racial equals. As Mr Curtis remarked of his wife: 'she took a drop in social standing when she married me. To most people she has married beneath her.' It was unsurprising, therefore, to find that a number of white respondents placed considerable emphasis, in their presentation of their partner's character, on aspects of their social identity – educational attainments and professional standing – which might be said to 'neutralise' a stigmatised ethnicity. Mrs Ademola (I), for example, was proud of her husband's education:

> 'My sister told me I was marrying beneath me and bringing disgrace on the family but I don't see it like that. I am beneath *him* in education, he is an educated person and, really, to tell the truth I am not, and my sisters aren't although they have all done well in their marriages... he comes from a good respectable family.'

'Respectability' could, indeed, help to allay the anxieties of kin. Mrs Birchall (GB), for example, recalled that her parents 'eased up quite a lot' when her husband-to-be left his clerical post for an administrative job that carried some public prestige. 'It reassured them, and at that time it reassured me. You did want to point out that he was different to the picture people had of coloured people.'

In a minority of cases, most notably those of the Curtises, the Hendersons, the Naylors and the Horaces, there were very real differ-

Table 5.5. *Research couples: socio-economic grade and level of educational attainment at time of first meeting*

	Male partner	Female partner	Compensatory pairings
Abbott–Pound	D/4	(E)/4	
Ademola	sA/2	C2(B)/4	CP
Birchall	C1/2	C1(B)/4	
Clough	C2/4	C2(C2)/4	
Collett	E/5	E(E)/4	
Curtis	C1/3	C1(C1)/4	CP (slight)
Gomez–Mackie	E/4	E(E)/4	
Handbury	B/1	C1(B)/4	
Henderson	D/4	B(B)/2	CP
Homer–Brettle	E/5	E(D)/4	
Horace	B/2	C1(C1)/4	CP
Jay	E/4	C2(C2)/4	
Kalipha	C2/4	(C2)/4	
Lowe–Simmons	C1/4	E(B)/4	
Naylor	D/4	C2(B)/3	CP
Ojo	E/3	E/4	CP (slight)
Oluwole	C1/3	B(A)/1	
Rich	D/4	E(E)/4	
Rowlands	E/4	E(E)/4	
Sidey	A/1	C1(A)/4	

Socio-economic grade assessed by criteria for social classification used by Research Services Limited. Occupation of female partner's father placed in parentheses after her own; where male partner a student at time of first meeting, indicated by s preceding projected occupation at that time.
Level of educational attainment:
5: functionally illiterate
4: basic education only
3: basic education plus either technical qualifications or O-level passes
2: education to A-level standard/vocational training qualifications
1: university degree or its equivalent

ences, in terms of socio-economic status, between the black and white partners (see Table 5.5). There was, however, a noticeable tendency for the white respondents to exaggerate the extent of such differences. In several cases where, in objective terms, the partners' educational level and level of socio-economic status were equivalent, or even weighted in favour of the white partner, the black partners' aspirations and intentions led their partners to regard them as their social and intellectual betters. Thus, Mr Clough (WI), Mr Ademola (Y) and Mr Ojo (Y) were all failed students without significant qualifications, but their respective wives still clearly thought of them as their educational superiors. Similarly, Mr Oluwole (Y) was still, almost ten years after his arrival in England, in the process of studying for professional qualifications part time, while working by day at a relatively humble clerical job; nevertheless, in the eyes of his wife, a teacher, he was her social equal.

To emphasise the black partner's achievements in those fields of endeavour to which social approval is, in general, awarded, should be seen both as an effective strategy to counteract stereotyped views of black inferiority and as a justification, on the part of the white respondent, of the decision to enter into a socially stigmatised relationship. How far this may be taken to reflect, in addition, an individual's *past* motivation is a point impossible to establish, although in some cases it seemed reasonable for me to make this assumption. Mrs Horace (GB), for example, was the second of four children. Family circumstances had obliged her to leave school at fourteen, despite promising academic achievements, and to take a job as a shop assistant.

> 'I wasn't keen on marriage at all. I had plenty of boy-friends, but none of them were serious – I didn't feel any of them were what I was looking for, none of them had prospects, they were just good fun and that was that. One or two of them had money but that was all they had. I wasn't that interested.'

When she met Mr Horace, however, she felt that he was, 'a cut above the rest. That interested me.'

The marriages of the Horaces, and possibly the Curtises, the Hendersons and the Naylors, could thus perhaps be described, in Merton's terms, as 'reciprocal compensatory pairings', in which the black partner's high socio-economic status rendered him, or her, an attractive partner despite a stigmatised ethnic identity. For most couples, however, as we have seen, objective status differences were insignificant; indeed, in many cases, the black partner appeared to have little to offer an individual concerned with the calculation of marital advantage. Two men, Mr Collet and Mr Homer (both WI), were illiterate and thus able to seek only a restricted range of employment; others had only very limited industrial skills. Discrimination in the labour market further restricted their chances; in the words of one English wife, 'There's no denying that an English husband would be able to give you a better job.' Why, then, were these women prepared to enter into a relationship which, at first sight, had so little to offer?

A striking feature of many of the personal histories of the white respondents in the research set was the extent to which they themselves were socially disadvantaged. Mrs Rowlands, for example, had attended a school for the educationally subnormal, and was very conscious of her need for help in dealing with some aspects of everyday life. Mrs Ojo, Mrs Brettle and Mrs Simmons were women coping with the aftermath of a failed marriage; all three were in financial difficulties, and two had dependent children to support. Mrs Collet was to find herself in a similar position when, shortly after her first meeting with her future husband, her common-law partner was sent to prison, leaving her to cope singlehanded with their three children. Janet Mackie, too, had an illegitimate child to support, and both she and Susan Pound had criminal records and histories of violence and prostitution. Such women, lacking the skills and resources that make female independence possible, were the casualties of a social system in which women expect, and are expected, to depend upon men for their financial and emotional security. The social stigma attached to divorced women, those with illegitimate children and those whose sexual and personal morality fails to conform to accepted standards – even where not compounded, as in some cases, by personal inadequacies – left such women both socially isolated and economically vulnerable. The immediate effect of the situation in which such women found themselves was to create a pressing need for a partner with whom some of these social burdens could be shared. This, however, was not simply a need for practical assistance – although in some cases this was, indeed, a matter of urgency – but was also a need for companionship and support in the emotional and social isolation which resulted from their position. Under such circumstances women were prepared to enter into relationships which, otherwise, they may well have rejected as socially disadvantageous.

Kathleen Ojo, for example, was born in 1935 and grew up in Peckham, the fifth of six children of a poor family. Her father, a private soldier, had been absent during much of her early childhood and then was 'invalided out' at the end of the Second World War; her mother – whose family were described by Kathleen as of a 'higher social class' and had little to do with her after her marriage – had to struggle hard to keep her family 'respectable'. Money was 'very short indeed' and accommodation cramped. Kathleen, like her sisters, married young; she was pregnant at the time. The marriage, however, was not a success. This first child died in early childhood , and in 1960 her husband 'walked out', leaving Kathleen to bring up their second daughter, Rosanne. Despite her mother's help, Kathleen found it hard to manage on her own; she had little money, and was obliged to return to work to make ends meet. The 'backbiting and nastiness' of some of her neighbours was an additional strain; after an attempt at suicide, she moved away, into a smaller and cheaper council flat, which meant that her daughter spent the weeks with her grandmother, and Kathleen only saw her at weekends.

It was at this time that she met her second husband. Her mother 'minded' small children, and Kathleen had struck up a friendship with the mother of one of these, Mr Ojo's sister. Several times, over a period of about a year, Mr Ojo phoned her mother's house to ask Kathleen out, but despite her mother's encouragement she 'thought of Rosanne' and refused. One weekend, however, when she and her daughter were stuck in her tiny flat with not enough money to go out, or even to buy something for a decent Sunday tea, she decided to phone him; he came round right away, and after than 'gradually it drifted...he did fascinate me'.

Like Mrs Ojo, for Mrs Brettle, Mrs Collet and Mrs Simmons, and, to a lesser extent for Mrs Rolands (all GB), the relationship with their present partner seemed to offer an escape from the exigencies of their position, and the possibility of achieving some measure of personal security. Expediency, rather than any interest in West Indian or West African culture or commitment to a black social world, determined their decision. This, however, was not necessarily the case among all the white respondents.

Marginality and rebellion

I have already indicated how, among the black respondents, a sense of detachment from their primary communities and of alienation from their cultures of origin could be linked to the experience of family disruption in childhood. Among a minority of the white respondents, too, similar disruption could be found. Janet Mackie, herself an illegitimate child, had been brought up largely in institutions; Susan Pound and Carole Rich were both products of 'broken homes', where the mother's remarriage had created considerable tension within the household; Mrs Horace and Mr Naylor had both lost parents in childhood. Mrs Birchall and Mr Handbury were both adopted children, while Mrs Ojo and Mrs Oluwole, because of the Second World War, had spent substantial portions of their childhood away from their families.

Such experiences often served, as among the black respondents, to detach the individuals concerned from family and kin. There were, however, less straightforward considerations which played their part in the decision to enter into an interracial relationship.

While for some respondents, like Mrs Oluwole (GB), relations with their black partner developed in a period when the individual concerned was already emancipated from the racial attitudes generally held by English people, there was evidence that, for others, association with black partners acted as a focus for rebellion against social convention, and was regarded as daring and exciting. In some cases, black culture was seen in romantic terms as 'more natural' or 'less restricted' than the English way of life. Mrs Birchall, for example, an adopted only child, had grown up in a peaceful suburb, once an autonomous village, on the outskirts of south London. Her father worked for the Post Office, and had worked his way up to a responsible executive position; her parents were active members of the local community, who, through careful management of their resources, had built up a solid, if not exceptional, economic security. Their daughter, however, in the terms of this rather narrow social world, was a failure. She was a messy and untidy child who suffered from asthma and did poorly in school; her adolescence was a period of frenetic socialising, repeated changes of job, and bouts of depression. Mrs Birchall did not make any explicit criticisms of the world in which she grew up. Nevertheless, it was clear, from her comments on Brixton and the people who lived there, that for her West Indian culture represented a degree of freedom from the conventions which ordered her parents' lives, and which – they had hoped – would order hers.

Other respondents, however, were not very interested in the characteristics of West Indian or West African culture. Rather, they seemed to be reacting against the prejudices of individuals or instututions from whose authority and control they were attempting to free themselves. For Janet Mackie and for Susan Pound, whose personal careers included periods in remand homes, informal and formal prostitution, as well as many acts of petty violence, association with black men was undoubtedly a political act, an aspect of a wider rejection of the values and goals of mainstream society, as well as a pragmatic response to personal insecurity. Then, there were the cases of Mrs Jay and Mrs Rich, whose parents were described as 'very prejudiced', as well as that of Mrs Simmons, whose estranged husband had, in fact, taken her to live in South Africa because of his racial attitudes: 'He could never even stand to see a black man and woman holding hands in the street, let alone a mixed couple.'

Interpretation of such data is a delicate matter. Mr Handbury, for example, another adopted only child, was, by his own account, devoted to his parents, and 'never went through a rebellious stage'. His father was an unsuccessful shopkeeper; his mother, who had 'married beneath her', resented her husband's failure and invested her considerable emotional energies in charitable works for her local church – concerned, for the most part, with West Indians in need – and in her son. He was sent to a local private school, then went on to university, but never left home; he described his parents as 'very powerful people...they only had me to bother with and I got the full weight of it'. His mother disapproved strongly of his first girl-friend, an English girl, whom she saw as her son's social inferior. She attempted to divert his attention from this girl by urging him to 'be kind' to a West Indian girl whose family she had met in church – his future wife – by taking her to the theatre. She was, however, 'horrified' when he announced his intention of marrying her; West Indians were the appropriate recipients of charity, not suitable partners for marriage. For Mr Handbury, his behaviour was explicable entirely in romantic terms; I would suggest, though, that other, albeit unacknowledged, considerations played their part. Significantly, Mr Handbury, like the other individuals discussed above, had enjoyed no friendly relations with black individuals of his own sex before meeting with his present partner; for these respondents, involvement in an interracial union did not develop naturally from the texture of everyday life, but represented a breaking of a pattern of avoidance.

Concluding remarks

From the foregoing, it is evident that, given initial contact, a variety of factors – demographic, social and psychological – operated to facilitate the interracial unions discussed above. Only rarely can we speak of individuals free from the prejudices and preconceptions which shape attitudes towards members of other races; far from indicating emancipation from the racial attitudes of the wider society, such relationships reflect, only too clearly, a structure imposed by the system of race relations of which they form a part.

Firstly, there were a number of couples, seven in all, whose relationship conformed very closely to those described in the studies made of the 'coloured quarters' of English cities in the 1940s and 1950s. Here, the men were, for the most part, proletarian West Indians with poor social resources, who had failed, or who did not wish, to acquire a mate from their own ethnic group. Their partners were women whose backgrounds sometimes, but not always, combined effective social disadvantage with a history of deprivation, rejection, and rebellion. For some, the very stigma attached to such relationships made them an appropriate focus of rebellion; there were, however, more practical considerations in such choices, and such relationships often had in them a strong element of expediency, on both sides. Nevertheless, the disadvantaged position shared by the white partners in this category masked a variety of personal differences which we might expect to have significance in their future conjugal lives. On the one hand, there were those who had found themselves in a socially marginal position through, in the terminology of popular morality, 'no fault of their own' – through the accidents of personal circumstance. But there were others who had more complex problems, as was apparent from their personal histories.

The second group concerned couples slightly higher in social status, and conformed to Merton's category of 'reciprocal compensatory pairings'; these involved black men of higher socio-economic or educational status than their white partners. Here, it was the black partner who was detached from the mainstream of his ethnic group by virtue of his aspirations or life-style, a detachment often reinforced by social isolation. However, it should be pointed out that, as in the first category, both partners often tended towards social marginality. In this category, perhaps, could be placed the two Anglo-Rhodesian Coloured unions, although it should be borne in mind that the context within which these relationships evolved was very different from that of England.

Concluding remarks

There remain six relationships in which personal and psychological imperatives were dominant, although these included two couples, the Handburys and the Sideys, where the black partner came from that stratum of West Indian society in which marriage to a white or light-skinned partner was a desirable goal. As I have tried to indicate above, however, these imperatives cannot be understood, for the most part, outside the complex of attitudes respecting colour, sex and ethnicity which are dominant in the wider society. In this, as in so many other aspects of their lives, these interracial couples were not so much flouters of social convention, as the exceptions which prove, and reflect, the racial rules of English society at large.

6 Coping with opposition: the reactions of family and friends

Family and kin

I have noted that some members of the research set had already drifted apart from their families of origin at the time of their meeting with their present partner; indeed, it has been suggested that in several cases this played some part in their decision to enter into what was, in the eyes of others, a socially stigmatised relationship. Nevertheless, only six respondents, three white and three black, all living in common-law unions, did not inform their kin of their union (see Table 6.1). The attitude of the black respondents in this category, all West Indians, may be summed up in the words of one of them, Mr Homer: 'I was born and grow in Jamaica, I have family in Jamaica, but them and me is strangers now...I have thought about writing a letter, but it is no good poking a dead fire, ennit?' Of the white respondents, only one, Mrs Brettle, did not tell her family for fear of their reaction; for Janet Mackie and Susan Pound, family reaction was a matter of complete indifference to them. These however, were the exceptions; for most individuals, the approval of their families, no matter how remote, was important to them, and they often went to considerable lengths to secure family approbation.

On the whole, the families of the black respondents reacted favourably to the news, although in a minority of cases there were objections, based upon stereotyped notions of the kind of white person likely to become sexually involved with a black man or woman. Mrs Naylor (RC), for example, recalled that, when she began bringing her future husband home, her parents were 'dubious' about the relationship, for at that time (1950), 'there were plenty of illegitimate babies from whites...whites didn't *marry* Coloured girls...at first, they asked themselves: "Is he playing the fool?" but then they realised he really did want to marry me'. Mr Rich's (WI) kin were even more dubious about his relationship with Carole.

> 'At first me Auntie didn't like it at all. She told me I should stop messing about with white girls because it was only the bad white girls would go with a coloured man. Then Carole get thrown out of the house and the baby come...and she soften up a lot.'

Table 6.1. *Reaction of respondents' families of origin*

Reaction	Black partner	White partner
Immediate acceptance by all immediate family	Ademola Clough Birchall Collet Curtis Handbury Henderson Horace Jay Kalipha Lowe Ojo Sidey	Collet [Simmons] Sidey Rowlands Naylor
Immediate acceptance by most immediate family/ostracism by sibling		Clough Ojo
Initial opposition, then acceptance	Naylor Oluwole Rich Rowlands	Birchall Curtis Handbury Henderson Horace Jay
Period of total ostracism, then reconciliation		Oluwole
Permanent ostracism		Rich Ademola
Kin not informed	Abbott Gomez Homer	Pound Mackie Brettle

Name in brackets indicates a case where only partial information was supplied to kin.

Mr Oluwole pointed out that similar stereotypes were current among Nigerians: 'My last night in Lagos they [his kin] took one hour advising me not to marry a white woman.' He added, in explanation, that 'There had been examples of very bad women who had [married Nigerians and] come to Nigeria, who became promiscuous openly so that everyone saw

Table 6.2. *White respondents' involvement with kin at time of first meeting*

White partners	Co-resident with kin	Financially/ practically dependent on kin	Extensive social contact with kin
Abbott–Pound			
Ademola	X	X	X
Birchall			X
Clough	X	X	X
Collet			
Curtis	X		X
Gomez–Mackie			
Handbury*	X		X
Henderson*			
Homer–Brettle			
Horace	X		X
Jay	X	X	X
Kalipha	X	X	X
Lowe–Simmons			
Naylor*			
Ojo		X	X
Oluwole			X
Rich	X	X	X
Rowlands	X	X	X
Sidey*			

* Indicates cases where male partners were white.

it.' Nigerians were also critical of such women's 'manners to their mothers-in-law...they were very rude'. Not surprisingly, he felt, his mother's first reaction to the news of his impending marriage was 'a simple "Don't"'. However, after further letters from her son, and one from his intended wife's parents – who had themselves, for a long time, been opposed to the match – she replied to say that she had been praying to God to make her son change his mind if the match were unsuitable, and, since he was still determined, she must take this as a sign of 'God's will'.

The reaction of the kin of the white partners tended to be much less favourable; of the seventeen respondents who informed their families, only six gained immediate support and approval. Others faced, from all or a number of their kin, either an initial period of opposition and hostility, or long-term rejection. There were, of course, a small number of cases in which the circumstances in which kin were informed were enough, in themselves, to provoke a hostile reaction. Both Mrs Jay and

Mrs Rich, for example, only told their parents of their relationship when they found they were pregnant. Undoubtedly, however, most hostile reactions were rooted in prejudice. Thus, family attitudes often shifted quite noticeably when it became clear that the relationship in question was not simply friendship, but 'something serious', and parents and siblings were forced to come to terms with the permanence of what they regarded as an unpleasant situation. Judith Oluwole, for example, had taken Paul Oluwole to meet her parents, who 'were very hospitable, as they would have been to anybody'. But when he became a regular visitor, 'the penny dropped and they were really upset'. 'My father is... a cosmopolitan person. In his view, the sooner the world is shades of brown the better. This was all very well until it was me.' Similarly, Mrs Birchall remarked, 'You know how parents are – all very liberal if they are talking about other people – but when *their* daughter wants to marry a coloured man...'

Family opposition crystallised around a number of issues. There was, undoubtedly, an element of practical concern in the objections of several parents, all of whom were keenly aware of the difficulties their offspring were likely to encounter as the spouse of a 'coloured' person. As Mrs Oluwole remarked, 'They were full of fear for me because I didn't know what I was doing.' Her parents also insisted that she could never have children, because of the problems these would face. Seven other families also made this point, two of them on eugenic grounds. 'My Mum was bad but he [her step-father] was worse,' recalled Mrs Rich; 'he carried on as how I was a race traitor, he called me some filthy names, I can tell you, then he started on about the baby, he said it shouldn't be allowed to live. Then he threw me out of the house.'

On the whole, however, objections centred on the conjectural unsuitability of black people as spouses for whites. Some of these unfavourable attitudes, especially among kin born before the First World War, were rooted in 'colonial' prejudices against Negro 'savages', reinforced by the way in which black people were presented in the European and American communications media. Mr Henderson, for example, remembered that when he wrote to his family, his father, who 'had travelled' and 'knew the world', said nothing, but his mother was 'very shocked'. She wrote saying that she hoped his future wife was 'not one of those black girls you see in the pictures'; when she heard that she was 'a professional woman' she was reassured. 'She didn't know what to expect', commented Mr Henderson, 'she thought I was marrying some Zulu woman done up in beads.' Mr Horace (Y) recalled being asked if he wore clothes in Africa and if he lived up a tree; 'like Tarzan', he remarked ironically. Other slightly more sophisticated objections in similar vein were that Africans were 'not mature', that black people were 'naturally cruel', and that they were 'civilised only skin deep'.

The unfavourable attitudes of others were drawn from the stereotyped image of the 'immigrant'; several families were concerned with the black partner's level of education, his 'home standards' and his moral character. 'Mother was rather hostile at first', recalled Mrs Curtis, 'she was worried about what the neighbours would think – and she did get one or two nasty remarks... she had all the usual ideas to begin with, but she could see that Warren wasn't the average Jamaican you get in Brixton.' As in the Hendersons' case, or that of the Birchalls, kin could often be reassured by personal contact with the black partner, or by information respecting his, or her, educational or professional qualifications. Such shifts in attitude did not, however, necessarily mean the disappearance of prejudice altogether. One of Mrs Ojo's brothers, for example, together with his wife, was 'shocked at first' when he heard of her plans for marriage. However, 'once they'd met Ade [her future husband] they changed their minds'. Now, 'they don't count Ade as coloured' but they still 'don't like other coloured people'. This kind of solution to the problems of cognitive dissonance was one which some black partners could tolerate more easily than others.

To separate the black partner from the mass of 'coloured' people was, of course, one strategy for dealing with the family's anxiety about loss of status in the eyes of friends and neighbours. Indeed, in six cases hostile family members asked variations on the question 'What will the neighbours say?' and emphasised the 'disgrace' that such a relationship brought upon them.

The impact of family hostility upon the couple concerned varied with the degree of each individual's involvement, both practical and emotional, with the family of origin. At the time of first meeting, all but two of the black respondents and twelve of the white respondents were independent of their families in practical terms, while a substantial minority had only low-intensity relations with their kin, or did not see them at all (see Table 6.2). Rejection by kin, and especially by parents, was nevertheless distressing for most: as one woman put it, 'you like to feel you have your family's goodwill behind you even if you never see them'.

Such sentiments could operate both ways, for while children are certainly bound emotionally to their parents, parents are tied, equally strongly, to their children. In all but two cases, parents eventually abandoned their attempts to bully their children out of their decision when they realised that the end result would be complete loss of contact. Judith Oluwole (GB), for example, had not seen or spoken to her parents for a year when she rang up to tell them that she and Paul were getting married and to ask them to come to the wedding. Her father's first reaction was to 'burst into tears'. But, a couple of days later, her parents rang up to say that 'we've had a talk and we've decided that the only people we are punishing are ourselves – we are losing our darling daughter and our grandchildren. So we want to come to the wedding and we'll pay for it.' By contrast, where kin were prepared permanently to ostracise an individual after the decision to enter into an interracial union, relations were usually already poor. Thus, the decision to enter into an interracial union tended to be a symptom of, and a contributing factor to, the breakdown of relations between an individual and his or her kin, rather than its original cause.

Friends and acquaintances

On the whole, the reactions of friends were not felt, by the respondents, to be of the same significance as the reactions of kin. A number had only a few friends in any case; others had friends who were, themselves, already involved with black people. Only one individual, Mrs Clough (GB), reported losing most of her friends and suffering significant changes in her social life, and she married in the 1940s, in the narrow social world of lower middle-class south London. Others, certainly, suspected that certain acquaintances did 'drift away', as one woman put it, 'as if there was a bad smell under their noses'. Most friends, however, like many kin, accepted the black partner as 'not really coloured', and, therefore, not to be rejected, although, as in so many other fields, the situation of the Anglo-Rhodesian Coloured couples was different; there, public segregation was the norm and private relations difficult.

The wider community

From the evidence of the couples studied here it appears that, in England, public attitudes towards interracial couples have grown more tolerant over time. In contrast to those whose first meeting with their partner dated back to the 1940s and 1950s, couples whose relationships were more recently established reported few unpleasant incidents in the street. Those that did occur were usually directed at the white woman concerned. 'I can only remember three occasions,' remarked Mrs Birchall (GB), 'and never with a sober man.' Insults usually concerned the kind of woman who 'went with blacks'; English men married to West Indian women reported no problems.

That such negative attitudes were not necessarily limited to whites was indicated by several of the black respondents. Remarked Mr Clough (WI):

> 'The Negro...is brainwashed into believing that it is only white trash that will associate with him. So he thinks that a white woman who goes with him will go with all his friends as well. A Negro will always make a pass at a white woman married to a Negro...because he thinks she is that sort of woman.'

Another West Indian respondent recalled how a friend had told him that, 'people were very upset that I had decided to go with "white rubbish" instead of finding a nice black girl'.

In some cases, the couple's developing relationship was subject to the scrutiny and comments of workmates. Mrs Rowlands (GB) remembered that, in the factory where both she and her future husband worked, 'most of the people were all right, the West Indian girls were very nice about it, but some of the others – there was one English woman there who kept on and on, I don't see why Ellen goes out with him'. Mrs Birchall met with a stronger reaction. Both she and her future husband were working for the same community organisation which catered for the needs of an ethnically mixed local population. The English organiser had previously expressed her disapproval at what she had taken to be Mrs Birchall's 'involvement' with a Jamaican musician, and was 'furious' when she discovered that she and Rex Birchall were going out together. 'That was the last straw...she went to Rex and told him what kind of girl she thought I was.' Mrs Birchall was also asked to leave her job.

Again, it should be noted that it was the white woman, not the black partner, in these relationships who encountered social disapproval. Similarly, it was only white women who reported hostility from neighbours, usually expressed covertly in withdrawal from friendly social interaction, or sometimes indirectly, through unfavourable comments to kin. Mrs Rowlands (GB) was still living at home when she met her future husband; during their courtship, he often used to come home for meals,

> 'But the people in the Flats didn't like it. Of course in those days [1962] it was quite unusual to see coloured people in the Flats, and when I took Josh home some of them got a bit nasty...there was one woman lived downstairs who wouldn't talk to me...Of course my Mum got it worse – there were lots of little niggles, but she's like me, not the kind to notice. It's all blown over now.'

Such hostility did, indeed, usually 'blow over'; yet it could only serve to increase the sense of difference felt by most interracial couples, and, especially, by the white female respondents. It was upon them that the full weight of familial and social disapproval fell, and, because of the importance of kin, neighbours and friends in the management of the domestic domain, it was they who suffered most from the withdrawal of external support.

Of these twenty households, six found themselves without immediate kin on whom they could call for help and with whom they could spend their leisure time. All but one household, the Riches, who had found an alternative network of support through the secondary kin of the black partner, felt the lack of kin support most strongly. Practical problems deriving from the lack of human resources were especially acute in poorer families who were obliged to rely heavily upon state agencies to meet their basic needs; these were the respondents, for example, who said that their children would have to go into care if the female partner fell ill, or was in hospital for the birth of a baby. Where marital solidarity was high, couples were able to cope with the burdens imposed by isolation; but where the conjugal relationship was, of itself, fragile, the kinless households were especially vulnerable to external crises and internal problems. Undoubtedly, in some cases, the vulnerability of such households led individuals to think in terms of abandoning a difficult situation. On the other hand, the isolation in which such households found themselves in times of stress often led to a strong, if resented, sense of dependency. There was, for example, an association within the research set between long-term common-law unions, in which women found themselves dependent upon optional male support, and cases where the white partner, in each case female, was alienated from her family of origin.

Most households, however, were able to maintain some kind of contact with their kin. In some cases, this reflected a real sense of affection and interest; in others, a sense of duty or of self-interest led individuals to bury their differences and construct a pattern of carefully managed social interaction. These relationships are discussed more fully in Chapter 8 below. Whatever the quality of kin relationships, however, the existence of a network of kin acted to anchor the interracial household in 'normal' social life, and to reduce the sense of difference felt by many individuals in the research set.

7   The construction of a domestic world

This chapter is concerned with what has been termed 'the private sphere of existence' (Berger & Kellner, 1964), the domestic domain within which couples seek to construct a satisfying and viable personal world. Although not all the couples in the research set were legally married, they all accepted the existence of certain 'conjugal' rights and duties towards each other; and the establishment of a common household under one roof indicated a willingness, on the part of both partners, to pool their social resources and construct some kind of life together – a process of accommodation and adaptation which, for some couples, appeared easy and, for others, difficult or even impossible. On one level, this process concerned straightforward, pragmatic choices as to how domestic life should be organised. On a second level, however, it concerned the social construction of a shared domestic reality, and the attempt – not always successful – to realise, within the conjugal relationship, the expectations which each partner had of the other.

All these couples acknowledged that, as interracial couples whose cultural backgrounds tended to be very different, they were likely to face particular problems in the construction of a life together. Individuals varied a good deal, however, in their sensitivity to the issues involved. Compare, for example, these two very different responses given, in the absence of the other spouse, by British women married to Yoruba men:

> 'Well, there was the food – I had to learn that. I suppose he has got one or two funny ways, but I can't really say I think about it. He's a good husband and that's enough for me.' (Mrs Ademola (I))

> 'I've not been to Africa, I've never seen him in his own context. I know he's not typical. People who uproot themselves aren't typical...he must have adapted a tremendous amount, but I only see the ways in which he hasn't adapted...he's terribly forthright, rude really – he never opens doors for me or carries a parcel, he's very firm about "I am the man and you're the woman" although he won't treat me as a second-class citizen...We have many different assumptions but I don't think it's all cultural. We're both very awkward people.' (Mrs Oluwole (GB))

For some individuals, as I have already indicated, the decision to enter into an interracial relationship was taken *faute de mieux*. Many such respondents, poorly educated and with limited experience of the world around them, had only the vaguest notions of cultures other than their own and of the difficulties they might face. For others, the dynamic of their relationship was such that they gave little serious consideration to the problems of adjustment that would follow.

Mrs Jay (GB), for example, herself pointed out that at the time when she met her future husband, she 'really hated' black people. Yet she was strongly attracted to him, and married him despite the hostility of her family. Once married, however, and with two small children to care for, 'we began to drift apart...we basically had nothing in common apart from the sex thing, and once that all died down there was nothing else'. Neither partner showed much sensitivity to the other's needs. There was friction over money and over leisure time; Mr Jay (WI) expected to continue in an independent social life centred on clubs, pubs and parties, while his wife expected him to spend time at home with her. Yet, as Mrs Jay herself remarked, 'On reflection I probably didn't help much.' She would not cook West Indian food, and refused to accompany her husband to West Indian parties or clubs: 'I just didn't like the atmosphere.' After five years of marriage, the couple separated. Reviewing her past, Mrs Jay asserted that

> 'I'd never even go out with another West Indian bloke, let alone marry one...I'd want a bloke that was going to be a real husband to me, not just going out all the time...I can manage better on my own.'

She felt very strongly that 'They *are* different. It's just a different way of life and I couldn't get on with it.'

The Jays were an extreme case in their absolute failure to find any kind of common ground within their relationship, but the problems of accommodation and adjustment that defeated them were faced to a greater or lesser extent by all these couples. Two factors were important in this respect: the expectations which each partner brought to their union concerning the desirable relationship between husband and wife; and the ability of the respective partners to negotiate the nature of domestic life as it developed over time – their ability, in other words, to translate expectations into reality.

Husbands and wives: models and reality

> It was about four o'clock on a chilly winter's afternoon, and Kathleen Ojo and I were chatting in front of her living-room fire. Her youngest daughter was asleep in the other room, and Rosanne, the oldest – her child by a previous marriage – was

staying on late at school. Ade came in with his other daughter. He had been out to the bank and to collect a TV licence, and, since Kath was feeling 'a bit under the weather', had gone to pick the child up from school on the way back. He sat down for a few minutes; then Kath said, 'Make us a cup of tea, will you, love?'

We sat in front of the fire, eating cake and drinking tea, while Ade played with the children. Kath remarked how different this was to her life in the past.

'Ade and I talk everything over, not like my first husband. With him you never got an explanation for anything. Ade might say to me, "We're a bit short of money this week, so go easy", and we'll sit down and talk about it – '

Ade interrupted, laughing, 'It doesn't make difference if I say go easy or not, you still – ' 'Oh, you know what I mean! There was no discussion in my first marriage, none at all. Ade and I don't ever quarrel, neither of us can bear to see the other miserable for long. It's a bigger amount of give and take.'

At other times, of course, Mrs Ojo did not see her marriage in such a favourable light. Nevertheless, her comments indicate what she, in common with many English people today, felt to be the ideal conjugal relationship: one of mutual trust, companionship, partnership and affection (Fletcher, 1966; Young & Willmott, 1973).

As many sociologists have pointed out, marriage in contemporary Britain is an institution which carries a heavy complement of social meaning. The conjugal relationship is the key relationship in the private sphere of existence, a source of emotional support, security and fulfilment (Berger & Kellner, 1964): furthermore, the premiss of stable conjugality that underpins the structuring of adult social life ensures that such needs are hard to satisfy outside marriage (Hart, 1976). Moreover, as many members of this research set were themselves aware, economic security outside marriage is equally hard to achieve. The opportunities of the wage system are founded upon the premiss of stable conjugality, and upon a division of labour in which men are expected to support their wives and children and women to supply unpaid labour in the home (Klein, 1965; Oakley, 1974; Secombe, 1974; Barker & Allan, 1976a and 1976b; Mitchell & Oakley, 1976).

None of the English respondents questioned these fundamental assumptions. Most had, themselves, been brought up in homes where the father 'provided' and the mother 'managed', although, like many women in the research set, mothers were often also in paid employment. While in some respects they held views in opposition to those of their parents, the latter's conjugal lives, although recognised as imperfect, still acted as a point of reference for them. Even those whose families of origin could only be described as disorganised accepted these ideals – and, indeed, tended to blame their own failure to live up to them upon their parents' precedent failure to do so.

English respondents thus brought to their conjugal relationships high expectations – expectations which were admittedly tempered, especially among the less affluent women in the research set, by a pragmatic and unromantic sense of the importance of money and economic security in married life. For such women, some of whom, like Mrs Ojo, had endured periods of real poverty as the result of the withdrawal of male support, a 'good husband' was a man who provided regular and adequate support for his wife and children; companionship, affection and shared social interests were highly valued but, in the last resort, not absolutely essential.

It would thus be misleading to suggest that marriage held the same meaning for all of the English respondents in the research set. Evidence suggests that, over the past thirty years, as more and more women have entered the sphere of paid employment, attitudes towards the patterning of behaviour between husband and wife have been changing from an ideal of segregated and complementary role relationships[1] towards a more flexible and egalitarian ideal. (Young & Willmott, 1957; Willmott & Young, 1960; Young & Willmott, 1973; Goldthorpe & Lockwood, 1963; Klein, 1965; Rosser & Harris, 1965). At the same time, important variations have been suggested between the ideals prevalent within different segments of the English population (Bott, 1957; Young & Willmott, 1957; Willmott & Young, 1960; Rosser & Harris, 1965; Turner, 1967). The expectations of British members of the research set varied, as one might expect, with age, socio-economic status, and regional origin.

> 'I thought it was unmanly to help around the house. Where I come from [Scotland] people laughed at a man with a shopping basket.' (Mr Henderson (GB), 39 years)

> 'I wouldn't expect any help in the home. He's the breadwinner, the house is my job – and the children, of course.' (Mrs Horace (GB), 50 years)

> 'I did the heavy jobs... did the painting and decorating. I'd lend a hand at weekends, or if Lorraine was coming in late. After all, she was working too.' (Mr Handbury (GB), 26 years)

---

[1] This terminology is, of course, derived from concepts first suggested by Herbst (1954), and elaborated by Bott (1957) in her work on London families. On the one hand are couples with what Bott termed a *segregated* conjugal role relationship. These may be divided into those with a *complementary* conjugal organisation, where 'the activities of husband and wife are different and separate but fitted together to form a whole', and those with an *independent* organisation, where activities 'are carried out separately by husband and wife without reference to each other, in so far as this is possible'. On the other hand, there are couples with a *joint* conjugal role relationship, where husband and wife carry out tasks together or interchangeably.

The expectations of the black partners were less easy to analyse. In the broadest sense, they were identical to those of the English respondents, in that they too were founded upon the premiss of an underlying division of labour, interest and concern between men as providers and women as managers of the domestic domain. Nevertheless, there were important differences of emphasis.

Thus, the expectations concerning the quality and scope of the conjugal relationship that West Indian men from peasant or proletarian backgrounds brought to their unions were very different from those of the younger British respondents. In the words of Carole Rich (GB):

> 'It takes a bit of getting used to. Coloured men expect a lot of time to theirselves, it isn't like an English bloke who'll do a bit around the house...Michael's off out all the time if I let him. Linton [Michael's] cousin is the same. Beverley [Linton's WI wife] isn't like me, though, she couldn't care less, she's out every night herself...she's used to it, I suppose.'

Such expectations reflect the much lower level of investment in and commitment to the conjugal relationship which was common among West Indian households in Brixton, as it was in the Caribbean.[2]

A significant proportion of the West Indian respondents, however, like the two Rhodesian Coloured respondents, came from segments of their own society which placed a high value upon family solidarity and upon a style of family organisation which has variously been termed 'Victorian' or 'patriarchal'; similarly, the four Yoruba respondents came from a culture where, at least until recently, marriage was universally desired and domestic organisation founded upon a rigid segregation of domestic roles that, while emphasising the domestic authority of the husband over his wife, allowed both men and women considerable independence (Ward, 1938; Izzett, 1961; Marshall, 1964; Lloyd, 1965; Bascom, 1969). However, as we have already indicated, a significant proportion of these black respondents had rejected some aspects of the conjugal values of their cultures of origin in favour of what they perceived as English mores. Mrs Sidey (WI), for example, had rejected what she described as 'a Victorian upbringing in the tightness of an Eastern hand' and her Chinese father's views on the proper role for women; she herself would not consider marrying a Chinese husband, since they were 'too authoritarian'. Thus, several black respondents explicitly or implicitly contrasted their own ideals of marriage with those of their cultures of origin.

[2] For example, the Bureau of Statistics of the Jamaican Government (1973, Tables 23 and 45), recorded that in 1964 only 53% of the total live births for the island were legitimate, and that, according to the 1960 census, 42% of women co-resident with a sexual partner were living in consensual unions. M. G. Smith (1962, p. 239) has estimated that in peasant communities in the Caribbean between half and two-thirds of all children were likely to be living with their mothers alone. See also, Clarke (1951 and 1957); R. T. Smith (1956 and 1963); Davenport (1961); Blake (1961); M. G. Smith (1962 and 1966); Horowitz (1967); Gonzalez (1969); Foner (1979).

'When I see those West Indian children at Dyott Road School I am thankful that I kept my wife at home where she belongs.' (Mr Clough (WI)).

'In Africa the polygamy thing poisons the relationship between man and woman. Without trust there cannot be love. A man will always cheat on a woman and a woman will deceive a man. Fidelity is important in a marriage.' (Mr Horace (Y)).

When examining the success enjoyed by individuals in translating their expectations into domestic practice, it is, therefore, important to remember that the attitudes of the racially intermarried do not necessarily reflect the values of their cultures of origin. To repeat the words of Mr Oluwole: 'I am not a typical Yoruba man, I am not a typical anything.'

Domestic culture

On the whole, it is women who control most aspects of domestic culture, and who invest most heavily, in terms of time and interest, in the domestic domain. Most of the women under study were English, and those that were not came from families strongly oriented towards English mores; it is hardly surprising, therefore, to record the over-whelming 'Englishness' of the domestic worlds these couples had made. In the domestic decor of the fourteen Anglo-Caribbean couples, for example, there was a conspicuous absence of the baby pinks and blues, the plastic flowers arranged carefully in vases surrounded by frills of brightly coloured nylon net, the rows of family photographs on the wall, which characterised the rooms of endogamously married West Indian couples living in Brixton. The rooms of these interracial couples reflected the style and taste of English people of their age and class position – with, perhaps, the addition of a few 'African' items of decoration not to be found in an English home, but rarely, either, in a West Indian one.

Cuisine, too, generally reflected English, rather than exotic tastes. Only one Anglo-Caribbean household (Gomez–Mackie) cooked in the style common among West Indian households in Brixton, although in a minority of households (the Collets, the Kaliphas and the Riches) 'exotic' dishes formed the basis of adult diet. In others, where families ate together, difficulties over children's tastes, or a mother's belief that such food was fattening or over-spiced, limited the extent to which such dishes were prepared, and in ten households such food was cooked either not at all, or 'as a treat'. Mrs Jay (GB), for example, never cooked Caribbean food for her husband. 'If he wanted it, he had to cook it...I sometimes made a feeble attempt at rice.' Mrs Rowlands (GB) was thankful that her husband was 'the kind of man who doesn't mind eating English food, I don't like spicy things at all...Besides, their food is so dear.'

In most cases, it was again English practice that dominated in the field of language use. None of the four English women married to Yoruba men could speak or understand any Yoruba dialect, although one, Mrs Oluwole, had tried unsuccessfully to learn, and intended to try again. Similarly, among those households where the West Indian partner normally spoke some kind of patois or dialect, in only one case, that of the Riches, did this act as the general medium of communication for all household members. Mr Collet, for example, was a St Lucian whose first language was a French-based patois and he could speak only 'broken English'; although his wife could understand him, she could not speak patois herself, apart from some of the 'rude words'. Their children also could not speak it: 'well, that's only natural, it's him as should learn English really'.

The assumption, often unstated, that it was up to the black partner to adapt to what were perceived as English mores could also be discerned in the respondents' comments on bringing up children. Mrs Ojo (GB), for example, stated emphatically that her children were being 'brought up English'; she felt that Yoruba child-rearing practices were 'all wrong for a child'. While staying with her husband's 'cousin', she had been 'horrified' by the levels of submissiveness and discipline demanded of this woman's children. They were, according to her, expected 'to fetch and carry all day long – well, it's not right, kiddies need to play'. She accordingly felt it right to sabotage her husband's attempts to get their eighteen-month-old daughter to fetch and put away his slippers and pyjamas, and to treat the cousin's children, when they stayed with her, 'like kids and not like bloomin' robots'.

Other, equally unfavourable, comments were made by English mothers about West Indian child-rearing practices, although here complaints tended to focus on erratic, rather than excessive, discipline. There were, of course, dissenting voices: Mrs Birchall (GB), for example, found herself in conflict with her parents over the behaviour of her children:

> 'They find them a bit much really, they try to send them off to bed early and oh! they do go on about how they must learn better manners... we'd rather have two noisy children than two well behaved robots... they want the children to be like other English children, they can't see any advantages in the West Indian attitude to life.'

Whatever a mother's views, however, the very fact that she herself was English, or strongly oriented towards English culture, ensured that her children grew up in a way not very different from their white peers. In this respect, fathers, absent for much of a child's waking day, often spending their leisure time outside the home, were in no position to influence domestic policy; most were content to leave such matters to their wife. Others, who looked back with some bitterness on their own childhoods – and who tended to blame the practices of their cultures of origin for this – were anxious that their children should be brought up differently.

On the whole, in the field of domestic culture, the choices of the interracial couples evidenced a pragmatic flexibility and a mutual willingness to adapt to new experiences – although there were, of course, exceptions. If most adaptations were towards English mores, the black partners were, in general, content with this situation or positively approved of it; the only complaints which were made repeatedly came from black men who could not persuade their wives to cook them West Indian or West African food. The situation was rather different, however, with regard to conjugal roles. For if women exercised control in the domain of domestic culture, it was men who determined the character and scope of this aspect of domestic life.

Financial affairs

> 'Men are the hunters and providers...a woman's place is in the home with her children...an army can only have one commander, isn't it?' (Mr Clough (WI))

All the men in the research set, British, West Indian or Yoruba, like Mr Clough, accepted their obligation to support their wives, either legal or common-law, and their children. Only one other man, however, shared his strong views on 'a woman's place'; in most households whether or not women were in paid employment was determined by the financial circumstances of the household, its stage of development, and the wishes of the women themselves. Apart from Mrs Clough (GB) and Mrs Horace (GB), both women in middle age who had not worked since marriage, Mrs Sidey (WI), who was in very comfortable circumstances, and Susan Pound (GB) and Janet Mackie (GB), neither of whom had ever held down a proper job, all the women in the research set were either in paid employment or intended to be so as soon as their children were all at school (see Table 5.2). Not surprisingly, with the exception of the minority of educated women in professional occupations, financial considerations, rather than job satisfaction, were the reason for women engaging in what one called 'the hard grind', although several welcomed the opportunity for escape from a narrow domestic routine.

Unlike many ordinary West Indian women encountered in Brixton, these wives, with two exceptions, did not keep what they earned for themselves, but used their wages for housekeeping or paid them into a joint bank account (see Table 7.1). Such behaviour was occasionally remarked upon by West Indian women; in the words of one middle-aged Jamaican, 'These white women, they will work for a man and give him all their money. No Jamaican girl would do that for him.' In the eyes of these women themselves, on the other hand, the way they chose to

Table 7.1. *Research couples: financial arrangements*

Financial arrangement	Husband only working	Both partners working
Earnings paid into joint bank account; daily expenses in hands of wife	Birchall (WI/GB) Clough (WI/GB) Sidey (GB/WI) Horace (Y/GB)	Curtis (WI/GB) Handbury (GB/WI) Oluwole (Y/GB)
Earnings under sole control of wife		Collet (WI/GB) Kalipha (WI/GB) Henderson (GB/RC)
Earnings under control of husband, wife given fixed housekeeping allowance	Homer–Brettle (WI/GB) Jay (WI/GB) Rich (WI/GB) Rowlands (WI/GB) Ojo (Y/GB)	Ademola (Y/GB)
Both partners retain earnings, wife give fixed housekeeping allowance		Naylor (GB/RC)
Both partners retain earnings; wife given cash as needed		Lowe–Simmons (WI/GB)
Wife given cash as needed	Abbott–Pound (WI/GB)	

Ethnic identity of partners in parentheses, male partner first.

The Gomez–Mackie household has been excluded from this Table, since both partners, who were unemployed, independently received social security payments.

dispose of their earnings reflected their view of the conjugal relationship in general; they were working, not for themselves, but 'to make a bit extra for the family'.

There was, however, considerable diversity in the way in which family finances were organised. It may be seen from Table 7.1 that in half these households men either handed their earnings over to their wives, who acted as bankers for the household, or paid their earnings into a joint bank account to which both partners had access. For the more educated individuals in the research set, such arrangements 'just seemed the natural thing to do', as one man put it, and were typical for people of their age and background. Other men regarded this arrangement as a reflection of their personal trust in their wives. Mr Clough, for example, stated that 'at this stage' of his marriage he simply banked his wages and his wife drew out what she saw fit: 'but I direct the household finances and every so often I say, "Come, let's have a check" and we will sit for one entire evening for her to account to me for everything'. There were, however, other cases where men relied on their wives to keep their own tendencies to extravagance in check; as Mr Henderson (GB) remarked, 'If I had the money I'd be broke all the time – I can go out and spend it and get nothing for it.'

On the other hand, there were ten households where the men chose to retain control over their earnings. In three of the common-law households, the man only handed over small sums for specific purchases at any one time, an arrangement which laid an especially heavy emphasis on the optional nature of the male partner's support. Most, however, gave their wives a lump sum each week for housekeeping and for certain specified bills and expenses.

As long as men handed over adequate sums at regular intervals, and were prepared to do their best to meet demands for cash for irregular but necessary purchases, their partners were satisfied with these arrangements. Most came themselves from traditionally-run English homes where it had been normal practice for husbands to hand over a fixed weekly housekeeping allowance to their wives, and they interpreted their husbands' behaviour, not in terms of alien values, but as conforming to acceptable, if rather old-fashioned, English norms.

Mr Ojo (Y), for example, gave his wife a weekly housekeeping allowance, with a supplement on Mondays if she needed it. However, he liked her to ask for the money formally, just before she went shopping on Saturday morning. He also expected to organise major financial decisions. In September 1971, Mrs Ojo's daughter by her first marriage needed a new pair of shoes urgently, so Mrs Ojo approached her husband and suggested that, if he gave her two weeks' housekeeping money together, she would be able to buy a pair straight away. He was angry – not at the demand, which he could see was reasonable, but at the way in which the demand had been made. In his view, his wife should simply tell him that the girl needed a new pair of shoes; it was up to him to decide how best to find the necessary cash.

Mrs Ojo found such attitudes tiresome, but she was prepared to 'humour' her husband, as she put it, because 'Ade may be a bit old-fashioned, but he puts the family first.' Similarly, on another occasion: 'Here, what there is is for the family...he's never mean where the family's concerned – he'd rather go without himself than see us want for anything.'

In this way, couples like the Ojos were able to construct 'working misunderstandings' which permitted individuals to interpret the transactions of conjugal life – and the behaviour of individuals often rooted in very different cultural imperatives from their own – in terms of the values and norms of their own cultural experience. 'Working misunderstandings' of this kind enabled couples to circumvent the problems of conflicting conjugal expectations, but such problems sometimes surfaced nevertheless. Mrs Ojo, for example, was very shocked when, some months after the incident described above, she discovered that her husband had been earning not £22 a week, as he had told her, but £32, and that he had a bank account about which she knew nothing. To Mr Ojo, this was simply none of her business: he had been saving that £10 a week for the family's return to Nigeria. To Mrs Ojo, it suggested that, 'He's not as English as he makes out if he can hide a thing like that.'

Thus, as long as men continued to meet their domestic obligations, their English partners tended to dismiss what were, in fact, quite significant differences in conjugal expectations as individual idiosyncracies. Where men failed to meet their obligations, wives often chose to interpret their failure as deriving from their ethnic origin.

'He's like all West Indian men', remarked Carole Rich (GB) bitterly, one night when she had run out of housekeeping money and her husband refused to give her any more, 'greedy and selfish...an English husband puts his family first but coloured men are always trying to get out of doing anything.'

Domestic tasks

In all interracial households, the management of the domestic domain was considered, by both partners, to be a woman's responsibility. There were no households where the majority of household tasks – cooking, cleaning, shopping, laundry and minding the children – were performed equally by husbands and wives. Nevertheless, there was considerable variation in the extent to which men participated in these tasks.

Whether or not women were engaged in paid employment outside the home was, obviously, an important consideration; husbands with working wives realised, often reluctantly, that their social situation did not permit them the luxury of a traditional domestic division of labour. The Hendersons, for example, had arrived in this country from Rhodesia in 1965. Before that date, although his wife had always worked, Mr Henderson (GB) 'never used to help' around the house. In England, however, there were no cheap servants and what he could earn seemed insufficient for his family's needs. His wife enrolled in Training College and, reluctantly, he realised that 'a man in Britain, if he does have a working wife, must play a part in the home'. He began by performing certain unskilled tasks about the house: vacuuming carpets, making the beds and so on. There was a certain amount of pressure on his wife's part to get him to do the washing up. When his wife completed her course and started work, he began doing the food marketing, since his working day ended early, at 2 p.m. He refused, however, to go to Brixton Market, preferring Sainsbury's supermarket: 'There are more men there and I don't get so embarrassed.'

In some cases, a husband's help was essential for the survival of the household, for there were no kin who might be expected to help out under difficult circumstances. Mrs Collet (GB), for example, when asked whether her husband (WI) helped her in her domestic duties, replied simply, 'He has to.' The household included seven children, ranging in age from fifteen to three years, and Mr Collet's labouring job brought in, in 1971, only £17 a week. Since he could neither read nor write there was little hope of anything better, and Mrs Collet's economic contribution was thus absolutely essential. She found an evening cleaning job which paid her 33 pence an hour. Because of their work routine, the Collets 'only really see each other on the weekends'. Mrs Collet minded the youngest children during the day, did the shopping and most of the housework, gave the children their tea and part-prepared her husband's supper for his arrival home at about 5.30 p.m., when she left for work. He then 'got his supper', washed up the tea and supper things, put the children to bed and tidied up the flat before her arrival home at 10.30 p.m. On Saturday night, they bathed the children together.

It was evident that many working wives deliberately sought work that would interfere as little as possible with their domestic roles. Nevertheless, in eight of the ten households where women were in paid employment, husbands took on some share of domestic responsibility, if not always as much as their wives would have liked. In only three of the ten households where women did not work was this the case. As in the case of financial matters, women whose husbands fulfilled what their wives perceived to be their obligations – an adequate level of support for their household – saw nothing wrong with this arrangement. 'It's my job,' as Mrs Horace (GB) said, 'and I do it as well as I can.' Where men proved to be poor or erratic breadwinners, however, or were especially authoritarian in the domestic sphere, there was considerable dissatisfaction. Again, this was sometimes expressed in terms of invidious ethnic comparisons.

At the time of interview, for example, Mr Lowe (WI) and Mrs Simmons (GB) had been living together for six months. Their relationship, however, was already beginning to show signs of strain, and Mrs Simmons was full of complaints. Mr Lowe was, in her eyes, a 'good provider' – he paid the rent for their flat, provided housekeeping money, and bought her all the clothes she needed – but in return expected her undivided attention and a high standard of domestic service.

> 'When I first started going out with George he was so well-mannered...Now it's just "do this" and "do that" and he has such a temper I just daren't disobey him...coloured men are more bossy, no doubt about it. They're less mature.'

Leisure

When I interviewed them in 1971, Mr and Mrs Rowlands and their two children did very little together as a family. During the week, Mr

Table 7.2. *Research couples: leisure activities*

Joint		
	Leisure time spent, with rare exceptions, together	Ademola (Y/GB)
		Collet (WI/GB)
		Curtis (WI/GB)
		Horace (Y/GB)
		Ojo (Y/GB)
		Sidey (GB/WI)
	Majority of leisure activities (two-thirds or more) enjoyed together ·	Clough (WI/GB)
		Oluwole (Y/GB)
	Mixed; both segregated and joint activities	Abbott–Pound (WI/GB)
		Birchall (WI/GB)
		Gomez–Mackie (WI/GB)
		Handbury (GB/WI)
		Henderson (GB/RC)
		Lowe–Simmons (WI/GB)
	Majority of leisure activities (two-thirds or more) enjoyed independently	Rich (WI/GB)
	Leisure time spent, with rare exceptions, separately	Homer–Brettle (WI/GB)
		Jay (WI/GB)
		Kalipha (WI/GB)
		Rowlands (WI/GB)
		Naylor (GB/RC)
Independent		

Ethnic identity of partners in parentheses, male partner first.

Rowlands (WI) left for work by 6.30 in the morning and returned about 9 o'clock in the evening. After supper, he usually went out again, presumably to the pub: 'At least I suppose that's where he goes, he doesn't say.' Occasionally, in his wife's words, 'he brings a bottle of something in for both of us', and 'once in a blue moon' Mrs Rowlands would herself go out with him to the pub. Otherwise, she spent her evenings alone with the childen, since Mr Rowlands never babysat for her. 'West Indian men won't stay in and look after the children...white men will give their wives an evening out now and again. Joshua won't let me go out...of course it's all right for him to do what he likes.'

Mrs Rowlands did not, however, resent this too much: 'I don't mind, long as I've got *that*,' pointing to the television in the corner, 'it's company, at any rate.' Her own socialising was confined to the daytime; she visited her mother nearly every afternoon, attended a mother and baby club, took the children to the park and so on. She and her husband saw relatives together occasionally on Sundays, and in the summer they had spent a couple of days out with a brother of Mr Rowlands, who also had an English wife and small children.

The Rowlands were one of six couples whose leisure time was spent, for the most part, in independent pursuits (see Table 7.2). In all but one case – the Naylors – the husband was a working-class West Indian, and there were small children; and it was the arrival of children that ended the courting period during which, like most other couples in the research set, they had spent most of their leisure time together. Like Mr Rowlands, and in common with many West Indian men in Brixton, the husbands in these households spent a good deal of their leisure time 'boozing' as Mr Kalipha put it; several 'liked a game of darts', a game of dominoes, or simply the conversation of male companions. 'How you can talk about football or cricket or any kind of thing like that to a woman?' remarked Mr Rich (WI). 'Woman talk house, house, house, money, money, money.'

Unlike many West Indian women in Brixton, however, the English partners of these men did not expect to spend most of their leisure time independently of their menfolk. Like Mrs Rich's sister-in-law (see above, p. 82), many West Indian women looked to female kin, friends and neighbours for companionship, and, although they too resented the fact that often their husbands refused to babysit for them, what they wanted was not more time with their husband but more time away from the house to pursue their own leisure interests. The English women felt differently, and the amount of time their husbands spent outside the home was a source of friction and dissatisfaction, seen by these women as a selfish and often expensive neglect. Women like Mrs Brettle (GB), cut off from kin and with no friends, certainly felt the absence of conjugal companionship most keenly; but dissatisfaction was marked even in those cases where, like Mrs Rowlands or Mrs Kalipha, the women concerned had a network of kin living nearby, or, like Mrs Jay, an extensive network of friends. This dissatisfaction was an undercurrent even in the four additional households where a West Indian male partner spent only part of his leisure time in independent pursuits. What such women wanted was, in Mrs Jay's words, 'a bloke that was going to be a real husband to me, not just going out all the time'.

On the other hand, there were three couples in the research set where an awareness of divergent interests had led to the development of a pattern of independent activities. Significantly, perhaps, the two cases where such arrangements were mutually satisfactory both involved Rhodesian Coloured women married to English men. Mr Henderson (GB), for example, although he described his family as 'close-knit', also remarked: 'You see, me and my wife...she's got her ideas and I've got mine. We move along different paths.' Mrs Naylor (RC) was even more emphatic: 'Our likes and dislikes are entirely different, we're like chalk and cheese...we go our own ways.' Unlike the English women in the research set, these Rhodesian Coloured women were quite content in their independence; in the words of Mrs Naylor: 'I think we Coloured women are more independent than most of the English I have met. Women in my family have always worked for themselves. You just didn't expect things to be otherwise.' Both couples, now in early middle age, had come to realise that their partnership did not include many shared tastes or interests, but were happy to continue in it, nevertheless; and there were indications that one or two of the younger couples in the research set, notably the Kaliphas and the Rowlandses, would in time develop similar attitudes. For others, however – the Jays and, for different reasons, the Handburys – independent leisure activities were both a cause and an index of the lack of common ground in their conjugal relationship, and offered signs of its coming dissolution.

In contrast, seven couples in the research set spent all or most of their leisure time together. With the exception of the Sideys, who were able to afford the services of a paid babysitter and had kin close at hand, this meant a much reduced social life, especially for the male partner. In the words of Mrs Collet (GB): 'He never goes nowhere. Sometimes I wish he would, sitting here all the time.' Mrs Collet's response was, however, unusual, for most of the women, all English, approved strongly of their partners' home-centredness, which, in their eyes, distinguished them from the mainstream of their respective ethnic group.

Mr Ademola (Y), for example, worked all morning in the grocery that he and his wife ran jointly, went off to do the buying in the afternoons, and remained in the shop until he locked up at 9.30 at night. He always returned home directly after he had locked up and organised the day's takings. As his wife remarked, 'I can tell the time by him, marvellous for a West African man – you know how they are. He never was no trouble.'

Similarly, Mrs Curtis commented that her husband was

> 'A great family man, which is very surprising for a Jamaican...they aren't often like that, from what I can see. Warren has always preferred to be at home – any free time he has he spends with us.'

These men clearly derived considerable pleasure from spending time with their wives and children; it should not be assumed, however, as their wives tended to do, that this inevitably reflected a sense of alienation from their cultures of origin. While one of the women married to a Yoruba suggested that this family-centredness was a 'reaction against polygamy and the kind of families they grew up in', and it was noticeable that five of the seven had been amongst the eleven black respondents with disrupted or unhappy childhoods, there was also evidence to suggest that, at least among the Yoruba respondents, a concern for one's family was perceived as a continuation of ideal Yoruba attitudes expressed in a rather different way. Mr Ademola, for example, said firmly that,

'My family comes first with me and they always have done. My people believe that a man's children are the most important thing that he has, but in Nigeria it is too easy to forget that, because there are too many children and you cannot do your best for all of them...Here I can do the best for my two and give them a good early background...I don't believe in going out, it takes the parents away from the children.'

Accommodation and adaptation

From the foregoing, it is evident that there was a considerable degree of overlap between the expectations which these respondents, from very different cultural backgrounds, brought to the conjugal situation. In terms of practical problems of adjustment, the most serious problems occurred in households where English women were living with West Indian men committed to a pattern of strongly segregated conjugal role relationships and independent leisure activities. Although the domestic balance of power permitted wives to impose their views of what was, or was not, desirable in the domain of domestic culture, they had considerably more difficulty in persuading reluctant spouses to 'opt in' to the responsibilities of domestic life. The outcome of this conflict of interests varied. In three cases – the Jay, the Lowe–Simmons and the Abbott–Pound households – the couples concerned had separated by January 1975, and, as we have indicated above, each partner's refusal to compromise on what the other felt to be important issues was, at least in part, responsible for this. In two cases, the Kaliphas and the Riches, there was a perceptible, if reluctant, shift in behaviour by the black partner towards greater participation in the domestic domain. Two couples, the Rowlandses and Mr Homer and Mrs Brettle, continued very much as before; in both cases the female partner disliked the strongly segregated nature of their conjugal role relationship but was in too weak and vulnerable a position either to change it or to consider terminating the relationship.

Other couples handled potential conflicts of orientation rather differently, by developing what I have termed 'working misunderstandings'. Over time, we would expect such couples to show a gradual convergence in the direction of genuine shared understandings. But for some, the fragile consensus predicated upon the ignoring of important differences in outlook and interest could be threatened by changing circumstances. In several households, for example, we have suggested that the white partners concerned chose to regard their partners as black Englishmen or women. Three of the four Anglo-Yoruba households planned to settle eventually in Nigeria; but only one of these, the Oluwoles, had any grasp of what problems this would entail for them.

The Ojos, for example, left for Nigeria in January 1973, leaving Mrs Ojo's daughter by her first marriage behind to finish her studies in London. Six months later, Mrs Ojo and her other two daughters were back in England. Nothing had been as she had expected. She had never travelled before and found she could not stand the heat and humidity of Lagos. The noise, dirt and disorder of the city frightened her and she worried constantly about her children's health. She missed the comfortable routines of English life; servants did the work with which she filled up her days at home and she felt 'useless' and lethargic. She could not accept, nor indeed fully comprehend, the role expected of her as a junior wife in a close-knit Yoruba family; even more disturbing was the realisation that her husband, whose 'Englishness' had seemed to her an integral part of his character, was in fact rooted in another culture whose imperatives she could not understand. Her husband, for his part, could not understand why his wife, always so loyal and efficient in England, should let him down in this way; like his wife, he had made assumptions concerning the underlying meaning of his partner's behaviour which were, as it turned out, misguided.

8 The construction of a social universe

It has been suggested (Bott, 1957, p. 99) that 'the immediate social environment of urban families is best considered not as the local area in which they live, but rather as the network of social relationships which they maintain'. Unlike the construction of a domestic world – a process which, although evidently influenced by considerations external to each interracial household, was essentially a transaction between husband and wife – the construction and maintenance of this 'immediate social environment' involved the interracial couple with the imperatives of a racially polarised social universe. Couples were in this manner directly confronted with the problems inherent in their own ambiguous ethnicity.

Much of the literature concerned with interracial families suggests that, in a racially divided society, the construction of social networks will inevitably be difficult. In the United States, for example, the social constraints imposed upon such couples were – at least prior to the liberalisation of race relations in the 1960s – considerable. In Drake and Cayton's blunt terms (1945, pp. 129–73), unless an interracial couple in Chicago moved in intellectual or 'bohemian' circles, such a union resulted in the 'sociological suicide' of the white partner. Golden (1954) similarly observed that in Philadelphia a white woman who married a black man would be ostracised by her family and friends and would become 'a negro socially'. Further difficulties awaited the interracial couples within the black community; middle-class American black men often faced social disapproval for marrying a partner who, it was assumed, would be his inferior in education or in socio-economic status (Drake & Cayton, 1945, pp. 129–73).

Evidence from Britain is less easy to interpret. Hill (1965), for example, has suggested that isolation is the typical pattern, but, as we have already indicated (above, pp. 6–7), in the 1950s in some areas white spouses appear to have been incorporated into the local black community and to have served significant functions within it. Patterson, on the other hand, found that the interracial couples that she knew in Brixton in the same period had, despite some constriction of their social universe, maintained or developed a circle of white friends, and that their children had perpetuated this 'assimilationist' orientation by marrying white spouses; Craven (1968, pp. 56–7, 68) found the same process operating among long-term African settlers in London.

Isolation, incorporation into a localised black community, or assimilation into the mainstream of white society each represent distinct and different strategies through which the interracially married might attempt to resolve their ambiguous ethnicity. The very existence of such couples, in the context of Brixton, challenged the categories with which individuals ordered the social world around them, as well as presenting practical difficulties in the ordering of interaction. As in America, there was the additional problem of the stigma which attached to the racially intermarried, especially to the white women who chose to enter into such unions. In the words of Mr Clough (WI):

> 'A mixed couple face hostility from both white and coloured people. If they live in a house owned by black people, the wife will be mocked behind her back...they believe the white man's propaganda about her.'

In order to gain social acceptance, then, these couples were faced with the problems of managing what Goffman (1968) has termed a 'spoiled identity'. The strategies they adopted reflect, however, more than straightforward practical considerations. They also reflect the orientations and aspirations of the respondents themselves, and their often highly ambivalent attitudes towards race, colour and ethnic identity.

The management of a spoiled identity

All the research couples were aware of the stigma attached to being black in English society, and of the negative stereotypes concerning interracial couples current among the local population. Pauline Kalipha and Sheila Jay, both married to West Indians, had, for example, joined with other English neighbours to form a small mother and baby club. As Mrs Kalipha put it, there had been

> 'no trouble, though some of them used to say "we don't count Tim [Mr Kalipha] as coloured", which is a bit daft, I always think...Oh, and one once passed a remark about Sheila, she said, "She doesn't look that sort of girl, does she?" That was before she knew that I was "that sort of girl" as well.'

The impact of such attitudes varied. Professional standing, the outward signs of education and the possession of the external indications of middle-class status all acted to neutralise the stigma attached to blackness. As Mr Clough (WI), himself an electrician, put it, recalling his own past:

> 'I was once thinking of training to be a barrister, after the war. The English lower middle classes are prepared to take in a lodger if he is a doctor or lawyer or something like that. It washes his colour out.'

The opprobrium that attached to white women who married black men did not attach in so great a measure to black women who married whites. For the Sideys, for example, linked through Mr Sidey's occupation to a liberal, cosmopolitan and affluent section of the London population, there were few problems attached to the fact that Mrs Sidey came from Jamaica rather than Esher. Others, however, faced greater difficulties.

As we shall see below, individual respondents varied considerably in the extent to which they sought, or felt the need to seek, acceptance within mainstream white society. Public disapproval is a difficult burden to bear, however, and many respondents, especially the white partners, sought, in their presentation of themselves and of their partner, to dissociate themselves from commonly held notions concerning the 'typical' interracial couple. In some cases, this manifested itself in anxiety over 'appearances'. Mr Lowe (WI), for example, insisted that Mrs Simmons (GB) should not smoke in the street 'like a common tart', and would not allow her to wear either mini-skirts or the then fashionable floor-length skirts which, he felt, made her 'look like a whore'. And Mrs Simmons herself, although she resented Mr Lowe's authoritarian attitudes, confided that she had become worried that she looked like 'a coloured man's woman'.

Similarly, Mrs Birchall (GB), in the course of a general conversation on Brixton, remarked that

> 'it's always the Irish women, isn't it, who seem to marry West Indians, or at least to have half-caste babies, and they're always the dirtiest babies too, dressed up in any old thing. I didn't notice it so much before I had children of my own but now I do. I try to make sure my children are extra neat and clean...so many half-caste children do look so uncared for.'

Here her husband interjected: 'I think you only notice the dirty children if they are half-caste – white Irish children are often just as dirty. You just notice the half-castes more.'

There was also, as we have already noted, a tendency among some respondents to detach themselves or their partners from what they regarded as a justifiably stigmatised ethnic group. Some chose to do this on the basis of class. 'People just lump all West Indians together,' complained Mrs Handbury, 'but there is a world of difference between someone from a middle-class background like myself and the kind of West Indian you find living in this area.' At other times, respondents sought to displace discreditable characteristics onto another section of the local black population:

> 'Things are worse now between the races. It's not surprising, look at the riffraff that has come into this area from the West Indies.' (Mr Horace (Y))

'I think Nigerians are a better class of people than the West Indians you get around here – most of them come here for their studies...but some of these Jamaicans, they can't even read and write.' (Mrs Ademola (I))

'You know, the worst landlords in Brixton are West Africans. To the English we all look alike, though, so we get blamed for what they do.' (Mr Curtis (WI))

'St Lucians are nice quiet people, most of them. Jamaicans and Barbadians are always fighting and quarrelling, leastways round here.' (Mrs Collet (GB))

'We Guyanese are like the English, but Jamaicans are terrible people, just peasants really. They are not good stock...There are too many Jamaicans in Brixton, that's why the area is full of thieves and boys who don't work – you see, their island is next to Cuba.' (Mr Lowe (WI))

This tendency towards scapegoating was to be found in even the most sophisticated of the interracial households. Mr Oluwole (Y), for example, despite his militant views on racial justice, regarded West Indians as responsible for the position in which they found themselves in Britain; they were the descendants of slaves who had been, in his phrase, 'drawn from the dregs of the population' in West Africa. While his wife scoffed at this expression of genetic determinism, she too was critical of West Indian culture:

'Their thing is so frail...they have patois and a few things like steel bands but you can't call that a culture – they come here and they're just floundering. But an African has his culture intact.'

To Mrs Birchall (GB), however, married to a West Indian, matters appeared rather differently: 'They [Nigerians] are all such snobs...I think it is pathetic the way they try to look as English as possible.'

Such scapegoating was a common enough phenomenon in Brixton. However, for certain members of the research set, scapegoating served another function: namely, to deflect the respondents' own ambiguous feelings about colour, race and ethnic identity onto 'safe' third parties and away from their respective partners. Mr Lowe (WI) and Mrs Simmons (GB), for example, had both disliked living in Brixton, and moved to another part of London shortly after interview. Brixton had frightened Mrs Simmons. She would not go out at night unescorted, and refused to travel alone after dark on the train between Paddington and Brixton. She also disliked the house in which she and Mr Lowe lived, describing it as 'nothing but coloured people'. As we have seen, Mr Lowe – a Guyanese – blamed Jamaicans, not black people in general, for Brixton's problems; similarly, he described the house in which he lived as, 'run by Jamaicans of the rough type – you know, not my scene at all'.

Residence and neighbourhood

In their comments on the social world around them, and, more specifically, in their attitudes towards Brixton and towards the people who lived there, these couples revealed something of their feelings about colour, race and class. At the time of interview, all were living in Brixton or in the districts which surrounded it, although each household's circumstances varied with their economic resources and the conditions under which they had entered the housing market. Six couples, among the poorest in the research set, rented rooms in multi-occupied houses in areas of heavy black settlement. Three were in various forms of public housing in Brixton itself, and a further three had GLC lettings in the ethnically mixed districts which surrounded Brixton proper. Two were able to afford privately rented flats in Tulse Hill and Clapham, while the remainder owned their own houses: two in areas of heavy black settlement, one on its periphery, and three in predominantly white areas (see Table 8.1). All couples were agreed, in broad terms, in their comments on the character of the area in which they lived; they differed a good deal, however, as one might expect, in the evaluation of this character.

The Sideys and the Handburys, for example, were 'professional people' who regarded residence in a working-class district such as Brixton as inappropriate for people like themselves. Other couples, eight in all, also wished to dissociate themselves from what they took to be the 'typical' Brixton resident. The Horaces, Cloughs and Curtises, all long-established households with fewer resources than the Sideys and the Handburys, had struggled hard to find somewhere to live outside the main area of black settlement. The Cloughs, for example, had bought their house in a quiet part of Tulse Hill in 1956, after failing to gain access to Lambeth Council's housing list. Mr Clough (WI) reckoned that he had paid £800 more for the property because he was black; yet both he and his wife felt that the financial hardship involved was worthwhile. Similarly, Mr Horace (Y) observed: 'I refused to live in Brixton. This cost this family money, but it was money well spent.'

What these couples resented was, as Mr Curtis (WI) put it, 'being all lumped together with everyone else, same skin colour so we all supposed to be the same'. More recent arrivals in the area expressed similar views. In 1965, for example, the Ademolas bought a house in the vicinity of Loughborough Junction – an area which Mr Ademola (Y) preferred to describe as 'Camberwell'. They had previously been living in South Kensington, but Brixton, according to Mrs Ademola, 'was the only place he could buy a house, being coloured. We tried Streatham, Tooting, but things were more difficult in those days.' The

Table 8.1. *Neighbourhood and residence, all households*

	Neighbourhood		
Type of tenure	Area of heavy black settlement	Area of moderate black settlement	Predominantly white area
Owner/occupier	Ademola Birchall	Curtis	Clough Horace Sidey
GLC letting		Collet Naylor	Kalipha
Council letting	Jay Ojo		
Housing Trust letting	Henderson		
Private letting, self-contained		Handbury Oluwole	
Private letting, not self-contained	Rowlands Abbott–Pound Gomez–Mackie Homer–Brettle Lowe–Simmons Rich		

Ademolas felt that they had little in common with their neighbours, and Mr Ademola would not allow his children to play with local black children: 'their home life is not suitable – I don't want them coming under that influence'. A similar sense of social superiority dominated the comments of the Naylors and the Hendersons, who regarded their residence in poor neighbourhoods as the unfortunate outcome of economic necessity. Unlike Mr Abbott and Mr Lowe (both WI), whose principal objection to Brixton was that it compared unfavourably with areas of black settlement north of the river, such couples resented, in the words of Mrs Oluwole (GB), being 'propelled towards the Ghetto'. Unlike Mrs Oluwole, however, such individuals could see no benefit in living in an area where interracial couples were common enough to excite little public attention.

Other couples with lower expectations simply accepted living in Brixton, with all its disadvantages, as a fact of life for people like themselves. Mrs Ojo (GB), for example, who had grown up in a working-class neighbourhood in Peckham, recalled that she was 'nervous' when she and her Yoruba husband moved to their council maisonette in the Railton Road area. 'I had never lived so far into the middle of Brixton before and you heard dreadful stories.' She found, in fact, that the people there were 'no different to people anywhere else'.

Most of the poorer couples were realistic: as Mr Rich (WI) remarked, 'Carole say she would like a better place, Clapham or Tooting way, but flat expensive up there you know. Brixton not too bad.'

At other times, Mr Rich, together with various other working-class West Indian men (Mr Gomez, Mr Homer, Mr Kalipha, Mr Jay and Mr Rowlands), expressed more positive attitudes; for Brixton, despite its problems, was a familiar environment which provided a range of much-needed goods and services. Mr Kalipha (WI), for example, admitted that he felt 'uncomfortable' when there were no black faces around him. One year he had taken his family to the Isle of Wight for a holiday, and he had felt 'strange for the first couple of days...it's nothing really but you can't help it. I don't believe in dispersal and all that – I want to live near enough to mix a bit.' As distinct from families like the Curtises or the Ademolas, who looked outward to the values of the wider white society to provide the framework within which they evaluated themselves and others, such men looked inwards, to the social world of black, and, more specifically, West Indian Brixton for validation and support.

A minority of white respondents also held positive attitudes to Brixton. Mrs Birchall, for example, was occasionally teased by her husband (WI) for her rather romantic views of the area and its residents – views which were, in a sense, a mirror image of those held by interracial couples concerned with respectability and status. Of the couple's move from East Dulwich to Brixton – in itself an eccentric decision, in south London terms – she remarked:

> 'If I'm going to live in a working-class area, I'd rather live in a proper working-class district like Brixton. I didn't like East Dulwich, it's too snooty there. Working-class, but upper working-class. It's a lace curtain area, you know what I mean?...the people are more friendly here. I lived in Dulwich for six months and I never spoke to any one except for one couple across the street.'

Mrs Jay and Mrs Kalipha also liked the friendliness that they had discovered in Brixton. Because of her poor health, Mrs Kalipha and her family had 'jumped the queue' and been rehoused by the GLC, on a pre-war estate whose residents were mainly elderly and white; she had immediately put in for a transfer back to her old neighbourhood of Angell Town. 'It's a great community round here,' she remarked of this area; 'of course it's breaking up now'. It was clear, however, that Mrs Kalipha's point of reference was the local white community, not the black Brixton world that was the focus of her husband's loyalties. The same could be said of Mrs Jay; and it was also true of Mrs Rowlands, who had been born and brought up in Brixton and whose relatives and childhood friends, living locally, formed the core of her social network.

The diversity of attitudes towards Brixton and the people who lived there held by these respondents indicates important differences in social orientations and aspirations. On the one hand, there were a number of couples who felt themselves to have little in common with the residents of Brixton and were anxious to dissociate themselves from them. Significantly, these included not simply all but one of those households where the male partner was engaged in a 'middle-class' occupation, but also households like the Ademolas and the Cloughs where the couple's aspirations and self image, if not their actual socio-economic status, oriented them firmly towards the middle classes. Mr Ademola, for example, still regarded himself as a student rather than as a small shopkeeper, while Mr Clough placed considerable emphasis on the intellectual pursuits which distinguished him from the ordinary run of skilled manual workers: 'we try to associate with people who could pull us up more intellectually'. On the other hand, there were those who felt able to identify themselves with some segment of the local population. While such individuals either rejected or ignored the 'outsider's view' of Brixton, even here there were important differences of orientation: there were those who identified primarily with the local white community and others who identified primarily with the black Brixton world.

Such aspirations and orientations cannot, however, be considered in isolation, for the translation of such preferences into concrete social relations must also take account of the social resources available to each household. In constructing a social world, these interracial couples had, in theory, access to both black and white social fields, a richer complement of social resources with which to realise social goals than was normally available to Brixton residents. In practice, as we shall see below, matters were rather different.

Kin resources

The number of kin with whom each respondent was in effective contact varied widely,[1] from Mrs Ojo (GB), who maintained active links with thirty-two relatives, to the seventeen individuals, eight black and nine white, with effective kin sets of three or less (see Table 8.2). In comparison both with the kin resources of endogamously married West Indians in Brixton, and with what is known of English urban kinship patterns (Firth, 1956; Firth, Hubert & Forge, 1969; Young & Willmott, 1957), the effective kin sets of the research couples seemed very small. They reflected the fact that the interracially married tended to bring to their unions a denuded or attenuated kin network – occasionally as the result of their marriage to a stigmatised outsider, but often as one aspect of the geographical and social isolation which had detached these

---

[1] 'Effective' kin are defined in this context as those with whom the respondent had some degree of contact – by telephone, letter, or in face-to-face interaction – during the course of one year. For the purposes of computing each couple's effective *social network*, a more restricted definition of 'effective' has been used (see n. 2 below).

Table 8.2 *Size of each individual's 'universe of kin' and effective kin set, all respondents*

| Household | Black partner | | | White partner | |
	Universe	No. in UK	Effective kin set	Universe	Effective kin set
Abbott–Pound	[46]	1	0	54	0
Ademola	117	1	3	77	0
Birchall	n/a	12	14	n/a	13
Clough	n/a	1	0	23	11
Collett	n/a	11	6	74	0
Curtis	53	16	6	19	3
Gomez–Mackie	[61]	30	1	48	0
Handbury	n/a	4	14	11	2
Henderson	53	11	10	44	17
Homer–Brettle	49	0	0	67	0
Horace	26	0	0	42	6
Jay	n/a	5	0	67	21
Kalipha	[40]	2	2	32	17
Lowe–Simmons	n/a	18	6	37	3
Naylor	105	4	7	43	25
Ojo	[32]	6	11	43	32
Oluwole	n/a	21	4	21	15
Rich	46	24	24	29	2
Rowlands	n/a	24	26	33	6
Sidey	n/a	9	11	n/a	5

n/a indicates respondent unable or unwilling to provide information.

Brackets indicate incomplete information.

For definition of 'effective' kin, see n. 1.

individuals from their families of origin, their countries of origin, and the association of their ethnic peers.

All the black partners were migrants whose kin were scattered over two or three countries. Nine wrote 'home', if only sporadically, to parents and grandparents, five to siblings; only three had ever returned home for a visit, and only four households – the Ademolas, the Oluwoles, the Ojos and the Birchalls – had definite plans to leave England. The accidents of migration played their part in determining the number of kin that each individual had resident in England (see Table 8.2); it so happened, for example, that Mr Rowlands (WI) had four brothers and their families living in London, while Mr Ademola (Y) had only a single cousin in the south of England, and Mr Horace (Y) no relatives here at all. Where kin were only distant relatives with whom the respondent had no previous friendly contact, there was little incentive to develop social relations. Mr Jay (WI), for example, had a cousin, his mother's brother's daughter, who was a primary school teacher in Scotland; they had met only once or twice, however, in the ten years he had been in England. But there were other cases where ties with close kin had been allowed to lapse. Mr Clough (WI), for example, knew that he had a brother living in London, but the last time they had met was in 1945, when they were both in the RAF. Mr Clough considered that he had become 'a Prussian officer in uniform' and did not see him again. Mr Collet (WI) had lost contact with his brother, who had simply stopped visiting – 'why, we don't know'. Mr Abbott (WI) and Mr Kalipha (WI) had similarly drifted apart from siblings. There were also other men who avoided contact with large networks of kin. Mr Gomez, for example, had nothing to do with his extended network of kin living in the West Midlands, while Mr Oluwole had 'about twenty' relations living in London, all relatively affluent people of good standing within the Nigerian expatriate community, whom he refused to see since 'it would look like creeping'.

There was thus a good deal of selectivity in what kin individuals chose to see, and this applied equally to the white partners. As among the black respondents, geographical distance was a reinforcing factor but not a sufficient cause to explain loss of contact. Both Janet Mackie and Ian Henderson had most of their kin living in Scotland, but whereas Mr Henderson was in regular contact with them, and went north to stay with his mother or sister at least once a year, Miss Mackie had not seen her mother or any other relative in ten years. Equally, four of the nine respondents who had kin within five miles enjoyed either minimal contact or none at all. In only one case – that of Mr Handbury – was this the inevitable outcome of an unusually small kin universe. Rather, lack of contact reflected the alienation, willed or otherwise, of these individuals from their kin.

By the time of interview, however, there were only two couples – Mr Abbott and Miss Pound and Mr Homer and Mrs Brettle – who had no contact whatsoever with the kin of either partner. For the rest, however, the significance of kin in daily life varied a good deal. In the six weeks prior to interview, the Rowlandses, for example, had seen, between them, Mrs Rowlands's (GB) mother and father, her sister, sister's husband and their small daughter, a paternal aunt, her maternal grandmother and maternal aunt, as well as two of Mr Rowlands's (WI) brothers, their wives and children – a total of seventeen kin in all, distributed over six households. In contrast the Collets had seen just one relative in the same period, Mr Collet's (WI) mother's brother's son, who dropped in on the family approximately every two weeks. Although he and his family lived only about two miles away, the Collets had not seen his wife and children since they spent the day with them some five months previously.

The meaning of kin relationships for each household depended, not simply on the number of kin seen – either in absolute terms, or as related to each household's total social network – nor on the frequency of interaction with them, but also on the category of kin involved. The expectation of mutual help and concern was strongest between parents and children and weakest between secondary kin. Again, the Rowlands and Collet households may serve as an example. Mrs Rowlands (GB) saw her mother nearly every day and the two women were involved in a constant exchange of goods and services. This was not the case with her sister: 'You can ask more of your mother than what you can of a sister, though that's not to say we wouldn't help one another out if we needed it.' Similarly, although Mrs Rowlands saw a lot of one of her husband's brothers in particular, she would not go to that household for help in an emergency: 'I'd ask my Mum first.' Nor would she trouble her elderly aunts or her grandmother. Mrs Collet, in contrast, had no one she felt she could rely upon, not even her husband's cousin: 'I wouldn't ask any help there – if it was one of my own family it would be different.'

For nine other households, as for the Rowlandses, contact with the parents of one – or less commonly both – partners played a crucial role in the maintenance of kin relationships. In most cases, primary kin were those of the white partner; for only the Birchalls and the Handburys had both sets of parents living in England. Where parents lived nearby, contact was easily maintained. Mrs Kalipha (GB), for instance, saw her mother at least once a week, during the day when her two children were at school; her parents lived only a short bus ride away, so, 'either she comes down or I go up, it doesn't take long', or, alternatively, the two women met in Brixton to do their shopping jointly and have a cup of coffee together afterwards. For others, meeting was more difficult. Mrs Birchall's (GB) parents, for example, lived about thirty miles from inner London, and her mother 'travelled up' every fortnight to spend the day with her daughter and grandchildren, while every so often, and especially in the summer, the Birchalls would spend the weekends with them. Similarly, Mrs Oluwole (GB) and her small daughter made the awkward journey out to Hertfordshire to see her parents at least once a week in school holidays and fortnightly during the term, when Mrs Oluwole was at work.

It was clear that social relations between the households of parents and offspring tended to pivot on the mother–daughter relationship, especially where grandchildren provided a focus for common concern. Mothers offered day-to-day companionship, practical assistance, and could provide help in life crises and sudden emergencies. This was especially important for less affluent households. By contrast, in several households where one partner came from a middle-class family, fathers had also been able to offer substantial assistance, providing expensive presents for grandchildren, loans for holidays, or even the deposit for a house.

Parents also frequently provided the main point of contact between their adult children and between those children and their aunts, uncles and cousins. Mrs Jay (GB), for example, had one brother, living in Croydon. He had only visited her once since her move to Brixton in 1965, but she saw him occasionally at her parents' house in Plaistow over Sunday lunch. In the same way, Mrs Oluwole (GB) saw a whole range of collateral kin – aunts and cousins – who arranged to visit her parents' house when they knew that she and her daughter would be there. In only one case, that of the Riches, did collateral kin provide the kind of help and companionship that primary kin felt was an aspect of relations within 'one family' – and Mr Rich's 'auntie' was, on his own admission, 'a mother' to him. More typically, the content of relationships with such kin was confined to formal visiting, the exchange of Christmas and birthday cards, and what one respondent called 'big family beanos' – weddings, anniversaries, and christenings. Nevertheless, participation in such networks did serve the important function of what might be termed 'normalisation'. In the words of one woman, 'they just think of us as relatives, not as black people or half-caste people'. Differences of opinion or orientation were swept under the carpet. Such contacts, thanks to the ideology of obligation that informed them, survived where other, voluntary, contacts did not, and acted to anchor the interracial family firmly in a white social field.

The quality of relationships with siblings was much more variable. In some cases, a close-knit family network had survived the death of one or both parents. Mrs Ojo (GB), for example, had five siblings. None of them lived in Inner London at the time of interview, and, in terms of their achieved socio-economic status, all had done rather better than herself; one sister was married to a skilled craftsman, and two others to supervisory white-collar workers, while one brother was an inspector for the Gas Board. They all owned, or were in the process of buying, their own homes. There was one other brother, who had broken off relations with his parents and siblings when his mother began to 'mind' West Indian children, but the other four remained, despite geographical separation and economic inequalities, a close-knit family, even after the death of their mother who had, in everyone's opinion, 'held the family together'. For Christmas and bank holidays they usually congregated in two households, and there was a constant flow of information and gossip, and a constant exchange of 'hand-ons' and items of household furniture between them. In contrast, the Cloughs saw relatively little of their respective siblings. Mr Clough (WI) had three brothers, but had lost contact with all of them. Mrs Clough was the youngest of eleven siblings. The oldest of these was no longer alive, and she and her husband were in close contact with only two of those remaining, a brother and sister who shared a joint household a few miles away, and who were seen or telephoned every fortnight or so. These were Mrs Clough's 'favourite' siblings and, economically, the least successful members of the family. Five siblings lived in Kent, the Midlands and outer London, and maintained friendly, if more distant, relations, sending Christmas and birthday cards but rarely visiting. Three siblings were not seen at all, including one who had broken off relations because of Mrs Clough's decision to marry a West Indian.

Yet even where siblings were not involved in an extensive exchange of services, nor formed part of an extended network of kin, such relationships could play a valued part in the social lives of these couples. Mr Curtis (WI), for example, saw his brother, an electrician, and his family about once a month. He described their relationship as, 'not quite friendship...we get along all right, the children enjoy going over there, but...if Lindon wasn't my brother I don't think I would be seeing him so often...I do not have many friends in this country and I suppose a brother fills a need there.' Similarly, Mr Lowe (WI), who regarded his accountant brother as 'too square' for his tastes, was pleased to be able to spend Christmas and bank holidays with him and his family. In some households, like the Ademolas or the Collets, kin provided virtually the only durable social relations the household enjoyed; in others they formed a significant portion of the social network.

'Real friends'

Four couples, the Cloughs, the Collets, the Horaces and the Ademolas, claimed they had no friends. Certainly, as far as could be ascertained, in each case no one apart from kin – and, in the case of the Ademolas, Mrs Ademola's priest – visited the house. While these households did enjoy some casual, low-intensity relationships with outsiders, they lacked the enduring and highly valued relationships which stood at the core of the social networks of most households, contacts which were described as 'lasting relationships', or 'real friends'.

Eleven of the white respondents and fifteen of the black respondents were still in contact with friends whom they had known before they met their present partners, individuals who formed a highly valued link between the present and the vanished past. Most of these were childhood friends, or, in the case of the black partners, friends from 'back home'; Mr Lowe (WI) and Mr Abbott (WI) also had close friendships forged in the hardships of immigrant life in England in the 1940s and 1950s. Such relationships often played only a minor part in the everyday social life of these individuals. Mrs Kalipha (GB), for example, saw her closest childhood friend perhaps only twice a year, when she visited London from Swansea; nevertheless, she described their relationship as, 'a good friendship...you don't see her for six months but when you do it's just the same as if it was last week'. Such relationships, in short, provided an important sense of continuity for the individual concerned.

More rarely, respondents had made durable friends of people encountered at work or through neighbourhood contacts in the course of adult life. Some of these were cross-ethnic friendships. Mr Abbott

(WI), for example, counted as his 'best friend' at the time of the interview an English garage owner whom he had known for six years: Mr Sidey's (GB) closest friend was his Indian business partner; Mrs Rowlands (GB) had kept up with a West Indian woman whom she had met at work before she was married. Most such friendships, however, like those friendships made early in life, were with individuals of the same ethnicity, and the same sex, as the respondent.

Some couples, nine in all, had other friends made after they had entered into their present interracial union. In five cases – the Curtises, Oluwoles, Sideys, Jays and Kaliphas – these were friendships with whites only; in four other cases – the Birchalls, Riches, Handburys and Hendersons – these were ethnically mixed. Despite, then, Mr Clough's assertion that, 'friendship is hard to gain when you are a mixed marriage', most of these couples demonstrated both range and flexibility in their choice of friends. And all but one of the households with any friends at all enjoyed social relationships with both black and white people.

In a way, however, this overall picture is misleading, since couples did not necessarily hold their friendships in common. There were, for example, six households where segregated leisure patterns were matched by a corresponding segregation in friendship association. The Kaliphas, for instance, saw few friends jointly. Until recently, Mr Kalipha (WI) had been in the habit of spending six nights a week in the pub, while Mrs Kalipha stayed in with the children. It was in his 'local' that Mr Kalipha saw his mates and any old friends from Guyana who wished to look him up; it was rare for any such friends to come to the flat and rare for the Kaliphas to spend an evening jointly with them. Mrs Kalipha, on the other hand, saw her friends during the day; some of these were old neighbours, while others were people who worked with her in a local community project and who knew her husband only slightly. In a few months prior to interview, they had seen only one friend jointly, an old school friend of Mrs Kalipha's with whom they had gone out for a meal.

A similar segregation prevailed in the Jay, Homer–Brettle, Rich and Naylor households. In all but the last of these, the male partner was a working-class West Indian who continued to participate in a network of male friends, spending time in pubs and clubs while his partner was tied to the home by small children. Withdrawal from such interaction was, however, for at least some of these women not simply a temporary inconvenience, but a positive choice. Mrs Rowlands (GB), for example, spent much time with her family of origin, a preference which she neither expected nor demanded that her husband share. Mrs Jay and Mrs Kalipha (both GB) both disliked certain aspects of West Indian social life and refused to participate in it – even when they had the chance to do so – preferring to spend the time with English female friends. Similarly Mr Naylor (GB) refused to associate with his wife's

Rhodesian Coloured and West Indian friends, and the couple spent little time together. The implications of this pattern will be analysed in more detail in the chapter that follows. For the moment, it will suffice to point out that, where a couple have a segregated friendship network, it is possible for them to pursue separate, or even conflicting, friendship strategies. Mrs Kalipha's friends, for example, were all white and female; her husband's, all black and all male.

In other households, there was a tendency to transform the friends of one partner into the friends of the household, which suggested, in itself, some consensus of social orientation. Naturally, in such cases, friends who failed to 'fit' tended to be discarded. Mr Ojo (Y), for example, had three male Nigerian friends whom, in the period before his marriage, he had seen with equal frequency. At the time of interview, two of these were still close friends, who dropped in regularly on the Ojos or who were visited jointly by them. The third, however, had married a Nigerian wife who, according to Mrs Ojo (GB) was 'not very clean'. At first, Mr Ojo continued to visit him, although he did not take his wife; as time passed, however, these visits became more and more infrequent.

In a minority of households – the Curtises, the Ojos, and the Handburys – both partners contributed friends to a joint network; in other cases, it was evident that one partner's friendship choices dominated the overall network, although the other partner had very largely accepted these friends as his or her own. The factors involved in this process were complex, and varied with each household; individual personality, pre-existing social resources, and the accidents of occupation, residence and everyday life all played their part. In some cases, as in the case of the Gomez–Mackie household, or the Lowe–Simmons household, the dominance of the friends of one partner reflected social dislocation in the network of the other. The implications of this will be discussed in more detail below.

Neighbours

It was women, for the most part, who initiated and maintained neighbouring relationships, although occasionally men in adjoining households became involved in the exchange of help or advice. These were relationships started casually, though chance encounters in multi-occupied houses, the street, neighbourhood clubs or through children's activities; they revolved around the shared routines of domestic life – shopping, minding small children, quick breaks for cups or tea or coffee – and catered for a variety of short-term, individual needs. Although such relationships could develop into durable friendships they typically did not survive geographical separation. When I interviewed Mrs Collet (GB), for example, the woman that she described as her 'best friend' on the estate where she lived, and who had been a witness at her wedding, had moved away some eight months before interview; the woman had not been in contact since. Similarly, Mrs Birchall and Mrs Ojo (GB) were neighbours who saw each other every day, spent much time together, and rendered each other many small services; yet when the Birchalls were on the point of moving to another part of London, Mrs Ojo observed, realistically, that although Mrs Birchall would 'always be welcome' if she visited Brixton, she herself did not intend to travel to see her. The distinction between neighbours and 'real friends' was indicated most clearly by Mrs Jay (GB), when she spoke of an ex-neighbour of hers with whom she had enjoyed a close relationship for eight years. Now they had both been rehoused, in different parts of Brixton, and saw each other less often: 'I'd have called her a friend, but I'm not so sure now.'

Such relationships nevertheless played a valued part in the lives of most of these women. All had some contacts with neighbours, although in two cases this was confined to the exchange of greetings in the street. The pattern of association which can be discerned is an interesting one. It is hardly surprising that, for women like Mrs Sidey (WI) or Mrs Clough (GB), living in areas with only a small black population, the neighbours with whom they were friendly should be English. Yet it also proved to be the case that even where households were located in areas of black settlement, the female partner saw either no black neighbours at all or very few of them – even where she was, herself, black.

In some cases, as we have already noted, interracial households in 'rough' neighbourhoods were reluctant to develop contacts with people whom they considered to be their social and educational inferiors. Mrs Henderson (RC), for example, an educated woman married to a white-collar worker, remarked of the dilapidated neighbourhood where she lived: 'We don't mix...most of our friends live outside the area.' Other families, like the Cloughs and the Curtises, who lived on the periphery of Brixton in areas of increasing black population, identified firmly with the long-established white residents of their immediate neighbourhoods rather than with the black, proletarian, newcomers. Mr Clough (WI), for example, stated that he did not intend to move house 'unless the street deteriorates...this used to be an area of the pretentious middle class but these people are moving out, and this you can see in the change in the schools and in the Youth Club'. 'There are some people now,' his wife added, 'like the ones down there [at the West Indian, multi-occupied end of the street] you wouldn't want to live next to.'

Other respondents, however, related their reluctance to associate with black neighbours to ethnic, not status, differences. Mrs. Collett, for example, lived on an estate with a high proportion of black residents, but the only neighbour she counted as a friend was an English woman who lived next door. 'I'll tell you straight, I don't get on with coloured women – the fights I have with coloured women when their kids pick on mine.' Similarly, Mrs Jay (GB) remarked that 'I don't much like West Indian women – they are always so aggressive, they're always on the offensive, or maybe it's the defensive – I don't know.'

These women tended to blame their difficulties upon the hostility of black women to interracial unions. As Mrs Collet (GB) put it: 'Being married to a coloured chap, they hate me for taking their men.' Certainly, antagonisms of this kind did exist among West Indian women in Brixton; and such antagonisms were sometimes reinforced, unwittingly, by the personal character of the woman in question. Mrs Collet, for example, was a woman who found social interaction difficult and avoided it when she could. 'I don't mix much, I never have done...keep myself to myself...I don't speak to women unless they speak to me first.' It was not surprising to find that her black neighbours interpreted this behaviour as evidence of an unwarranted sense of superiority.

In fact, most of the women who had no social contact with their black neighbours did feel that they adhered to one set of standards and their black neighbours to another. Mrs Birchall and Mrs Ojo (both GB), for example, were neighbours in the same Brixton street, at the heart of a dense area of black settlement. They had, however, developed their social relations with neighbours in very different directions. Mrs Birchall enjoyed the company of West Indians, and was on visiting terms with four Jamaican families in the neighbourhood, two of whom were living in miserable conditions in overcrowded multi-occupied houses. She was neither disturbed by the disorganised nature of these households nor moralistic about values very different from those of English convention – attitudes which earned her the esteem of her West Indian neighbours. Her friendships with her black neighbours did not, however, lose Mrs Birchall her contacts with whites, for her evidently middle-class origins and her husband's occupation testified to her 'respectability'.

Unlike Mrs Birchall, Mrs Ojo had grown up in poverty and placed a high value upon good domestic management. Dirt and disorganisation were anathema to her, and she was intolerant of people who, in her opinion, did not 'try to pull their families up'. She disapproved strongly of what she took to be the predominant West Indian attitude towards family life: 'I can't understand people who don't put their children first, even if it means going without yourself.' Even West Africans, whom she felt to be 'more responsible people than West Indians', she found wanting in this respect; and she felt that she got on with her Yoruba husband's family only because they had 'been brought up in the English way...I don't usually get on with coloured people.' These ethnocentric attitudes were reflected in her choice of neighbouring relationships: of nine, only one, a Ugandan woman – met, in fact, through Mrs Birchall – was not English.

Neighbouring relationships, then, offered a channel through which the interracially married could develop a sense of rootedness. They required, however, a careful management of the household's social identity. Relationships flourished with local English residents, for example, where the woman in question was able, through the presentation of a conventionally 'respectable' social profile, to convince her neighbours that she was not 'that sort of girl'. 'She's married to a coloured chap, you know', remarked one of Mrs Ojo's English neighbours, 'though you wouldn't have thought it. Her kiddies are always spotless.'

The casual nature of neighbourly contact, which did not require the involvement of other members of the household, permitted even the 'prejudiced' neighbour to engage in such relationships without confronting the contradictions inherent in his or her attitudes. Here, as in other situations, it was always possible to handle the problems of cognitive dissonance by turning the black partner into an exception: as Mrs Collet (GB) observed laughingly of her next-door neighbour, 'She is really colour-prejudiced, but my husband is different, for some reason.'

Workmates and associational contacts

The women in the research set who were engaged in manual or clerical occupations tended to work 'unsocial hours', and it was not surprising that most – four out of six – saw nothing of their fellow workers outside work. For those men who were engaged in similar occupations, however, friendship with co-workers served much the same function as did neighbouring relationships for their wives. Eight such men had 'mates', invariably of the same sex and ethnicity as the respondent, with whom they spent time in activities outside the home: visiting pubs or drinking clubs, or going to football or wrestling matches. Indeed, men who had no interest in such masculine activities rarely developed friendships at work.

For a significant number of the men, nine in all, drinking in pubs or drinking clubs was an important element in their leisure activities, although the time spent thus varied considerably from Mr Clough's fortnightly visits to the six nights a week spent drinking by Mr Jay, Mr Rich and Mr Rowlands. Mr Clough (WI) and Mr Naylor (GB) preferred to drink alone, but for most this was a social occasion. Men sometimes drank with their workmates, or with neighbours, but often their companions were others who simply happened to visit the same pub or club.

Naturally enough, then, the respondent's choice of drinking place directly affected the kind of companions he acquired. Mr Lowe (WI), for example, preferred 'smart' pubs on the periphery of the area of black settlement north of the river near his place of work; his companions there were white. Other men, working-class West Indians like Mr Rowlands or Mr Rich, drank in the West Indian drinking clubs of central Brixton or in pubs with a substantial West Indian clientele; their companions were black. Miss Mackie (GB), the only woman to spend much time in pubs, also drank in these locations.

Like neighbourhood contacts for women, then, these locations acted as a channel through which the racially intermarried could maintain low-intensity, casual links with their 'own' ethnic community, and through which an individual could express his, or her, personal ethnic orientations.

For the eight individuals – three of them women – who were engaged in professional or vocational work, relations with colleagues and clients played a much more important part in their social networks, often providing some of the most satisfying of their social relationships. With the exception of Mr Birchall (WI), who was involved in community work, most of the contacts made in this way were with whites, no matter what the ethnicity of the respondent, for blacks tended to be excluded from the kind of occupations in which these respondents found themselves. Equally, their occupational status was, in itself, a guarantee of the 'respectability' which facilitated the development of relations with whites.

Only a minority of respondents, ten in all, were members of social clubs or societies, including five English mothers who attended local mother and baby clubs; two men who were members of sports clubs; and one wife who played a minor part in her local church's musical society. Such contacts tended to reinforce the racially intermarried individuals' links with a white rather than a black social field. Similarly, none of these households attended any of the West Indian – or West African-run churches that flourished in the Brixton area, but four had active links with local Anglican or Roman Catholic congregations, and one couple, the Handbury's, recruited a large proportion of their personal friends from the body of young clergy and welfare workers in the area.

A significant proportion of these respondents were involved with community organisations: two, Mr Birchall (WI) and Mrs Oluwole (GB), with groups concerned with race relations; two, Mrs Kalipha and Mrs Jay (both GB), with a local community project; and three, the Handburys (GB/WI) and Mr Clough (WI), with youth work. This involvement reflected, perhaps, a consciousness of social issues which may have been stimulated by the individual's decision to enter into an interracial union. Again, however, for the most part such work brought these individuals into contact with whites rather than blacks.

Constraints and orientations

Table 8.3 sets out the size and composition of each couple's effective social network, defined rather more narrowly than in the discussion of

Table 8.3. *Size and composition of effective social networks, all households*

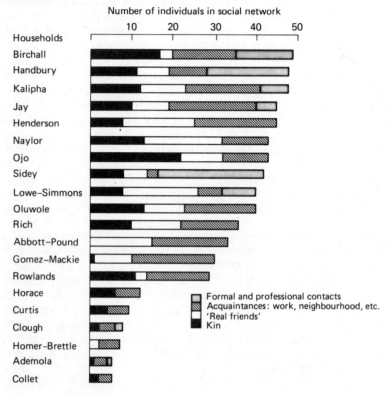

kin presented above.[2] We have seen that couples brought to their interracial relationships very different social resources. There were those who brought with them extensive networks of kin and a wide range of durable social relationships, and those whose disrupted and unstable histories were reflected in the paucity and fragility of their social contacts. There were those whose occupational and geographical

[2] In a study of this kind, it is impossible to avoid a subjective element in the definition of 'effective' social network. By this term, I indicate the field of significant social relationships that each couple had constructed, comprising every adult (of sixteen years or more) with whom respondents enjoyed an independent social relationship. In compiling each household's effective social network, I have chosen to include:

(a) All adults with whom respondents had regular, face-to-face informal contact at least once very three months, contact ranging from routine but frequent casual interaction to less frequent but more extensive visiting or contact.

(b) All adult kin seen at least once every three months.

(c) Any relationships which the respondents themselves felt to be of personal importance to them, but which for various reasons (such as distance) involved contact less often than once every three months, but at least once a year.

circumstances made it easy for them to find friends and acquaintances whom they liked, while there were others who felt themselves to be isolated, having little in common with those with whom they came into contact in the course of everyday life. Some households were thus firmly embedded in a network of social relations which provided them with considerable satisfaction and security, while others were confronted with the task of constructing a viable social world from scratch. If each household's social network may be viewed as an expression of that household's aspirations and orientations, this expression was undoubtedly constrained by the social resources available to the persons concerned, as we shall see in the following chapter.

9 Living in a divided community

I have suggested, in the preceding chapter, that these twenty interracial couples were able to draw upon a wide range of social resources in the construction of their social networks; I have also noted that, in their comments on the area in which they were living and the people who lived there, they evidenced considerable diversity of orientation. This diversity is directly reflected in the structure of each household's social network.

As I have already indicated, the social choices of each interracial couple were, essentially, choices directed specifically towards the alternatives of interaction with the ethnic group of the white partner or with that of the black partner; it was unusual to find a household with friends drawn from a plurality of ethnic groups. In this respect, considerable differences are immediately apparent between the interracial households. Though all included some whites in their selected social field, the proportion of whites in each household's network varied widely, from 100% for the Cloughs to a mere 17% for the Riches (see Table 9.1). Thus, households could be divided into those with white-dominated, black-dominated, or racially balanced networks. As I have already argued, however, to assess households on the basis of overall network composition may be misleading in several respects. Only some of the couples whose social field comprised a roughly balanced mixture of black and white social contacts, for example, were participating jointly in a network which included both black and white households; in other cases, the racially balanced character of the network was derived from the inclusion of a high proportion of interracial couples, while others again were involved in segregated personal networks differentiated on ethnic grounds.

In the analysis which follows, households have been divided into several clusters sharing certain similarities in the deployment of black and white social contacts. Firstly, there were two households with what I have termed 'composite' networks, comprising a balanced proportion of both black and white households, and two others whose networks comprised a high proportion of interracial couples and which, for reasons that will be apparent below, I have termed 'interstitial' networks. In contrast, there were those households whose social networks evidence a strong commitment, by both partners, to interaction with one partner's ethnic group at the expense of the other. These

116

Table 9.1. *Ethnic composition of social networks*

	Segregated network	Joint network
Over two-thirds *black* individuals	Rich	Gomez–Mackie
Mixed (between one-third and two-thirds both black and white individuals)	Naylor Rowlands	Abbott–Pound Birchall Lowe–Simmons
Over two-thirds *white* individuals	Jay Kalipha	Handbury Henderson Oluwole Ojo Sidey
Networks too small to permit quantification	Ademola (1 black individual, 4 white) Clough (All white) Collet (2 black individuals, 3 white) Curtis (2 black individuals, 7 white) Homer–Brettle (6 black individuals, 1 white) Horace (all white)	

included two households with what I have termed 'black-oriented' networks, where at least two-thirds of all social contacts were with black people, and five 'white-oriented' households, where at least two-thirds of social contacts were with whites. Finally, there were three households where the social strategies of the individuals concerned were not consonant with those of their partners, giving rise to 'Janus' networks where segregation between the networks of the partners was correlated with strong differences in ethnic orientation.

Six households remain unaccounted for. These were cases where household networks were so small that they warrant special consideration. These 'isolate families' are treated separately, below.

Households with black-oriented networks

Both the Riches and the Gomez–Mackie household lived in the centre of Brixton, in neighbourhoods with very large black populations. The men, both West Indians, were manual workers from poor peasant families; their partners had grown up in the insecure world of the British urban poor.

Both men had been living in Brixton for a number of years, and had no intention of moving away; in all, 84% of one and 92% of the other couple's social contacts lived within a two-mile radius of Brixton town centre. Most of these were relationships made initially through the black partner. Both networks contained a relatively dense, highly localised cluster of male friends of roughly equivalent socio-economic status, all of whom spent much time in the drinking clubs, pubs, betting shops and cafés of central Brixton; indeed it was in these very locations that these two couples had first met. Mr Rich had, in addition, a number of relatives living locally whom he saw jointly with his wife. In short, both men were fully involved in the mainstream of Brixton West Indian life, and selected their friends from its social universe.

Mr Gomez and Miss Mackie engaged in much of their social life together, while the Riches saw many of their contacts separately. Nevertheless, in both cases, the women concerned shared the social orientation of their black partners. Both had minimal contact with their kin, Miss Mackie having incurred the hostility of her family many years previously, when she became pregnant in adolescence, and Mrs Rich losing touch with her family when they discovered her relationship with a West Indian. Both women had, as a result of their detachment from mainstream white life, few enduring social relationships. Miss Mackie had moved eight times in ten years spent in London, never stopping, as she said, 'long enough to get to know a lot of people'; Mrs Rich had lost touch with all but one of her many school friends living in the area: 'After the business with my family, they don't want to know me.' With no cohesive networks of their own, these women had been drawn into the social worlds of their partners, either participating in their partner's friendships or developing independent relationships with women in the neighbourhood whom they felt to be socially similar to themselves – women also involved in the black Brixton world, or others whose disadvantaged status rendered them, too, marginal to mainstream white life. Thus, Mrs Rich's personal network included an English unmarried mother whom she met at an ante-natal clinic, an English neighbour married to a Jamaican, an unmarried Jamaican girl with two children who lived in the same house, the Guyanese former girl-friend of one of her husband's cousins, and the Jamaican wife of one of her husband's workmates. The only school friend with whom she was still in touch was, in turn, married to a West Indian.

Though rejection by white society undoubtedly played its part in shaping the social field from which these couples recruited their friends, it was evident that these white partners, unlike many others in the research set, shared with their partners a liking for many aspects of West Indian life. They ate Caribbean food, liked reggae music, enjoyed West Indian parties and Blues dances, and preferred to spend their leisure time in pubs and discotheques catering for West Indian, rather than English, tastes. Mrs Rich had even adopted Jamaican patois as her usual manner of speech when in black company. These expressions of the strong sense of commitment to a black, rather than a white, Brixton

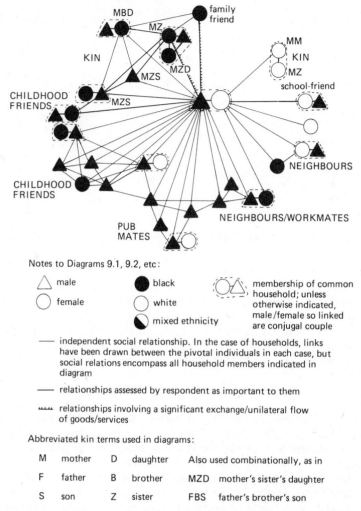

Notes to Diagrams 9.1, 9.2, etc:

△ male   ● black   ⬡△ membership of common
○ female   ○ white   household; unless
            ◐ mixed ethnicity   otherwise indicated,
                                male/female so linked
                                are conjugal couple

—— independent social relationship. In the case of households, links
   have been drawn between the pivotal individuals in each case, but
   social relations encompass all household members indicated in
   diagram

—— relationships assessed by respondent as important to them

⌣⌣⌣ relationships involving a significant exchange/unilateral flow
    of goods/services

Abbreviated kin terms used in diagrams:

M	mother	D	daughter	Also used combinationally, as in
F	father	B	brother	MZD mother's sister's daughter
S	son	Z	sister	FBS father's brother's son

Diagram 9.1. Household with black-oriented social network: the Riches.

world in themselves reinforced the barrier between these households and
mainstream whites, for it was exactly this kind of behaviour that local
whites identified as being typical of what they termed a 'black man's
woman', an immoral creature to be despised and shunned. As Miss
Mackie herself put it: 'they [white people] think you're all right if you
show you haven't gone over to the other side, like. They expect you to
live with a Jamaican like he was a bloody Englishman.'

On the whole, it seemed true to say that, in these households, the white
partners had indeed 'gone over to the other side' (see Diagram 9.1). Yet,

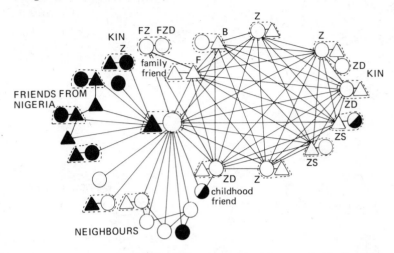

Diagram 9.2. Household with white-oriented social network (1): the Ojos.

even so, there were differences between these networks and those which seemed to be typical of endogamously married households in Brixton. In the latter, women's closest friends were usually kin, or other West Indian women; Miss Mackie's and Mrs Rich's closest friends were white, albeit white women living with West Indians. Thus, although these households were embedded in a black social field, they remained in some ways marginal to mainstream black life.

Households with white-oriented networks

These households included two of the four Anglo-Yoruba households, the Ojos and the Oluwoles, and three of the four households where the female partner was black, the Handburys the Hendersons, and the Sideys. The socio-economic status of these respondents was higher than that of those discussed above, with the husbands in professional, executive, and clerical occupations while the three wives who worked included a teacher, a nurse and a librarian. All the black partners came from families of relatively high status in their countries of origin; unlike the black respondents discussed above, all had received a formal education up to Ordinary Level standard and most had continued, or had attempted to continue, their studies to a higher level.

Unlike Mrs Rich and Miss Mackie, the white partners in these households had remained in touch with their families of origin and, through them, with a wider field of kin. However, only in one case – that of the Ojos – where the relatively dense cluster formed by the white partner's kin set comprised over half the couple's total social field, could this be adduced as a sufficient explanation for the dominance of whites

120

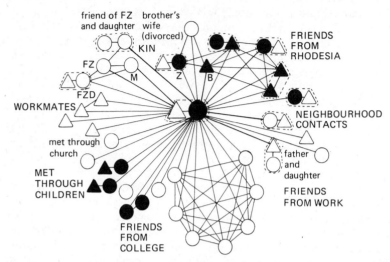

Diagram 9.3. Household with white-oriented social network (2): the Hendersons.

in these households' social fields. The Handburys, for example, had more black effective kin than white, while in other households, like the Sideys, kin contacts did not form a significant part of the total network. Again, it was only in the case of the Ojos that it seemed that a black partner with an attenuated social network had been drawn into the dense and localised social field of the other partner (see Diagram 9.2). The remaining couples all had rather low-density networks, made up of individuals encountered in a diversity of social contexts by one or both partners (see Diagram 9.3).

In these cases, it is important to note that white friends and acquaintances were recruited by both partners; the black partners' social horizons were not bounded by their respective ethnic communities. None of these couples had first met in a 'black' location, and only one through a black mutual friend. Several came from families with strong orientations towards English culture and mores, and two, in fact, had siblings who had also married English people. Both Mrs Handbury and Mrs Sidey had attended schools where the majority of pupils was white; Mrs Henderson, Mr Ojo and Mr Oluwole had all attended colleges of higher education in England; four were engaged, or had partners who were engaged, in occupations where, they felt, relationships between black and white colleagues were better than average. These households, then, had relatively strong links to mainstream white society.

By contrast, their attitudes towards the black partners' respective ethnic groups were characterised by some ambiguity. An extreme point of view was expressed by Mrs Ojo (GB), when she asserted that her

121

Yoruba husband had 'no need for Nigerian friends, he gets along so well with the English'; but, in fact, only one white partner, Mrs Oluwole, felt she would have liked to see more of members of her partner's ethnic group. The remainder all assumed, as did their black partners, that their choice of friends reflected the kind of people that they were. We have already noted how Mrs Handbury (WI), for example, felt she had little in common with 'the kind of West Indian you find living in this area'; like Mrs Handbury, others among these respondents often pointed to what they felt were important differences in ideals, aims and life-style between themselves or their partners and those in the social mainstream of their respective ethnic groups.

Such attitudes inevitably led to the curtailment of some social relations. I have already mentioned how Mr Ojo (Y), for example, allowed his friendship with a fellow Yoruba to lapse because the friend's wife did not share the same standards of domestic hygiene as his own English wife. Similarly, Mr Oluwole refused to let his small daughter visit the household of a married Yoruba friend because the children there were dirty, badly dressed, and were not given what he thought to be 'proper' meals. Mrs Henderson (RC) too controlled her children's social life; she would not let them visit a neighbouring West African household where, in her opinion, they were not properly supervised or made welcome, and she would not permit them to accept invitations from West Indian children at school 'unless I know the family'. Though she hastened to add that she would do this for all invitations, it was clear that she felt that West Indian children, more often than whites, were likely to come from 'undesirable homes'. In contrast, the West Indians that she did see were carefully differentiated from the rest; one couple were described as 'very fine people', while of West Indians in general she said, 'if they are educated people, they make very good friends'.

With the exception of the Ojos, then – where the black partner had been, at least temporarily, very largely incorporated into his wife's social field – these couples looked towards a wide range of occupational, associational and casual contacts through which they could meet people of similar social status and interests to their own. Their success in this respect reflected the extent to which these households were detached – and could present themselves to others as being so detached – from the black Brixton world which defined the social horizons of many other respondents.

Janus households

There were three households of this type in the research set: the Jays, the Kaliphas and the Naylors. Mr Jay and Mr Kalipha were both West Indians in manual occupations; their wives came from solid, working-class families, as did Mr Naylor. Mr Naylor, a semi-invalid, had a light

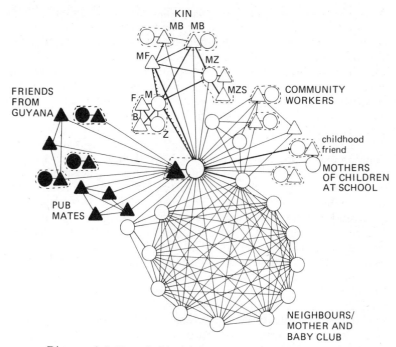

Diagram 9.4. Household with Janus network: the Kaliphas.

manual job, while his Rhodesian Coloured wife worked as a catering superintendent for a local firm. Until the summer of 1970 and the spring of 1971 respectively, when they were rehoused, the Kaliphas and the Jays have been living in Angell Town, an area with a substantial black population; the Kaliphas were moved to an estate in Stockwell, while the Jays went to central Brixton. The Naylors too had lived in Angell Town, but had then moved to Clapham.

In the Anglo-Caribbean households, both partners led active social lives, but with separate friends. However, unlike other couples who led independent social lives, the segregated personal networks of these couples were characterised by a striking ethnic differentiation. The men spent much of their leisure time outside the home with other West Indian men of similar socio-economic status to their own, while their wives spent much of their time with a clique of white female neighbours who had grouped themselves into an informal mother and baby club.

Neither partner knew very much about each other's friends, nor felt that they had much in common with them. The husbands' male companions rarely visited them at home, and those their wives made welcome were often understood to be rather different from the rest; Mrs Jay, for example, named an elderly Englishman and a church-going Barbadian couple, whom she described as 'very nice people', as being the only people in her husband's circle that she liked. Equally, these husbands hardly knew the friends that their wives had made among the English workers of the local community project with which they had become involved, or had much in common with the English women, unmarried mothers or the wives of manual workers, who comprised the mother and baby club. Both households were in touch with the families of the white partner, but here, as we might expect, the women were much more intensively involved than their husbands, who themselves had no kin in this country.

Evidence suggests that such segregated arrangements are not un-common in working-class households. Nevertheless, in these cases, the evolution of this particular pattern of social life had further implications. Before the arrival of children, these women had, indeed, participated in their partners' social network and spent much of their leisure time with their future husbands; unlike the English wives in the black-oriented households, however, they did not regret their withdrawal from these joint activities, for neither found a West Indian style of socialising congenial. Mrs Jay, in particular, found relations with both West Indian men and West Indian women very difficult. Both women preferred the company of English women like themselves, although Mrs Kalipha, in particular, did know a number of English women married to West Indian men: 'If you are one, you meet a lot, I don't know why it should be so, but I know four mixed marriages, not counting friends of my husband's who've married English girls.'

The Anglo-Rhodesian couple were a rather different case. Here, the white husband, even more than the wives in the two households discussed above, was reluctant to socialise with members of his wife's ethnic group – or, indeed, with any black people at all. As a result, only the most long-standing of Mrs Naylor's friends visited her at home: 'I go out to coloured friends...he just sits and glares. I tell them, don't mind Naylor, you'll get used to him.'

In Rhodesia, the couple had led segregated social lives, she within the Coloured community, he with his white peers. In England, 'always a loner', he had only a handful of acquaintances and a number of married siblings, living in Kent, whom he saw intermittently. She, in contrast, led an active social life with several sets of friends: Coloured Rhodesians known from 'back home', a scattering of white friends, and a clique of women, two Anglo-West Indian sisters and two English women married to West Indians, with whom she went to West Indian parties, clubs or 'Blues' dances on Saturday nights.

It was clear that in these three cases a segregated social network operated to minimise the tensions inherent in a marriage in which husband and wife were committed to very different social strategies, and held very different views on questions of colour and ethnic identity. It did not appear very likely that it was the precedent existence of the network itself which, through exerting pressure on the individuals concerned to conform to this segregation, caused this divergence in attitudes; nevertheless, such segregation evidently reduced the possibility of the couples' resolving these differences through change or convergence in attitudes or behaviour, since each was so effectively insulated from pressures towards conformity emanating from the other's social network (see Diagram 9.4). The Naylors' case demonstrates that such an arrangement could prove both durable and acceptable. It was evident, however, from conversations with Mrs Kalipha and Mrs Jay, that they regarded their present social arrangements as a poor substitute for a satisfying social life shared with a husband. Indeed, for Mrs Jay, the lack of common interests so evident in her relationship with her husband, and their commitment to irreconcilably different social fields, were the major reasons for their eventual separation. The Kaliphas, on the other hand, showed some signs, at the time of the interview, of moving towards a joint orientation. Mrs Kalipha, unlike Mrs Jay, was not especially hostile towards West Indians; she was particularly concerned that her children should visit her husband's country of origin and learn as much as they could about it. Mr Kalipha, for his part, was beginning to assume an increasing number of commitments in the home and to spent less time in the pub. The couple were hoping to buy a house from Lambeth Council. Gradually, Mr Kalipha found himself drifting away from his Guyanese friends. 'They move around a lot,' explained Mrs Kalipha, 'especially the ones who aren't married. You never know where to find them... well, Tim leads a bit of a different life from them, especially if they are bachelors.'

Households with interstitial networks

The Lowe–Simmons and that Abbott–Pound households both lived in neighbourhoods with a high black population, in multi-occupied housing where there were other interracial couples among the tenants. Both Mr Lowe and Mr Abbott were in middle age, long-term migrants from the Caribbean who had never settled down domestically in England. Their common-law partners were both considerably younger than themselves. All four were very much the 'black sheep' of their respective families. Mr Abbott had long ago lost touch with his kin, while Miss Pound had run away from home in adolescence after a troubled and unhappy childhood; Mr Lowe's relations in England were settled and conventional people, with whom he felt he had little in common, while Mrs Simmons felt that she and her parents led 'totally different lives' and that they blamed her for deserting her husband and her four children.

The women in these households were in much the same social situation as Mrs Rich and Miss Mackie, and for the same reasons; neither had been able to maintain a stable network of social relations through time, and both had been incorporated into their partners' social

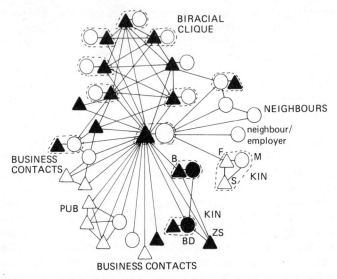

BIRACIAL
CLIQUE

NEIGHBOURS

neighbour/
employer

BUSINESS
CONTACTS

B.

F M

S KIN

PUB

KIN

ZS

BD

BUSINESS CONTACTS

Diagram 9.5. Household with interstitial network: Mr Lowe and Mrs Simmons.

fields. However, unlike Mr Rich or Mr Gomez these men spent much of their time with compatriots who, like themselves, consistently evidenced a preference for white women as sexual partners (see Diagram 9.5).

Mr Lowe and Mr Abbott had many friends in common, although, of course, their social networks did not exactly coincide. Mr Lowe, for example, spent some of his leisure time in smart pubs on the periphery of an area of black settlement, where he drank with English 'business contacts' and some of his clients; Mr Abbott had several English friends who were known to Mr Lowe only by name, and spent some of his leisure time with long-term Fante migrants, all of whom had white wives or girl-friends, but whom Mr Lowe avoided since he disliked West Africans. Nevertheless, both men participated, at least until the summer of 1971, in numerous shared social activities.

These two men, together with a third, a Jamaican, formed a trio of intimate friends who, with their white partners, spent much of their leisure time together, visiting each other's flats to watch TV, have a meal, or play records and dance. Occasionally, one or other of them threw a more formal party which brought together a wider set of similar couples. These were, for the most part, West Indian men in skilled manual or entrepreneurial occupations with white wives or girl-friends. Only rarely were active social relations maintained with a girl once she ceased to be attached to one of the men who formed this close-knit circle; similarly, friends of the white partner, who might be included in activities for a while, dropped out of the clique's social life when she did.

The most striking fact about this clique was its members' lack of contact with mainstream black life. Some, like Mr Lowe and Mr Abbott themselves, had arrived in England in the early days of black migration and had drifted into the enclosed world of hustlers, petty entrepreneurs, musicians and hangers-on that had developed in areas of black settlement in London. Others had arrived later, but either lacked the contacts through which they might have become enmeshed in mainstream black life or shared a taste for the 'hustler' life-style which set them apart from most other West Indians in London. Such men recruited their sexual partners from the pool of white women who, for various reasons, had themselves been drawn into this narrow social world.

Within this circle of acquaintances, sexual partners were often exchanged – not, of course, without trauma, but on the whole reasonably amicably. Mrs Simmons, for example, who, at the time of interview, was cohabiting with Mr Lowe, subsequently spent a year in Ghana with a classificatory cousin of the Fante who owned the house where she and Mr Lowe lived, and whose closest friend, another Fante, was also a friend of Mr Abbott. Miss Pound had been living with this second Fante before she moved in with Mr Abbott. Miss Pound's relationship with Mr Abbott, however, was not to last; after a period of continual quarrels and domestic violence Miss Pound was admitted to a mental hospital and her children placed in care. By this time, Mrs Simmons had returned from Ghana, and she and Mr Abbott developed a sexual relationship; the couple finally married, in 1974. Most of the women selected as sexual partners by these men, like Mrs Simmons or Miss Pound, had had a succession of black boy-friends, but little or no contact with West Indian women or West Indian family life. Indeed, they often maintained a series of unfavourable stereotypes concerning ordinary West Indians which received support from their partners' frequently adverse comments on the same theme.

These households thus occupied a position that was interstitial in relationship to mainstream black and white life. Here, as in the black-oriented households, it was the black partner who dominated the pattern of social life. However, unlike these black-oriented respondents, Mr Abbott and Mr Lowe found that they had little in common with most of their compatriots. We have already noted, for example, Mr Lowe's contempt for the black residents of Brixton, 'just peasants really'; equally, he had little sympathy with the life-style of his prosperous brother, an accountant who lived in Streatham: 'he's too square for me'. Unlike the West Indian respondents in white-oriented households then, the distinction that these men drew between themselves and other West Indians was that between 'straights' and 'swingers', and their attitudes towards mainstream white society and its values were markedly ambivalent. These men enjoyed black music, often visited black-owned clubs, cooked simplified West Indian food, and were fond of using black American slang, but their tastes, interests and even their linguistic usage differentiated them from their black peers as sharply as it did from conventional white society.

Households with ethnically composite networks

Both the Birchalls and the Rowlandses lived in central Brixton. This was a somewhat unusual choice of residence for the former since Mr Birchall (WI) had a semi-professional job; Mr Rowlands, more typically, had a semi-skilled manual job.

Unlike many other households in the research set, the Rowlandses and the Birchalls enjoyed good social relations with the kin of both black and white partners and had an extensive range of kin within reach. Kin comprised 37% and 41% of their social networks respectively, and thus played a significant part in determining the ethnically bilateral nature of their social field. However, even where non-kin were concerned these couples tended to have more cross-racial friendships than others in the research set. The women, for example, like Mrs Rich and Miss Mackie, had good relationships with black neighbours; but, unlike Mrs Rich and Miss Mackie, they also enjoyed amicable relationships with 'respectable' white neighbours.

In other respects, the social networks of these two households were very different. Apart from their relations with kin, the Rowlandses had few friends in common, Mr Rowlands spending much of his time with other West Indian men and Mrs Rowlands with various white and black female neighbours. In the Birchall household, many social relationships were joint, and many involved West Indian and English people working alongside each other in community work or in the field of race relations. At the same time, they also had friends who were not part of this essentially multiracial social set: local West Indians who had been involved, with Mr Birchall, in a political project some years before, neighbourhood contacts, and local entrepreneurs.

An obvious point is that in the Birchalls' case it was Mr Birchall's occupational status that enabled the household to draw so freely upon the social resources of both ethnic groups. A more interesting point emerges if we look at the social relationships which these households had with neighbours. Both Mrs Rowlands and Mrs Birchall were somewhat eccentric in terms of social identity, and, therefore, enjoyed a certain degree of tolerance from others respecting their friendship choices. Mrs Birchall was a middle-class woman, who not only lived in a proletarian area but was content to make friends across the boundaries of socio-economic status; Mrs Rowlands was considered to be 'a little bit simple' and it appeared that, for some time, she had been more readily accepted by West Indian women than by whites. Neither woman seemed to be especially concerned with public opinion respecting

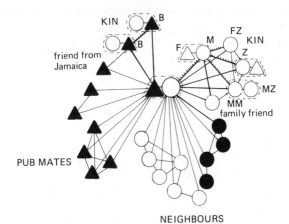

Diagram 9.6. Household with racially composite network: the Rowlandses.

her friendships, and both were noticeably non-judgemental in their relationships with others – attitudes which eased their relationships with black women in particular.

Nevertheless, as we may note from Diagram 9.6, even within the ethnically composite networks of these households there existed strong tendencies for ethnic segregation within clusters of high density in different areas of the network. Even where friends and neighbours were drawn from ethnic groups which in Brixton did not have much to do with each other socially, different social arenas still tended to supply an ethnically specific set of contacts, and the black and white contacts juxtaposed in the networks of these couples remained, to a very large extent, compartmentalised.

Isolate families

All the households described above had social networks composed of a minimum of twenty households. There were, however, six households where social interaction with outsiders was so reduced as to merit special consideration. Two, the Ademolas and the Collets, had a total social network of five households each; one, the Cloughs, had six; two, the Horaces and the Homer–Brettle household, had seven; and one, the Curtises, had nine. In terms of occupational status, these households ranged from some of the poorest in the set to some of the most affluent. Withdrawal from social life was evident in all areas of their social field: four couples claimed to have no real friends, five had no social contacts at work, while four had failed to maintain potential links with kin. In four households, the children also showed a similar failure to develop relationships outside the immediate family.

All this is well demonstrated by a consideration of the case history of one of these households, the Ademolas. Together, Mr Ademola (Y) and his wife (I) ran a small shop in the poor and decaying area around Loughborough Junction; one or the other of them was in the shop from 8 in the morning until 9.30 at night and on Sunday mornings as well. When asked about the neighbourhood in which she lived, Mrs Ademola replied that she knew 'nothing about the area, I'm too tired after a day in the shop to go round'. The couple's small amount of free time was spent at home; they 'never left the children' alone in the house and Mrs Ademola 'couldn't remember' the last time they went dancing, or to the cinema.

The couple had no friends. Mrs Ademola said that she had been a quiet, deeply religious child, who seldom went out and was 'very particular' about her friends; she had seriously considered becoming a nun. Today, 'I like my home and children, I like cooking. I have plenty of people I could ask in but I don't... I don't mix with the neighbours – oh, we're all very sociable in the street but that's all. I don't like people dropping in. I see the women at school and I see my priest – he visits us now and again.'

The children were also discouraged from forming outside friendships: 'They don't go out on the street playing, I won't have that. If they go out, they go out with me. They have everything indoors, there's no need for them to go out.' Mr Ademola, in particular, was anxious to stop his children associating with West Indians in the area; he felt they would be 'badly influenced'.

Neither did the Ademolas have much contact with kin. Although Mr Ademola maintained contact by letter with his father in Lagos, and their son went to visit his grandfather in 1970, the Ademolas had only one cousin in England, at Sandhurst, who visited them about once every six weeks. Mrs Ademola had no contact with her eleven siblings and their families, all of whom rejected her because of her relationship with Mr Ademola. Her parents in Cork had been more tolerant, but she had never gone home 'because of the others'; now both her parents were dead.

In short, neither Mr nor Mrs Ademola saw the need for extra-familial relationships. 'We are a close-knit family,' observed Mrs Ademola, 'we don't need other people. I don't think friends are necessary when you have a family, your family is your best friend.'

There did not seem to be any single cause for this tendency towards isolation. Although the black respondents in this group were cut off from their families of origin, either having no kin in England or refusing to see those that were here, this was also true of other respondents; similarly, Mrs Ademola, who had been ostracised by her kin, or Mrs Clough, who reported losing most of her friends as a result of her marriage, were not the only cases where the decision to enter into an interracial relationship had resulted in the disruption of an individual's social network. With one exception, all these couples had been living in the Brixton area for some time, and had had the opportunity to develop new social relationships.

It was clear, however, that many of the respondents in these isolate households had always had difficulty in making friends or maintaining social relationships. Mrs Collet (GB), for example, recalled that she 'never used to mix well at school – none of my family did', while Mrs Curtis (GB) and Mrs Horace (GB) both, like Mrs Ademola, described themselves as 'solitary' children with few friends. Childhood problems perpetuated themselves in adult life, as Mr Clough was well aware:

> 'I have always needed a friend. I was very sickly as a child...I used to lie in bed and watch the boys playing out in the road and wish I could talk to them...I never learnt how to deal with people.'

Many of these respondents, then, like Mrs Ademola, placed considerable emphasis on the satisfactions to be obtained from within the domestic group – and, by implication, the dangers of forming relationships with outsiders, as these extracts from field notes indicate:

> Mrs Collet (GB) said that she did not have much contact with her neighbours. 'Some women, you see them all the time sitting in each other's rooms having cups of tea. I'm not like that. I don't mix much, I never have done, keep myself to myself – out of trouble...I don't go looking for friends...my husband's like that too. He doesn't like to see me sitting around in other women's rooms drinking cups of tea.'

> Mr Clough (GB) explained that he did not believe in relying on other people: 'The outlook in this house is rather peculiar – kindness is inconvenient to repay and we'd rather manage without.'

> 'I don't enjoy socialising, it's a waste of time. We are a very close family and we prefer to be together here. My wife feels the same way...we prefer to keep ourselves to ourselves.' (Mr Horace (Y))

Withdrawal from social interaction was thus a predictable personal response for these individuals when they encountered problems contingent upon their situation as interracial couples. There were, however, other considerations. Unlike couples who had managed to work out some kind of *modus vivendi* within Brixton and the districts that surrounded it, these isolate households felt themselves to be irreconcilably at odds with their immediate social environment. In these households, more than in any others in the research set, social resources were inadequate or inappropriate for the social goals that these couples wished to attain.

The Cloughs, for example, were one of the four isolate households who had much in common, in terms of life-style and aspirations, with the white-oriented households discussed above. They owned their own house, in a neighbourhood peripheral to Brixton proper and on the fringes of a middle-class area; and Mr Clough, despite his skilled manual occupation, identified strongly with those he termed 'the educated middle classes', as distinct from those who were 'middle-class through money' or the 'pretentious middle class', amongst whom he placed most of his more affluent neighbours. Nor did the Cloughs feel they had much in common with the more recent arrivals in their street, poor families living in multi-occupied houses. They wished 'to associate with people who would pull us up more intellectually'. Unfortunately, neither through Mr Clough's work, nor through any other channels, were such social contacts available to them, as they were for those couples, like the Hendersons or the Handburys, who were involved in the liberal professions. In the past, Mr Clough had joined a number of societies concerned with intellectual discussion, but had always felt that, because of his relative poverty, he could not associate with fellow members in an egalitarian way; as Mr Clough himself admitted, his 'pride' had lost him what friends he could have made. By the time of interview, the Cloughs had withdrawn almost completely from what social contacts they had once had. They continued their self-education through systematic and intensive reading, and participated in a handful of local associations; their overwhelming concern, however, was with their children, and with their children's future.

Though individual circumstances varied, this theme of frustrated social aspirations could be discerned in the histories of most of these isolate households. Obviously, this is not an experience confined to interracial couples, although black men and women are more likely than their white peers to be denied the social place commensurate with their abilities and expectations. However, the readiness of others to blame the interracial household for any difficulties in interaction could only compound these households' problems; and several of these families, most notably the Ademolas and the Collets, had got themselves into a position in which the development of satisfying relationships with outsiders was virtually impossible.

The resolution of ambiguous ethnicity

In all but a few households, then, the social networks of these twenty interracial couples reflect the discontinuity between West Indian, West African and English social fields that characterised relations within the Brixton community as a whole. Such discontinuity evidently presented considerable problems for families whose social identity was, by virtue of their ambiguous ethnicity, not clearly defined, either for themselves or for those around them. On one level, these were practical problems. Couples were obliged to construct and maintain an adequate and satisfying network of kin, friends and acquaintances, within a social universe where an interracial household was an 'outsider' not just to one, but to all ethnic groups. But there were other considerations too. If Brixton residents at large placed considerable emphasis upon the implications of ethnicity, and allotted very different amounts of 'status honour' to different ethnic groups, so too did these individuals. In constructing the social world around them, and in their comments and attitudes towards it, these couples were seeking more than people simply with whom they could pass the time of day; they were seeking esteem, acceptance and a sense of belonging. The stigma attached to being interracially married presented more than external problems. These couples also had to resolve their own ambivalent feelings about ethnicity.

How they chose to do so was a complex process. There were the black-oriented households, where the white partners (both female) had committed themselves to a black social field, defined by their partners. In a sense, these were women who had little to lose by such a choice and much to gain; they were already pariahs in their own ethnic community. In interstitial households too, the women involved found themselves defined as 'black men's women' by the external world, but here, their partners had constructed an enclosed social universe of others like themselves. Within this restricted world they, the interracial couples, represented the 'normal', isolated from the mainstream of both black and white society. Ambivalent attitudes towards colour could, as a result, be channelled outwards, undestructively, onto others within the mainstream. Other households handled ambivalent attitudes towards colour rather differently, by constructing and maintaining segregated 'Janus' networks that left both partners firmly embedded in their own ethnic communities. In contrast were those households whose aspirations and orientations led them to pursue what we have termed an 'assimilationist' policy *vis-à-vis* white society. In some cases, where households had access to an active and accepting network of English kin or friends, or where socio-economic status might be said to neutralise the stigma of ethnic identity, such households were successful. In other cases, as we have seen from the unhappy histories of the isolate families within the research set, they were not. Each strategy, whether successful or not, involved both social costs and benefits. These costs and benefits were reflected especially clearly in the problems faced by the children of these interracial couples.

10 Parents and children

In Brixton, mixed-race children were sometimes referred to by whites simply as 'coloured', and it was clear that, in terms of seeking employment, accommodation and so on, the individual of mixed race, if identifiably 'coloured', met with much the same kind of treatment as his black peers. At the same time, the wide use of the term 'half-caste' by the English population reflected the commonly expressed opinion that such individuals were, somehow, 'betwixt and between' two races, and were thus likely to meet with rejection by both. In folk philosophy, those of mixed race could not be fully accepted by whites because they had 'coloured blood', but would resent being classified with blacks because of their 'white blood'. Studies of friendship choice among school children have suggested, however, that in fact mixed-race children were often more popular with their white peers than black children, and more popular with black children than were whites (Durojaiye, 1970). Their chances of acceptance by whites, at least in childhood, were especially good in areas with few black people (Pushkin, 1967; Marsh 1970; Laishley, 1971). In Brixton, the mixed-race child was more likely to be identified with the local black population. Thus, black youngsters asserted that the mixed-race child was 'just another brother'; some of them, however, added the significant rider, 'but some of them think them white, you know'. As in the case of black youngsters born in England, the full acceptance of the mixed-race child by his black peers was contingent upon his or her acceptance of a black identity, and some degree of overt commitment to black mores. For the mixed-race child, then, even more than for his or her parents, there were problems inevitably arising from an ambiguous ethnicity.

Parental attitudes

Eighteen of the research couples had one or more children, ranging in age from a few months to over twenty years. Although several had been urged by relatives not to have children because of the difficulties they would face, none had considered remaining childless for this reason; indeed, it was rare for these couples even to have discussed the issue. In fact, for a number of couples an unplanned pregnancy had been a significant factor in cementing their relationship. Nevertheless, all couples were aware, to varying degrees, of the difficulties their children were likely to encounter, and of the ambiguities of their position.

Table 10.1. *Ethnic identity of children, parental preference*

Preference	Black partner	White partner
English/Scots		Henderson
	Naylor (RC)	Naylor
	Sidey (WI)	Sidey
English, but 'coloured'		Collet
	Curtis (WI)	Curtis
	Horace (Y)	Horace
		Jay
'Half and half'		Ojo
		Ademola
	Abbott (WI)	Pound
	Gomez (WI)	Mackie
	Homer (WI)	Brettle
	Kalipha (WI)	Kalipha
	Ojo (Y)	
	Rowlands (WI)	Rowlands
'Coloured' first, English second	Birchall (WI)	Birchall
	Clough (WI)	
	Rich (WI)	Rich
Black partner's ethnicity	Ademola (Y)	
	Henderson (RC)	
	Oluwole (Y)	Oluwole
No comment/don't know		Clough
	Collet (WI)	
	Jay (WI)	

These ambiguities were reflected in the comments made by the parents themselves on the subject of their children's ethnic identity. As may be seen from Table 10.1, only two couples, the Naylors and the Sideys, agreed unequivocally that they preferred their children to consider themselves as English; it is, perhaps, significant that both were households where the male partner was English, and the children concerned could 'pass' as white. Again, only one couple, the Oluwoles, felt that they would prefer their children to think of themselves as belonging to the black partner's ethnic group, but even here there were qualifications. As Mr Oluwole put it,

> 'I would rather they say they are Nigerians, but that's as far as it goes – there will be no pressure from me. They can call themselves English if they want to make use of that...but I would prefer them to say Nigerian. There is no struggle then, nothing to lose.'

More typically, however, parents found this question difficult to answer, for they recognised that while culturally the mixed-race child might have much in common with his white peers, the fact of his colour distinguished him from them. In the words of Mr Curtis:

'Well, that really depends…they are British because they have been born here and they know the British way of life. But they will not be treated like British people with white skin. They will be different in that respect, so I can't really call them English. I don't know.'

Couples varied a good deal in the emphasis they chose to give to different aspects of their children's ambiguous identity. Many simply felt they were 'half and half'; others felt that they were, in the words of one West Indian father, 'coloured first and English second'. Others again felt their children were essentially English, albeit with special problems arising from their colour. These latter respondents attempted to handle the effects of prejudice upon the child as they arose, but made no attempt to acquaint him or her with the country from which the black parent had come, nor with its culture and history. There were other parents, however, who did make some effort to stimulate the children's interest and pride in their black heritage. The Kaliphas, for example, had two boys, aged eight and seven. When they were small, they used to watch films on television of 'savages' swinging through trees, and ask, 'Daddy, did you do that?'. Their parents would 'tease' them by answering yes. By the time of interview, however, their mother was trying to teach them more about Guyana, their father's birthplace: 'I wish I knew more about it myself.' She took the children on trips to the Commonwealth Institute and bought them Guyanese school textbooks to read; she felt that they were 'beginning to take an interest'. Mrs Kalipha would have liked to go to Guyana for a holiday, if it were financially possible, but had no wish to settle there, 'not because of the country or anything but because I couldn't fit in to the Indian way of life, the way women have to behave. But I want my children to keep in touch.'

However, parents' views were not necessarily unanimous, and they often disagreed, covertly or overtly, over this issue. Mr Henderson (GB), for example, felt that his children should think of themselves as British: 'I feel that if a person lives and works in a country he should give his allegiance to that country – if not, he should have the guts to pull up roots and get out.' More specifically, he regarded his children as Scots; his son insisted that he was 'coloured', but Mr Henderson thought this was 'silly', since 'I always understood that you took your nationality from your father not your mother.' At this point in the conversation his wife interrupted him, saying that she felt it was 'foolish to sweep questions of colour aside like that'. She herself felt very strongly that she was 'a Rhodesian first and a Briton second'; her elder son, by her first, Coloured, husband, was in Zambia for a year and she hoped her other children would also go to Africa one day.

Other parents, of course, intended to take their children to settle in the black partner's country of origin. Both Mrs Oluwole and Mrs Birchall had travelled outside Europe, and both had some notion of what this transition would mean for their children; it was evident, however, that Mrs Ademola and, especially, Mrs Ojo, had little idea of what to expect and had not attempted to prepare their children in any way for the future.

Most couples, however, envisaged their children's future in England, not elsewhere. Only Mrs Jay (GB), separated from her Jamaican husband, and the Horaces, who felt no commitment at all to any section of the black community, stated definitely that they hoped their children would marry English people; and only Mr Clough (WI), rather surprisingly in view of his household's isolation from the local black population, hoped they would marry blacks. Most would have echoed the words of Mrs Curtis (GB): 'I don't mind who they marry, as long as it's someone decent and kindly...they must marry the person who is going to make them happy.'

On the whole, the statements made by parents about their children's ethnic identity reflected their more general ideological orientations; these, in turn, could be broadly correlated with each household's effective social orientation, as expressed in domestic organisation and social network. It is unsurprising to find that those families that felt their children were English tended to be those with white-oriented or isolate networks where Caribbean or African influences in domestic culture were minimal; and that the reverse tended to be true of those households where an emphasis was placed upon the child's 'coloured' identity (see Table 10.2). Nevertheless, there was often a considerable degree of inconsistency between the effective, everyday orientation of the household as it impinged upon the child, and the ideal orientations of its parents. Mrs Kalipha (GB), for example, was strongly committed to an English social world, but attempted to provide some contact between her children and their Guyanese heritage; Mr Clough (WI) had no effective contact with black people at all, yet held militant views on race relations and wished his children to consider themselves as black. Mrs Oluwole (GB) was strongly aware of the inconsistencies in her daughter's social world and their impact upon her sense of identity:

> 'I am very anxious that she should have the black point of view...she's never going to be white so it's no use her looking upon herself as English...I want her to realise our hypocrisy. Of course, all her first contacts with white people – me, my parents, the lady who looks after her – are all very warm and she trusts them, but I want her to be aware of our qualities, both good and bad...I don't want her to be white.'

The fact that most mothers in the research set were white, and that few households were organised in anything other than an English way,

Table 10.2. *Parental ethnic preferences for their children and household social orientation*

Household	Parental preferences	Effective social orientation of household
Collet	White	Isolate
Curtis	White	Isolate
Horace	White	Isolate
Jay	White	Janus
Naylor	White	Janus
Sidey	White	White-oriented
Abbott–Pound	Mixed	Interstitial
Ademola	Mixed	Isolate
Gomez–Mackie	Mixed	Black-oriented
Henderson	Mixed	White-oriented
Homer–Brettle	Mixed	Isolate
Kalipha	Mixed	Janus
Ojo	Mixed	White-oriented
Rowlands	Mixed	Composite
Birchall	Black	Composite
Clough	Black	Isolate
Oluwole	Black	White-oriented
Rich	Black	Black-oriented

Parental preferences for their children have been assessed as 'mixed' either where both parents had described their children as 'half and half', or where they held conflicting opinions.

meant that the majority of the mixed-race children in these households were growing up, or had grown up – unlike West Indian children in Brixton – in a white-dominated domestic world. Moreover, in most households the child's earliest and most intimate relationships with adults other than his or her parents were, as Mrs Oluwole pointed out, with whites, not blacks; in only seven households did black visitors function as part of the routine, everyday social world in which these children grew up. It is hardly surprising to note, then, that, unlike West Indian or West African children growing up in Brixton, these children were, with one exception, culturally indistinguishable from English children of the same age. To regard such children as black, then, was to assign them an identity without content.

Nevertheless, the fact of their colour, and the attitudes respecting it held by a significant section of the English population, placed a barrier between the mixed-race child and his white peers. The problems of identity and of personal security that were the inevitable outcome of such contradictions were approached by parents with differing degrees of concern and interest. Some, as we have seen, attempted to give their children some sense of secure identity by cultivating pride in their black ancestry and knowledge of their black parent's country of origin; others tried, with varying degrees of sophistication, to establish defences against the prejudices that their children would encounter. Mrs Ojo (GB), for example, deliberately introduced terms of racial insult to her children in the context of affectionate family discourse: 'If I call her a "little wog" then she isn't going to be upset when she hears it in the street.' Others encouraged their children to be self-reliant. Mr Clough (WI), for example, admitted that

> 'My children are an obsession with me sometimes. I have no intention that they should be relegated. I don't want them to be like me, to suffer the fear of not being in a community...I want them to understand it and be above it, not to have to buy their place in.'

Accordingly, he tried to teach them self-reliance.

> 'I have made them learn music so that they can release tension when they are alone, without the need for other people. I teach them to occupy themselves, rehabilitate their minds through music, then they won't depend on friends.'

Other were simply unconcerned or baffled by the problem. As Mrs Rowlands remarked about her two sons, aged five and six: 'I have tried to tell them they are half and half, but they don't really understand how they can be.'

Whether or not the children of these interracial couples could come to terms with their ambiguous ethnic identity appeared, in large measure, to be dependent upon their parents' successful resolution of their own ambiguous and conflicting allegiances. More precisely, this was dependent upon the mother's resolution of these conflicting allegiances, for it was the mother who was primarily responsible for shaping the child's early world, and for establishing the cognitive categories though which he or she perceived it. Where the mother herself held unfavourable or ambivalent views about her black partner's ethnic group, then the child's difficulties were exacerbated. This may be seen very clearly in the following extracts drawn from the Collet case history.

> During an afternoon visit to Mrs Collet (GB), her five-year-old son, Paul, came running in from the yard below her flat, complaining that 'two blackies' had been throwing 'wee-wee' at him. He certainly smelt of urine, though he may simply have wet his pants and decided to divert his mother's displeasure. Mrs Collet remarked how 'spiteful' West Indian children were, always 'picking on' her children. She did not 'get on' with West Indian women and felt they resented her being married to 'one

of their men'. One point of friction with the women on the estate where she lived was the children; she had recently had a fight with a Barbadian woman because she had slapped Paul, who, she claimed, had hit her little girl.

'But you didn't, Paulie, did you?'

'No I didn't, Mum. They're always telling lies.'

On another visit, when Paul again was present, I asked his mother whether her mixed-race children considered themselves to be English or West Indian.

'Oh, they class themselves as English, at least they call all the other coloured children wogs and niggers.'

She added that, when Paul – the darkest of the four mixed-race children in the household – had his bath, he tried to 'get the dirt off' and wash himself white. Mrs Collet and her eldest daughter, Paul's white half-sister, found this comical. Turning to Paul, who had been following the conversation, his mother asked: 'What colour are you, Paulie?'

He replied instantly, 'I'm not black, I'm white.'

I added, 'Are you? I thought you were brown, like me.'

'No, I'm white.'

'What about the people who go and sunbathe up the park? What colour do they go?'

'Their faces go brown but they're still white.'

Paul, who seemed to be an intelligent child, showed other signs of disturbance. At five years old, he was still strongly attached to his bottle and had difficulty controlling his bladder. He was very violent, and often smashed crockery and furniture in his 'tempers'; during these interviews, he repeatedly grimaced and banged his head against a chair. He gave the impression of acting out laughter or tears. His behaviour – which his mother attributed to his being 'spoilt' – made his half-sister say, half jokingly: 'You'd better hurry up and have him baptised, Mum, and drive the devil out of him.'

Though Paul was the most disturbed of Mrs Collet's mixed-race children, all of them avoided contact with the black children on the estate; their 'best friends' were recruited from the white migrant population, and were Greek Cypriot or Irish. Paul occasionally played with a light-skinned Barbadian boy, but Mrs Collet did not like this boy's parents, and discouraged the association. Paul's three-year-old sister had one 'half-caste' playmate, but again Mrs Collet disapproved of the mother and did not encourage the friendship.

Mrs Collet, like a minority of other parents in the research set, was unable or unwilling to deal with her children's rejection of their own ethnicity. Even the most sensitive and thoughtful of parents, however, could not eliminate the impact of hostility and prejudice upon their children, which was reflected in the attitudes towards colour and ethnic identity held by the children themselves.

The development of an ethnic identity

A substantial body of research on race awareness among young black children in the United States has demonstrated that children as young as two and three years old have absorbed the idea of ethnic variation and are capable of identifying and labelling themselves, and others, in ethnic terms. From this age onwards, such children show an increasing awareness of the social implications of ethnic variation, and begin to internalise, and reproduce, the racial attitudes of their society. One of the most striking aspects of black children's behaviour in these research projects is what may be inferred as to their highly ambivalent feelings respecting their own ethnic identity, a significant proportion refusing to identify themselves as black and evidencing hostility towards their own ethnic identity (E. L. Horowitz, 1936; Clark & Clark, 1939 and 1947; Radke, Trager & Davis, 1949; Radke & Trager, 1950; Stevenson & Stewart, 1958; Morland, 1958 and 1963; Vaughan, 1963 and 1964; Goodman, 1964; Porter 1971). Analogous studies carried out in England have indicated a similar pattern among children of West Indian Migrants (Kawwa, 1965; Jahoda, Veness & Pushkin, 1966; Laishley, 1971; Richardson & Green, 1971; Milner, 1975). In the case of mixed-race children, the problem of achieving a viable and secure personal identity is further complicated by the ambiguous nature of their position in the system of ethnic classification that obtains in Britain; and it is hardly surprising to note that a significant proportion of the children in these twenty interracial households sought to define themselves as white.

The Jay family were a case in point. At the time of interview, Sharon and Julie Jay were six and four years old respectively. Julie, whom her mother described as a 'more placid type', did not, thus far, show any signs of concern over her ethnic identity. Her elder sister, however, the lighter in colour of the two, was, as her mother put it, 'a bit mixed up'. She accepted that she was 'half-caste', but vehemently denied that she was black: 'Julie's black, but I'm not.'

Sharon's rejection of her colour had been a problem with her for some time. At her pre-school play group it had been suggested that she should see a psychiatrist, for she had terrible temper tantrums. Since going to school, however, she appeared to have settled down, although she remained 'a bit undisciplined'. Her friends at school, a parochial institution where most of the pupils were English or Irish, were either white or very light-skinned; according to her mother, 'she says they don't believe her if she says she's black'. She avoided contact with black children: 'She doesn't like dark-skinned people'. She refused, for

Table 10.3. *Indications of rejection of a black identity, children aged three to sixteen years*

Overt rejection of black identity	Collet (4 children in 4)
	Jay (1 child in 2)
The 'washing' syndrome	Ademola (1 child in 2)
	Collet (2 children in 4)
	Curtis (1 child in 3)
	Gomez–Mackie (1 child in 2)
	Horace (1 child in 1)
	Ojo (1 child in 1)
Desire to change appearance to resemble whites	Collet (2 children in 4)
	Curtis (1 child in 3)
	Gomez–Mackie (1 child in 2)
	Horace (1 child in 1)
	Jay (1 child in 2)
	Ojo (1 child in 1)
Abusive behaviour towards black children	Birchall (1 child in 1)
	Collet (3 children in 4)
	Gomez–Mackie (1 child in 2)
	Ojo (1 child in 1)
Total number of children in research set age 3–16	27
Total number evidencing signs of disturbance	11

example, to play with, or even speak to, the Nigerian child who was being 'minded' by her mother. It was evident that she sought to avoid being identified as black; when a friend of her mother's showed her a picture he had drawn of her with frizzy hair, she burst into tears and tore the picture up.

Jane Curtis's mother first realised that her daughter was conscious of her colour when she found her scrubbing her hands in the bath. She was three and a half. She said that she was trying 'to get white like you'.

> 'I did my best to explain that that was just the colour she was, it wasn't dirt or anything, but she went on doing it. After a few weeks she just stopped of her own accord. Then it was her hair that was the trouble. I had to be very careful what I said, she was very sensitive about it. It didn't bother the boys at all, but she was very difficult. Now [at the age of ten] she is still very touchy. You can't tease her about colour at all.'

Of the twenty-seven mixed-race children in the interracial set, whose age at the time of interview fell between three and sixteen years, ten were reported by their parents to have some problems related to their ethnic identity, which typically took the form of attempts to deny or negate the fact of their colour. Five children, like Paul Collet and Sharon Jay, directly denied that they were black; others, like Jane Curtis, wanted to change their appearance so that they looked more like whites, or tried to wash off their 'dirty' brown skin. Six children habitually abused and shunned black children (see Table 10.3). Yet none of this hostility was overtly directed towards the black parents, who could, in a sense, be 'blamed' for their children's plight (although in one case, that of Sharon Jay, we might suspect that the child's hostility towards black people was in some sense generated by feelings of animosity towards the absent father). All the children questioned on this point knew very well that their parent was black – indeed, the most disturbed family, the Collets, even had a little rhyme, adapted from a pop song, about Dad being black and Mum being white – but hostility was either channelled outside the family, onto other children and onto strangers, or directed inwards, onto the child itself.

There was no correlation between relative skin colour and problems of identity, and only tentative evidence to suggest that girls might be more prone to reject a 'coloured' identity than boys. What was clear, however, was that disturbed children tended to be found in households where the parents had not themselves succeeded in working out a satisfactory social solution to the problems arising from their situation as interracial couples. Thus, disturbed children could be found in four of the six isolate households; in only one of the five households with white-oriented networks; in one of the two Janus households; and in one of the two households with black-oriented networks.

Friendship choice

We have already noted that there was a strong tendency for mixed-race children who evidenced ambivalent feelings towards their own ethnicity to avoid any contact with black children and to select their friends from the white ethnic groups to be found in Brixton. On the basis of what is, admittedly, incomplete information,[1] it appeared that most of the children in the research set had white, rather than black, friends. In those households where the parents' social field was predominantly white, or where the family lived in neighbourhoods with a low black population, such a pattern was an understandable reflection of the household's social circumstances. Indeed, in households pursuing what might be termed an 'assimilationist' strategy with respect to mainstream white society, one could reasonably expect that the children would be committed to similar goals; and that they, like their parents, would achieve them where social resources, or factors such as educational success or occupational mobility, permitted them to do so. Among the older children of such couples, however, there were occasional instances where the child himself had chosen to define himself as 'coloured' rather than 'English'. Among younger children, there were few who had even

[1] Material on friendship choice among children was based upon information given by parents.

Table 10.4. *Ethnic patterns in friendship choice, children aged 5 years and above*

Mixed black and white	Predominantly white	Almost exclusively white
	*Kevin Ademola (7)	
	Mary Ademola (5)	
		Philip Clough (17)
		Linton Clough (12)
		Raymond Clough (11)
		*David Collet (9)
		*Delia Collet (7)
		*Paul Collet (5)
		Michael Curtis (13)
		*Jane Curtis (10)
	Derek Curtis (9)	
		*Yvonne Mackie (8)
	Sharon Mackie (6)	
David Henderson (14)		
		Clare Henderson (12)
Stephen Horace (20)		
		Patricia Horace (17)
		*Robert Horace (14)
		*Sharon Jay (5)
	Darren Kalipha (8)	
	Simon Kalipha (7)	
		John Naylor (17)
		Roy Naylor (16)
		Leslie Naylor (13)
		Sheila Naylor (12)
		*Bisi Ojo (5)
	Thomas Rowlands (6)	
	Sean Rowlands (5)	
		Richard Sidey (6)

* Overt identity problems.

Children's ages given in parentheses.

a minority of black friends, even though some children were attending schools whose black population was over 80% of the total. Such selectivity bears eloquent testimony, not merely to the strong sense of similarity that these children felt between themselves and their white peers, but also to the corrosive effects of racism. In a racially divided society, where differences of ethnic origin are of primary significance in establishing social identity, the future lives of such children must, inevitably, be fraught with difficulties.

11 Concluding remarks

In 1971, there were nearly one and half million people of 'New Commonwealth' and Pakistani descent living in Britain. Between 80,000 and 120,000 of these people – around 9% – were in fact of mixed parentage, with only one parent of 'New Commonwealth' or Pakistani ethnic origin (Office of Population Censuses and Surveys, 1975b, p. 4 and 1978, p. 5). The General Household Survey has confirmed the existence of a significant number of interracial households within the British population (see above p. 14), and it has been estimated that, in recent years, around one-fifth of all births involving 'New Commonwealth' or Pakistani parents in England and Wales have been to mixed unions (Office of Population Censuses and Surveys, 1975b, p. 3). In the context of the total black population of Britain, interracial unions may well be, as I have argued earlier, of diminished importance. Nevertheless, in terms of absolute numbers, they involve a substantial segment of the United Kingdom population.

In the present climate of race relations, however, the precise status of this segment of the population remains highly ambiguous. Government statisticians, for example, have conventionally regarded those of ethnically mixed descent as part of the West Indian, African or Asian populations from which one of their parents was drawn – despite a recognition that this must, in the words of one publication by the Immigrant Statistics Unit, 'lead to growing methodological problems in the future' (Office of Population Censuses and Surveys, 1975b). Some indication of the difficulties involved was provided in another Immigrant Statistics Unit publication concerned with projections of the future 'New Commonwealth' and Pakistani population:

There is no firm basis for defining people of mixed descent as part of an ethnic minority: some of those of mixed descent will be identified with or will themselves identify with the ethnic minorities while others will be associated entirely with those of wholly UK descent. There is no agreement on whether six (or four, or two) NCWP great grandparents out of eight should be the criterion for classifying someone as part of the NCWP population'. (Office of Population Censuses and Surveys, 1979, p. 26)

These misgivings about the 'correct' classification of those of ethnically mixed parentage reflect certain broader difficulties which official sources prefer to ignore. The careful use of socially meaningless terms–'the New Commonwealth and Pakistani population', 'the ethnic minorities'–circumvents any discussion of the rationale underlying this classification of United Kingdom residents; the emphasis given to the need for 'correct' and 'accurate' estimates of this 'New Commonwealth' and Pakistani population asserts the premiss of objectivity, and lends tacit support to the assumption that categories are distinguished on the basis of significant social and cultural differences. Yet, confronted by the existence of a population of mixed ethnicity, the underlying contradictions of this process of classification emerge. 'Objectively', there is no more reason to classify those of mixed descent with the 'New Commonwealth' population than with those of United Kingdom descent; indeed, to do so must lead to distortions in the social profile of culturally distinct groups. But the members of the Immigrant Statistics Unit–another euphemism there–know, just as people living in Brixton know, that to classify those of mixed descent with the 'New Commonwealth' population makes sense, no matter how irrational that seems. For those with parents from Asia, Africa and the Caribbean, at any rate, the fact of colour differentiates them from their English peers. The ambiguity that characterises their status is an ambiguity that arises, in large measure, from the tacit assumptions that lie at the heart of English racial attitudes, in which colour, as biological 'fact'; culture, as everyday behaviour, tastes and mores; and nature, as aptitudes and abilities, are linked within a broad if poorly articulated framework of genetic determinism. It is the assumptions that inform the well-known words of Mr Enoch Powell, MP, from a speech given to the Rotary Club of Eastbourne in November 1968:

The West Indian or Indian does not, by being born in England, become an Englishman. In law, he becomes a United Kingdom citizen by birth; in fact he is a West Indian or Asian still. (Quoted in Foot, 1969, p. 119)

Much of this book has been concerned, directly or indirectly, with racial divisions in contemporary England and with the attitudes that shape and are shaped by those divisions. I have suggested that, in Brixton at least, it is misleading to see the difficulties faced by Anglo-Caribbean and Anglo-African couples and their children primarily in terms of their being 'between two cultures'. Problems arising from differences in cultural practice there certainly were – in some cases, quite serious problems – but these were on the whole less significant than the problems that derived from the anomalous status of these families in a racially divided society. This would not, of course, necessarily be equally true of Anglo-Indian, Anglo-Pakistani or Anglo-Bangladeshi families. In Brixton, however, colour as much as culture determined the segmented nature of local social relations, and identities assigned by others on the basis of assumed similarities were as important as shared cultural understandings in differentiating one individual from another. It is too easy, and too comfortable, to drift towards a view of contemporary Britain as a 'plural society', in which neatly defined 'communities' – or 'ethnic minorities' – are allotted unproblematic corporate identities. I hope that the preceding chapters have given some indication of just how problematic such identities are.

Casual observers of whatever shade of opinion have tended to view interracial unions as a flouting of the racial conventions of English society. Certainly, for each of the twenty couples in this research set, the decision to enter into such a union involved the conscious breaking of a well understood pattern of avoidance and separation. This was a decision taken by individuals, whose motivation can only fully be comprehended in terms of idiosyncratic circumstances, aspirations and sentiments. These individual choices, however, cannot be understood in isolation from the wider social context that inevitably constrains and shapes individual decision. If interracial couples are, in one sense, individuals who refuse to conform to the rules, at another level of analysis their personal careers and everyday lives only make sense in the light of the imperatives of the society in which they live.

First, and most obviously, individuals who enter into an interracial union must live in a racially divided society, in which ethnic identity is an important principle of association and dissociation. One theme of the preceding chapters, then, has been the ways in which these couples tried to handle what might be termed the external or objective difficulties of their situation – the hostility of family and friends, the problems that confronted them in building up a viable social network, or in bringing up their children. But these individuals were themselves a product of that racially divided society, and their values, attitudes and orientations reflected that fact. I have argued, for example, that the forces that drew certain people into an interracial union did not necessarily produce individuals emancipated from the racial values of the society in which they grew up, nor necessarily with the skills or the will to handle the problems that they would face. Some relationships evidenced a strong element of expediency, especially those that developed between migrant West Indians or West Africans, often lonely, often poor, and white women whose personal circumstances had isolated them from family and friends, or placed them in financial or emotional difficulties, or who were in some sense handicapped in their search for a partner. For some of the white respondents, involvement with black people was attractive precisely because of the racial attitudes of society at large, while for some of the black respondents an interracial union both reflected, and gave expression to, the sense of alienation that they felt from family, friends and culture of origin.

It is not surprising to find, therefore, that while there were individuals in the research set for whom race was not an important issue, for most a consciousness of race, of colour, and of their social implications held a place – acknowledged or unacknowledged – in their lives. Such a consciousness inevitably transformed the management and organisation of everyday affairs into a succession of inescapably political acts. A second theme of the preceding chapters, then, has been the way in which couples confronted what one could term the internal or subjective difficulties of their situation and the ambiguities of their attitudes towards colour and ethnicity.

I have argued that the relationship between, on the one hand, orientations and aspirations, sometimes shared and sometimes not, and on the other, social resources, is central to any understanding of the everyday lives of these couples. Broadly speaking, it is possible to see the choices facing an interracial couple in the Brixton area in terms of a continuum of possibilities. At one extreme will be those who seek, and gain, incorporation into mainstream white society. Although an extensive network of kin may well act to embed the interracial household in a predominantly white social universe, such assimilation is undoubtedly easiest for those couples whose status on other axes of social and economic differentiation – educational success or occupational prestige – permits the neutralisation of a stigmatised ethnic identity and the development of a wide range of associational contacts. At the other extreme will be those couples whose social world is defined by the parameters of the universe inhabited by the local black population: West Indian or West African men strongly committed to the black Brixton world, and white women, rejecting or rejected by mainstream white society, often alienated from their families of origin. At the centre of this continuum will be those couples whose broad orientations and flexible social resources permit them to straddle two social universes, both black and white.

As the preceding chapters indicate, however, there are other interracial couples whose solutions to the problems posed by their ambiguous ethnicity cannot be so straightforward. I have argued that, in a number of cases in the research set, social isolation was the outcome where social aspirations – essentially assimilationist, sometimes rooted in strong negative attitudes towards the local black population – were thwarted by a lack of appropriate social resources. In other cases, involving two partners equally alienated from their communities of origin, and again with highly ambiguous attitudes towards race and colour, interracial couples had constructed their own interstitial and parochial social world of other couples like themselves. Then there were couples where the partners, both still firmly committed to their communities of origin, both reluctant to adapt, remained embedded in essentially segregated social fields. In all these cases, it is possible to detect the impact of racial attitudes upon social strategies; and to detect, more specifically, the implications attached by individuals to associating with those whose ethnic identity is a social stigma.

All individuals in the research set were well aware of the meaning attached to colour and ethnic identity by society at large. For some interracial couples, such as those moving in affluent and cosmopolitan circles, the views on race and colour current in English society had little impact. Others, however, were obliged to confront them in the course of their everyday life. Some individuals responded by rejecting such views in their entirety; others sought to differentiate themselves or their partners from those so stigmatised by appealing to differences in socio-economic status, educational attainment or personality, or by 'laying the blame' on other segments of the black population. Such strategies were, on one level, attempts to deflect and contain the hostility of others. On another level, however, I have suggested that they reflect the ambivalent attitudes of many of the respondents themselves, and their attempts to handle the uneasy contradiction between values which they themselves shared and their own actions and behaviour.

Less directly, but equally significantly, I have tried to show in what way ethnic stereotypes came to play a part in the domestic lives of these couples. I have indicated the way in which respondents, again with some notable exceptions, tended to construct a model of conjugal reality in which their partners' behaviour was understood in terms of models of appropriate behaviour drawn from their own culture. Thus, couples who in fact held quite different opinions as to the basis of desirable domestic life were able to develop 'working misunderstandings' and a comfortable sense of common ground. In contrast, there was a tendency to associate conjugal failings with the real or imagined characteristics of the culture from which the delinquent partner had come. For many of those entering interracial unions, as for the English in general, it proved difficult to escape the predisposition to associate culture with nature, and nature with the fact of colour.

The perspective adopted in this book has been an unfashionable one. I have no interest in developing any 'theory' of interracial relations in England today, nor do I believe that it is either possible or desirable to do so. Any such theory must, inevitably, oversimplify and trivialise the complex relationship between social forces and individual decisions. I can only point to certain tendencies, certain factors, that shape and constrain the diversity of human action. The weaknesses of a study as small as mine are obvious; yet perhaps one advantage of a narrow focus is an inability to submerge the idiosyncratic in the general.

Nor has this book directly concerned itself with what are, undoubtedly, the critical issues that affect the life chances of black people living in Britain today. I have no new insights into the structuring of discrimination in employment and housing, or into the changing nature of the inner city. My intentions have been more modest. In the context of contemporary Britain, interracial families – and there are, as the census data show, quite a number of them – must inevitably be anomalous, in many ways peripheral to the central concerns of the society in which they live. Yet like all anomalies, they both challenge and illuminate the social order that defines them: Through a consideration of the histories and everyday lives of these interracial families, I have sought to elucidate the way in which concepts of ethnicity and race are reflected in the attitudes of individuals, and the impact of racial divisions upon the ways in which individuals organise their lives. I have examined the ways in which ethnic identity may be negotiated, and the limits set upon that process of negotiation by the character of British race relations. Unlike researchers of an earlier generation, I cannot see, in interracial unions, a 'solution' to the racism and hostility that characterise relations between black and white in Britain today. Rather, they reflect in microcosm all the tensions of a racially antagonistic society. But in the resolution, or perhaps more germanely, the neutralisation, of these tensions, these families offer, perhaps, some not insignificant insight through which these various forces may be more fully comprehended.

Appendix 1

The research project: development and methodology

Between January 1970 and October 1971, I lived in rooms in multi-occupied houses in Brixton. I spent much of my time, especially in the early stages of fieldwork, walking, watching and listening; sitting in cafés, pubs and drinking clubs; visiting local community organisations; and building up a network of personal relationships with people living in the Brixton area. The inner city environment is a daunting one for an inexperienced anthropologist committed to the canons of participant observation. No one in Brixton relished the presence of an inquisitive stranger; many harboured dark suspicions of links with the Home Office, the Special Branch, or the local Social Security office. Then, as many of the more articulate individuals I spoke to pointed out to me, 'research', in the context of Brixton, was at best irrelevant and at worst a tool in the hands of the enemy – the enemy, of course, varying with the personal perspective of the speaker. If one of the difficulties of fieldwork in an urban environment must always be the fragmented, fluid and impersonal nature of city life, working in Brixton presented additional problems; there was a good deal of hostility, mistrust and irritation with the notion of 'research'. Black people in particular were wary of the motives and activities of whites who wished to know more about them. To some extent, my own ambiguous ethnicity – claimed by virtue of an African grandparent – served as evidence of my good intentions; to most people in Brixton, personal interest seemed a much healthier reason for doing research than intellectual curiosity. Nevertheless, it is important to emphasise that in Brixton I remained a stranger – not, as might be the case in some remote part of the world, an exotic and unclassifiable stranger, but a stranger from another segment of English society, middle-class, educated, and essentially white.

It had originally been my intention to base my study of interracial families upon a sample of between fifty and a hundred couples, drawn from Africa and the Caribbean on the one hand and from the United Kingdom and the Republic of Ireland on the other. It soon became apparent that, given limited time and resources, a random sample would be impossible to achieve; a pilot survey in what seemed like a promising neighbourhood produced only two interracial households from a total of forty houses visited. Geographically scattered and indistinguishable in most respects from their neighbours, interracial households were not easy to find by any method. Differences in names were obviously a clue to the existence of Anglo-African households; a partial inspection of the Lambeth electoral register produced twenty such cases, only one of which, however, turned out to be an interracial pairing. Rather more successful was an inspection of the 1969–70 record of registrations of intention to marry, kept in Lambeth Registry Office, which detected nine cases of probable Anglo-West African marriage. Only four of these, however, could be traced to their current addresses. An inspection of the Lambeth records of registration of births for one quarter of 1970 – records which, since 1969, have included data on the country of birth of both father and mother – was the most promising procedure; this turned up six possible cases, of which four were in fact interracial pairings but only two involved partners actually sharing a joint household. Finally, Dr Esther Goody and Ms Christine Muir, at the time engaged in an extensive survey of West Africans in London, were kind enough to give me access to their own survey material from which two more households were contacted.

At this point, it would have been possible to apply for official permission to inspect the Lambeth registry records over a longer period, in the hope of constructing a larger sample. By this time, however, it had become clear that there were serious drawbacks in attempting to build up a research set through such methods. Most couples contacted as a result of these enquiries disliked the fact that their names had been discovered through an inspection of official files; the interest of an inquisitive stranger in their personal lives was regarded with suspicion. Some had good reason for not wishing their domestic arrangements to come to the attention of someone they feared might be connected with 'authority'; others were very sensitive about aspects of their lives, past or present, that would inevitably emerge in the course of interview. Most were reluctant to take part in what was, after all, a lengthy and intrusive research project. The rate of refusal and of incompleted interviews was high. This contrasted markedly with the good rapport I had managed to establish with interracial couples met through personal contacts. These were on the whole more willing to participate, and the rate of successfully completed interviews was much higher. I decided, therefore, to abandon any plan for a large sample and concentrate on exploring a smaller number of cases in depth.

How couples in the research set were recruited is set out in Table A1.1. Some couples became known to me personally, through informal contacts or through the personal introduction of individuals. I also asked local clergymen and community leaders if they knew of any couples who would be willing to be interviewed. Some names were suggested by other interracial couples. In no sense, then, can this research set be said to be representative of all those living in interracial unions in Brixton.

Interviewing was carried out in the main between October 1970 and

Table A1.1. *Recruitment of the research set*

Source of recruitment	Total number possible cases	Not traced	Not eligible	Refused	Incomplete interview	Complete interview
Household surveys	42	1	38	1	1	1
Electoral register	20	7	11	1	—	1
Registration of intention to marry	9	5	2	1	1	—
Registration of births	6	—	4	1	1	—
No personal introduction, total	77	13	55	4	3	2
Churches	10	1	2	1	1	5
Community organisations	11	1	4	4	—	2
Personal contact	17	—	3	3	—	11
Personal introduction, total	38	2	9	8	1	18
All sources	115	15	64	12	4	20

October 1971, although I continued to see many families after this date. After an initial visit, information was collected by means of an open-ended questionnaire, although this questionnaire was treated as a guide for the direction of conversation and for the subsequent organisation of information rather than as something strictly to be adhered to; respondents were encouraged to talk freely and to move from subject to subject very much as they wished. Naturally, the degree to which individuals talked spontaneously and without prompting varied a good deal; some interviews generated a mass of rich and interesting data, while others remained essentially question-and-answer sessions. The time spent in formal interviewing thus varied considerably between households, ranging from 5 to 13 hours, with eleven households falling in the 7- to 9-hour range and six households in the 10- to 13-hour range. Efforts were made to see both partners separately as well as together. Formal interviewing was supplemented by informal visits; in many cases where rapport was good this developed into extensive participation in the everyday lives of the households over a period of several years.

Appendix 2

The calculation of births by parental ethnic origin

Table A2.1. *Births where mother born in the New Commonwealth and father born elsewhere: percentage of total for each birthplace category where mothers estimated to be of New Commonwealth ethnic origin, 1971*

Mother's birthplace	Father's birthplace			
	UK	Republic of Ireland	Old Common-wealth	Foreign countries
India/Pakistan/ Bangladesh	5	5	35	50
African Commonwealth	20	10	65	60
Mediterranean Commonwealth	65	70	50	95
Remainder New Commonwealth	40	45	60	85

Owing to the subjective element in assessment, figures rounded to nearest 5%.

No calculations possible with respect to West Indian categories.

From personal communication, Office of Population Censuses and Surveys, March 1972. I have been informed that no more recent information on this subject is in existence.

Table A2.2. *Births where father born in the New Commonwealth and mother born elsewhere: percentage of total for each birthplace category where fathers estimated to be of New Commonwealth ethnic origin, 1971*

Father's birthplace	Mother's birthplace			
	UK	Republic of Ireland	Old Common- wealth	Foreign countries
India/Pakistan/ Bangladesh	35	50	40	70
African Commonwealth	60	85	70	85
Mediterranean Commonwealth	75	90	75	90
Remainder New Commonwealth	50	65	40	90

Owing to the subjective element in assessment, figures rounded to nearest 5%.

No calculations possible with respect to West Indian categories.

From personal communication, Office of Population Censuses and Surveys, March 1972.

Table A2.3. *Live births for England and Wales, 1971, by parental birthplace*

Birthplace of father	Birthplace of mother		New Commonwealth countries					Old Common- wealth	Foreign	Not stated	Total
	UK	Republic of Ireland	India/ Paki- stan	Africa	West Indies	Med. Common- wealth	Other New C'wealth				
UK	632,440	8,589	77	87	537	573	305	1,495	8,635	4,029	656,767
Republic of Ireland	9,697	10,733	2	1	27	22	11	32	225	31	20,781
India/ Pakistan	992	86	18,856	866	47	16	122	12	312	24	21,333
Africa	380	34	623	3,476	176	7	19	4	136	2	4,857
W. Indies	2,141	173	32	27	9,472	17	41	10	163	7	12,083
Med. C'wealth	841	74	7	4	6	1,903	5	5	137	7	2,989
Other New C'wealth	420	40	164	9	41	8	1,762	6	292	5	2,747
Old C'wealth	1,032	26	5	2	10	1	5	592	109	5	1,787
Foreign	8,960	356	81	31	123	108	103	140	9,120	47	19,069
Not stated (legit.)	4,440	34	13	2	3	6	5	5	60	299	4,867
Not stated (illeg.)	30,939	1,510	126	110	2,102	80	103	157	558	190	35,875
Total	692,282	21,655	19,986	4,615	12,544	2,741	2,481	2,458	19,747	4,646	783,155

Classification of birthplace; UK: England, Scotland, Wales and Northern Ireland. India/Pakistan includes Bangladesh. West Indies includes other Commonwealth countries in the Americas. Mediterranean Commonwealth (Med.) comprises Cyprus, Malta, Gozo and Gibraltar. Old Commonwealth comprises Australia, New Zealand and Canada.

From Registrar General's Quarterly Return No. 494 and amended, on basis of information in Tables A2.1 and A2.2, to reflect probable ethnic origin.

References

Published material

Adams, R. 1937. *Inter-racial Marriage in Hawaii*. New York: Macmillan.

Anstey, R. 1975. *The Atlantic Slave Trade and British Abolition 1760–1810*. London: Macmillan.

Anstey, R. 1976. The historical debate on the abolition of the British slave trade. In *Liverpool, the African Slave Trade, and Abolition: essays to illustrate current knowledge and research*, ed. R. Anstey & P. E. H. Hair, pp. 157–66. Historical Society of Lancashire and Cheshire, Occasional Series No. 2.

Atkins, John. 1735. *A Voyage to Guinea, Brazil and the West Indies; in his Majesty's Ships, the Swallow and Weymouth*. London: C. H. Ward & Chandler.

Bagley, C. 1972. Interracial marriage in England: some statistics. *New Community* 1, pp. 318–26.

Ballard, R. & Ballard, C. 1977. The Sikhs: the development of South Asian communities in Britain. In *Between Two Cultures: migrants and minorities in Britain*, ed. J. L. Watson, pp. 21–56. Oxford: Basil Blackwell.

Ballard, C. 1978. Arranged marriages in the British context. *New Community* 6, pp. 181–96.

Banton, M. 1955. *The Coloured Quarter: Negro immigrants in an English city*. London: Jonathan Cape.

Banton, M. 1959. *White and Coloured: the behaviour of British people towards coloured immigrants*. London: Jonathan Cape.

Banton, M. 1967. *Race Relations*. London: Tavistock.

Banton, M. 1977. *The Idea of Race*. London: Tavistock.

Barbot, Jean. 1732. A description of the coasts of North and South Guinea. In *A Collection of Voyages and Travels...*, compiled by John & Awnsham Churchill, Vol. 5. London.

Barker, A. J. 1978. *The African Link: British attitudes to the Negro in the era of the Atlantic slave trade, 1550–1807*. London: Frank Cass.

Barker, D. L. & Allan, S. (eds.). 1976a. *Dependence and Exploitation in Work and Marriage*. London: Longman.

Barker, D. L. & Allan, S. (eds.). 1976b. *Sexual Divisions and Society: process and change*. London: Tavistock.

Barnett, L. D. 1963. Interracial marriage in California. *Marriage and Family Living* 25, pp. 424–7.

Barron, M. L. 1946. *People Who Intermarry: intermarriage in a north-eastern industrial community*. Syracuse, New York: Syracuse University Press.

Bascom, W. 1969. *The Yoruba of Southwestern Nigeria*. New York: Holt, Reinhart & Winston.

Bastide, R. 1961. Dusky Venus, black Apollo. *Race* 3, pp. 10–18.

References

Benson, S. N. 1975. *Interracial Households in a Multi-Ethnic Community*. Ph.D. dissertation, University of Cambridge.

Berger, P. & Kellner, H. 1964. Marriage and the construction of reality. *Diogenes* 46, pp. 1–24.

Berghe, P. L. Van Den 1960. Hypergamy, hypergenation and miscegenation. *Human Relations* 13, pp. 83–90.

Best, George. 1578. *A True Discourse of the late voyages of discoverie, for the finding of a passage to Cathaya...also there are annexed certayne reasons, to prove all partes of the world habitable...* London: Henry Bynnyman. Reprinted under a slightly different title in *Principal Navigations...* compiled by R. Hakluyt. Second edition, Vol. 2, 1599.

Biddiss, M. D. 1976. The politics of anatomy: Dr Robert Knox and Victorian racism. *Proceedings of the Royal Society of Medicine* 69, pp. 245–50.

Biddiss, M. D. (ed.). 1979. *Images of Race*. Leicester: Leicester University Press.

Blake, J. W. 1937. *European Beginnings in West Africa, 1454–1578: a survey of the first century of white enterprise in West Africa...* Royal Empire Society Imperial Studies No. 14. London.

Blake, J. W. (trans. & ed.). 1942. *Europeans in West Africa, 1450–1560.* 2 vols. Hakluyt Society, Second Series No. 87. London.

Blake, Judith. 1961. *Family Structure in Jamaica*. New York: Free Press of Glencoe.

Blumenbach, J. F. 1865. On the natural variety of mankind. In *The Anthropological Treatises of Johann Friedrich Blumenbach...and the inaugural dissertation of John Hunter...*, trans. & ed. T. Bendyshe, pp. 65–276. London: Longman, Green, Longman, Roberts & Green. Originally published in Gottingen, 1775 & 1795.

Bolt, C. 1971. *Victorian Attitudes to Race*. London: Routledge & Kegan Paul.

Booth, C. 1891. *Labour and Life of the People in London.* Vol. 2. London: Williams & Norgate. Volume 1, entitled *Life and Labour...* had been published in 1889.

Booth, C. 1903. *Life and Labour of the People in London.* Third edition. Vol. 4. London: Macmillan.

Bott, E. 1957. *Family and Social Network: roles, norms and external relationships in ordinary urban families.* London: Tavistock. Second edition, with additions, 1971.

Boxer, C. R. 1963. *Race Relations in the Portuguese Colonial Empire, 1415–1825.* London: Oxford University Press.

Brah, A. 1978. South Asian teenagers in Southall: their perceptions of marriage, family and ethnic identity. *New Community* 6, pp. 197–206.

Brown, E. J. P. 1929. *The Gold Coast and Asiante Reader.* 2 vols. London: Crown Agent for the Colonies.

Burma, J. H. 1952. Research note on the measurement of inter-racial marriage. *American Journal of Sociology* 56, pp. 587–9.

Burma, J. H. 1963. Interethnic marriage in Los Angeles, 1948–1959. *Social Forces* 42, pp. 156–65.

Burnet, James, Lord Monboddo. 1773. *The Origin and Progress of Language*, Vol. 1. 8 vols. Edinburgh.

Burney, E. 1967. *Housing on Trial: a study of immigrants and local government.* London: Oxford University Press, for the Institute of Race Relations.

Burrow, J. W. 1966. Evolution and Society: a study in Victorian social theory. Cambridge: Cambridge University Press.

159

References

Carey, A. T. 1956. *Colonial Students: a study of the social adaptation of colonial students in London*. London: Secker & Warburg.

Carter, L. F. 1968. Racial caste hypogamy: a sociological myth? *Phylon* 21, pp. 347–50.

Christensen, H. T. & Barber, K. E. 1967. Interfaith and intrafaith marriages in Indiana. *Journal of Marriage and the Family* 29, pp. 461–9.

Clark, K. B. & Clark, M. P. 1939. The development of consciousness of self and the emergence of racial identification in Negro preschool children. *Journal of Social Psychology* 10, pp. 591–9.

Clark, K. B. & Clark, M. P. 1947. Racial identification and preference in Negro children. In *Readings in Social Psychology*, ed. T. M. Newcomb & E. L. Hartley, pp. 602–11. New York: Holt.

Clarke, E. 1951. Land tenure and the family in four selected communities in Jamaica. *Social and Economic Studies* 1, pp. 81–118.

Clarke, E. 1957. *My Mother Who Fathered Me: a study of the family in three selected communities in Jamaica*. London: Allen & Unwin.

Cohen, E. 1969. Mixed marriage in an Israeli town. *Jewish Journal of Sociology* 11, pp. 41–50.

Cohen, S. 1972. *Folk Devils and Moral Panics: the creation of the mods and rockers*. London: MacGibbon & Kee.

Collins, S. F. 1951. The social position of 'white' and 'half-caste' women in the coloured groupings in Britain. *American Sociological Review* 16, pp. 796–802.

Collins, S. F. 1957. *Coloured Minorities in Britain*. London: Lutterworth.

Community Relations Commission. 1974. *Unemployment and Homelessness*. London: HMSO.

Community Relations Development Project. 1969. *Working Paper* 4. London: YMCA (Mimeo.).

Count, E. W. 1946. The evolution of the race idea in modern Western culture during the period of the pre-Darwinian nineteenth century. *Transactions of the New York Academy of Sciences* 8 (Second Series), pp. 143–5 and 137–54.

Craven, A. 1968. *West Africans in London*. London: Oxford University Press, for the Institute of Race Relations.

Curtin, P. D. 1964. *The Image of Africa: British ideas and action, 1780–1850*. 2 vols. Madison, Wisconsin: University of Wisconsin Press.

Curtin, P. D., Feierman, S., Thompson, L. & Vansina, J. 1978. *African History*. London: Longman.

Dahya, B. 1974. The nature of Pakistani ethnicity in industrial cities. In *Urban Ethnicity*, ed. A. Cohen, pp. 77–118. London: Tavistock.

Davenport, W. 1961. The family system of Jamaica. *Social and Economic Studies* 10, pp. 420–54.

Davis, D. B. 1966. *The Problem of Slavery in Western Culture*. Ithaca, New York: Cornell University Press.

Davis, D. B. 1975. *The Problem of Slavery in the Age of Revolution, 1770–1823*. Ithaca, New York: Cornell University Press.

Davis, K. 1941. Intermarriage in Caste societies. *American Anthropologist* 43, pp. 376–95.

Department of the Environment. 1978. *National Dwelling and Housing Survey*. London: HMSO.

Doherty, J. 1969. The distribution and concentration of immigrants in London. *Race Today* 1, pp. 227–31.

References

Dover, C. 1943. *Hell in the Sunshine*. London: Secker & Warburg.

Drake, St. C. & Cayton, H. R. 1945. *Black Metropolis*. New York: Harcourt Brace.

Drescher, S. 1976. Capitalism and abolition: values and forces in Britain, 1783–1814. In *Liverpool, the African Slave Trade, and Abolition: essays to illustrate current knowledge and research*, ed. R. Anstey & P. E. H. Hair, pp. 167–95. Historical Society of Lancashire and Cheshire, Occasional Series No. 2.

Durand, J. B. L. 1806. *A voyage to Senegal...* in *A Collection of Modern and Contemporary Voyages and Travels...*, Vol. 4. London. Originally published in Paris, 1802.

Durojaiye, M. O. A. 1970. Patterns of friendship choice in an ethnically mixed school. *Race* 12, pp. 189–200.

Eggington, J. 1957. *They Seek a Living*. London: Hutchinson.

Fage, J. D. 1978. *A History of Africa*. London: Hutchinson.

Fanon, F. 1968. *Black Skin, White Masks*. London: MacGibbon & Kee. First published 1952, Paris, Editions du Seuil.

Firth, R. (ed.). 1956. *Two Studies of Kinship in London*. London: University of London, Athlone Press.

Firth, R., Hubert, J. & Forge, A. 1969. *Families and Their Relatives: kinship in a middle-class sector of London*. London: Routledge & Kegan Paul.

Fishman, J. 1972. Domains and the relationship between micro- and macro-linguistics. In *Directions in Sociolinguistics: the ethnography of communication*, ed. J. J. Gumperz & D. Hymes, pp. 435–53. New York: New World Books.

Fletcher, R. 1966. *The Family and Marriage in Britain*. Harmondsworth: Penguin.

Foner, N. 1979. *Jamaica Farewell: Jamaican migrants in London*. London: Routledge & Kegan Paul.

Foot, P. 1969. *The Rise of Enoch Powell: an examination of Enoch Powell's attitude to immigration and race*. Harmondsworth: Penguin.

Frazier, E. F. 1937. *The Negro Family in the United States*. Chicago: Chicago University Press.

Freyre, G. 1946. *The Masters and the Slaves: a study in the development of Brazilian civilization*. New York: Alfred Knopf.

Fyfe, C. 1962. *A History of Sierra Leone*. London: Oxford University Press.

General Register Office, London. 1967. *Sample Census 1966, England and Wales. County Report: Greater London*. London: HMSO.

Genovese, E. 1976. *Roll Jordan Roll: the world the slaves made*. New York: Random House. Originally published in 1972.

George, M. D. 1925. *London Life in the XVIIIth Century*. London: Kegan Paul, Trench, Trubner & Co.

Goffman, E. 1968. *Stigma: notes on the management of a spoiled identity*. Harmondsworth: Penguin.

Golden, J. 1953. Characteristics of the Negro–White intermarried in Philadelphia. *American Sociological Review* 18, pp. 177–83.

Golden, J. 1954. Patterns of Negro–White intermarriage. *American Sociological Review* 19, pp. 144–7.

Golden, J. 1959. Facilitating factors in Negro–White intermarriage. *Phylon* 20, pp. 273–81.

Goldthorpe, J. H. & Lockwood, D. 1963. Affluence and the British class structure. *Sociological Review* 11, pp. 133–63.

References

Gonzales, N. S. 1969. *Black Carib Household Structure*. American Ethnological Society Monograph No. 48. Washington: University of Washington Press.

Goode, W. J. 1959. The theoretical importance of love. *American Sociological Review* 24, pp. 38–47.

Goodman, M. E. 1964. *Race Awareness in Young Children*. Revised edition. New York: Collier Books. Originally published in 1952.

Gordon, M. 1949. Race patterns of prejudice in Puerto Rico. American Sociological Review 14, pp. 294–301.

Greve, J., Page, D. & Greve, S. 1971. *Homelessness in London*. Edinburgh: Scottish University Press.

Gutman, H. (ed.). 1975. *Slavery and the Numbers Game*. Chicago: University of Illinois Press.

Gutman, H. 1976. *The Black Family in Slavery and Freedom, 1750–1925*. Oxford: Basil Blackwell.

Hakluyt, Richard (comp.). 1589. The second voyage to Guinea, set out by Sir George Barne, Sir John Yorke, Thomas Locke, and Edward Castelyn, in the yeere 1554. In *The Principall Navigations, Voiages and Discoveries of the English nation...*, Part 1, pp. 89–97. London: George Bishop & Ralph Newberie. Reprinted in the second edition, and in the facsimile first edition published by Cambridge University Press for the Hakluyt Society & the Peabody Museum at Salem, 1965.

Hall, S., Critcher, C., Jefferson, T., Clarke, J. & Roberts, B. 1978. *Policing the Crisis: mugging, the state and law and order*. London: Macmillan.

Haller, J. S. 1971. *Outcasts from Evolution: scientific attitudes of racial inferiority, 1859–1900*. Urbana: University of Illinois Press.

Hargreaves, J. D. (ed.). 1969. *France and West Africa: an anthology of historical documents*. London: Macmillan.

Hart, N. 1976. *When Marriage Ends: a study in status passage*. London: Tavistock.

Hebdige, D. 1976. Reggae, Rastas and Rudies. In *Resistance Through Rituals: youth subcultures in post-war Britain*, ed. S. Hall & T. Jefferson, pp. 135–54. London: Hutchinson. Originally published as a Working Paper in Cultural Studies by the Centre of Contemporary Cultural Studies, University of Birmingham, 1975.

Hecht, J. J. 1954. Continental and colonial servants in eighteenth century England. *Smith College Studies in History* 40, pp. 1–61.

Heer, D. 1965. Negro–White marriage in the USA. *New Society* 6, No. 152, pp. 7–9.

Heer, D. 1962. The trend of interfaith marriages in Canada, 1922–1957. *American Sociological Review* 27, pp. 245–50.

Heer, D. 1966. Negro–White intermarriage in the United States. *Journal of Marriage and the Family* 28, pp. 262–73.

Henriques, F. 1974. *Children of Caliban: miscegenation*. London: Secker & Warburg.

Herbst, P. G. 1954. Conceptual framework for studying the family; Family living – regions and pathways; Family living – patterns of interaction. In *Social Structure and Personality in a City*, ed. O. A. Oeser & S. B. Hammond, pp. 126–79. London: Routledge & Kegan Paul.

Hernton, C. C. 1969. *Sex and Racism*. London: Andre Deutsch.

Hill, C. 1965. *How Colour-Prejudiced is Britain?* London: Gollancz.

References

Holland, Milner. 1965. *Report of the Committee on Housing in Greater London.* Cmnd. 2605. London: HMSO.

Home, Henry, Lord Kames. 1788. *Sketches of the History of Man.* Second edition. 4 vols. Edinburgh: A. Strathan & T. Cadell; Wm Creech. Revised and enlarged from edition first published in 1774.

Horowitz, E. L. 1936. Development of attitude toward the Negro. *Archives of Psychology* 28, No. 194.

Horowitz, M. 1967. A decision model of conjugal patterns in Martinique. *Man* 2 (New Series), pp. 455–53.

Hume, David: 1898. Of national character. In *The Philosophical Works of David Hume*, Vol. 3, p. 252. London. Originally published 1742; revised edition, Edinburgh 1753.

Hunter, John. 1865. An inaugural dissertation. In *The Anthropological Treatises of Johann Friedrich Blumenbach...and the inaugural dissertation of John Hunter, M.D., on the varieties of man*, trans. & ed. T. Bendyshe, pp. 357–94. London: Longman, Green, Longman, Roberts & Green. Originally published in Latin by Balfour & Smellie of Edinburgh, 1775.

Inner London Education Authority. 1968. *The Education of Immigrant Pupils in Special Schools for ESN Children.* Report No. 657, September.

Izzett, A. 1961. Family life among the Yoruba. In *Social Change in Modern Africa*, ed. A. Southall, pp. 304–315. London: Oxford University Press for the International African Institute.

Jahoda, G., Veness, T. & Pushkin, I. 1966. Awareness of ethnic difference in young children: proposals for a British study. *Race* 8, pp. 63–74.

Jamaica, Central Bureau of Statistics. 1973. *Facts on Jamaica.* Kingston.

Jeffery, P. 1976. *Migrants and Refugees: Muslim and Christian Pakistani families in Bristol.* Cambridge: Cambridge University Press.

Jobson, Richard. 1623. *The Golden Trade: Or, a Discovery of the River Gambra, and the Golden Trade of the Aethiopians...* London: N. Okes. Reprinted (ed. C. Kingsley) Teignmouth, 1904.

Johnston, J. H. 1970. *Race Relations in Virginia and Miscegenation in the South, 1776–1860.* Amherst: University of Massachusetts Press.

Jones, E. 1965. *Othello's Countrymen: the African in English Renaissance drama.* London: Oxford University Press.

Jordan, W. D. 1968. *White Over Black: American attitudes towards the Negro, 1550–1812.* Chapel Hill: University of North Carolina Press.

Kawwa, T. 1965. *A Study of the Interaction between Native and Immigrant Children in an English School with Special Reference to Ethnic Prejudice.* Ph.D. dissertation, Institute of Education, University of London.

Kiernan, V. G. 1969. *The Lords of Humankind: European attitudes towards the outside world in the imperial age.* London: Weidenfeld & Nicholson.

Klein, J. 1965. *Samples from English Cultures.* London: Routledge & Kegan Paul.

Laishley, J. 1971. Skin colour and race awareness in nursery school children. *Race* 13, pp. 47–64.

Lee, T. R. 1977. *Race and Residence: the concentration and dispersal of immigrants in London.* Oxford: Clarendon Press.

Linnaeus, Carl. 1758. *Systema Naturae...* Tenth edition. 2 vols. Stockholm. Originally published in Leiden, 1735.

References

Little, K. L. 1947. *Negroes in Britain: a study of race relations in English society.* London: Routledge & Kegan Paul.

Lloyd, P. C. 1965. The Yoruba of Nigeria. In *Peoples of Africa*, ed. J. L. Gibbs, pp. 547–82. New York: Holt.

Lomas, G. B. G. 1973. *Census 1971. The Coloured Population of Great Britain: preliminary report.* London: The Runnymede Trust.

London Borough of Lambeth (Directorate of Development Services). 1973. *Main Findings of the Greater London Report.* London: London Borough of Lambeth.

London Borough of Lambeth (Corporate Research Group). 1975. *Lambeth Community Profile 1975.* London: London Borough of Lambeth.

Long. Edward. 1772. *Candid Reflections Upon the Judgement lately awarded by the Court of King's Bench on what is commonly called "The Negroe Cause"* ... London.

Long Edward. 1774. *The History of Jamaica: or, general survey of the ancient and modern state of that island...* London: T. Lowndes.

Lorimer, D. 1978. *Colour, Class and the Victorians: English attitudes to the Negro in the mid-nineteenth century.* Leicester: Leicester University Press.

Lowrie, S. A. 1939. Racial and national intermarriage in a Brazilian city. *American Journal of Sociology* 44, pp. 685–98.

Marsh, A. 1970. Awareness of race differences in West African and British children. *Race* 11, pp. 289–302.

Marshall, G. 1964. *Women, Trade and the Yoruba Family.* Ph.D. dissertation, Columbia University.

Martinez-Alier, V. 1974. *Marriage, Class and Colour in Nineteenth Century Cuba: a study of racial attitudes and sexual values in a slave society.* Cambridge: Cambridge University Press.

Merton, R. K. 1941. Intermarriage and the social structure: fact and theory. *Psychiatry* 4, pp. 361–74.

Milner, D. 1975. *Children and Race.* Harmondsworth: Penguin.

Mitchell, J. & Oakley, A. (eds.). 1976. *The Rights and Wrongs of Women.* Harmondsworth: Penguin.

Monahan, T. P. 1970. Are interracial marriages really less stable? *Social Forces* 48, pp. 461–73.

Moore, Francis. 1738. *Travels into the Inland Parts of Africa; Containing a Description of the Several Nations for the Space of Six Hundred Miles up the River Gambia...* London.

Morland, J. K. 1958. Racial recognition by nursery school children in Lynchburg, Virginia. *Social Forces* 37, pp. 132–7.

Morland, J. K. 1963. Racial self-identification: a study of nursery school children. *American Catholic Review* 24, pp. 311–42.

Norton, M. B. 1973. The fate of some black Loyalists of the American revolution. *Journal of Negro History* 58, pp. 402–6.

Oakley, A. 1974. *Housewife.* London: Allen Lane.

Office of Population Censuses and Surveys. 1970. *Classification of Occupations, 1970.* London: HMSO.

Office of Population Censuses and Surveys. 1972. *Census 1971, Great Britain: Advance Analysis.* London: HMSO.

Office of Population Censuses and Surveys. 1973a. *Census 1971, Great Britain: Summary Tables (1% sample).* London: HMSO.

References

Office of Population Censuses and Surveys. 1973b. *Census 1971, England and Wales. County Report: Greater London.* London: HMSO.

Office of Population Censuses and Surveys. 1973c. *The Registrar General's Statistical Review of England and Wales, 1971.* London: HMSO.

Office of Population Censuses and Surveys. 1975a. *Census 1971, England and Wales. Economic Activity. County Leaflet, Greater London.* London: HMSO.

Office of Population Censuses and Surveys (Immigrant Statistics Unit). 1975b. Country of birth and colour 1971–1974. *Population Trends* 2, pp. 2–8.

Office of Population Censuses and Surveys (Immigrant Statistics Unit). 1978. Marriage and birth patterns among the New Commonwealth and Pakistani population. *Population Trends* 11, pp. 5–9.

Office of Population Censuses and Surveys (Immigrant Statistics Unit). 1979. Population of New Commonwealth and Pakistani ethnic origin: new projections. *Population Trends* 16, pp. 22–7.

Office of Population Censuses and Surveys. 1980. Births by birthplace of parents 1978. *OPCS Monitor* FMI 80/1. London: HMSO.

Patterson, O. 1967. *The Sociology of Slavery: an analysis of the origins, development, and structure of negro slave society in Jamaica.* London: MacGibbon & Kee.

Patterson, S. 1963. *Dark Strangers: a study of West Indians in London.* London: Tavistock.

Poliakov, L. 1974. *The Aryan Myth: a history of racist and nationalist ideas in Europe.* London: Chatto & Windus; also Heinemann for Sussex University Press.

Porter, J. D. R. 1971. *Black Child, White Child: the development of racial attitudes.* Cambridge, Mass.: Harvard University Press.

Pryce, K. 1979. *Endless Pressure: a study of West Indian life-styles in Bristol.* Harmondsworth: Penguin.

Pushkin, I. 1967. *A Study of Ethnic Choice in the Play of Young Children in Three London Districts.* Ph.D. dissertation, University of London.

Radke, M., Trager, H. G. & Davis, H. 1949. Social perceptions and attitudes of children. *Genetic Psychology Monographs* 40, pp. 327–447.

Radke, M. & Trager, H. G. 1950. Children's perceptions of the social roles of Negroes and Whites. *Journal of Psychology* 29, pp. 3–33.

Reade, A. L. 1912. *Johnsonian Gleanings Part II: Francis Barber.* London: privately printed for the author.

Research Services Ltd. 1966. *Lambeth Housing Occupancy Survey.* London: mimeo. Appendix dated 1967.

Rex, J. & Moore, R. 1967. *Race, Community and Conflict: a study of Sparkbrook.* London: Oxford University Press for the Institute of Race Relations.

Richardson, S. A. & Green, A. 1971. When is black beautiful? Coloured and white children's reactions to skin colour. *British Journal of Educational Psychology* 41, pp. 62–9.

Richmond, A. H. 1954. *Colour Prejudice in Britain.* London: Routledge & Kegan Paul.

Richmond, A. H., with Lyon, M., Hale, S. & King, R. 1973. *Migration and Race Relations in an English City: a study in Bristol.* London: Oxford University Press for the Institute of Race Relations.

Rodney, W. 1975. The Guinea Coast. In *Cambridge History of Africa*, Volume

References

4: *From c. 1600 to c. 1790*, ed. R. Gray, pp. 223–325. Cambridge: Cambridge University Press.

Rose, E. J. B. in association with Deakin, N., Abrams, M., Jackson, V., Preston, M., Vanags, A. H., Cohen, B., Gaitskell, J. and Ward P. 1969. *Colour and Citizenship: a report on British race relations*. London: Oxford University Press for the Institute of Race Relations.

Rosen, L. 1973. The social and conceptual framework of Arab–Berber relations in central Morocco. In *Arabs and Berbers: from tribe to nation in North Africa*, ed. E. Gellner & C. Micaud, pp. 155–74. London: Duckworth.

Rosser, C. & Harris, C. 1965. *The Family and Social Change: a study of family and kinship in a South Wales town*. London: Routledge & Kegan Paul.

Saifullah Khan, V. 1976. Pakistanis in Britain: perceptions of a population. *New Community* 5, pp. 222–9.

Secombe, W. 1974. The housewife and her labour under capitalism. *New Left Review* 83, pp. 3–24.

Shankland Cox Partnership, in association with the Institute of Community Studies. 1974a. *Inner Area Study, Lambeth: Changes in Socio-economic Structure. A report by the consultants*. IAS/LA/2. London: Department of the Environment.

Shankland Cox Partnership, in association with the Institute of Community Studies. 1974b. *Inner Area Study, Lambeth: Labour Market Study. By the consultants*. IAS/L/4. London: Department of the Environment.

Shankland Cox Partnership, in association with the Institute of Community Studies. 1974c. *Inner Area Study, Lambeth: People, Housing and District. Report by the consultants*. IAS/L/5. London: Department of the Environment.

Shelter. 1972. *Reprieve for Slums: a Shelter report*. London: Shelter.

Shyllon, F. O. 1974. *Black Slaves in Britain*. London: Oxford University Press, for the Institute of Race Relations.

Shyllon, F. O. 1977. *Black People in Britain 1555–1833*. London: Oxford University Press, for the Institute of Race Relations.

Smith, M. G. 1962. *West Indian Family Structure*. Seattle: University of Washington Press.

Smith, M. G. 1966. Introduction. In E. Clarke, *My Mother Who Fathered Me*. Second edition, pp. i–xliv. London: Allen & Unwin.

Smith, R. T. 1956. *The Negro Family in British Guiana: family structure and social status in the villages*. London: Routledge & Kegan Paul.

Smith, R. T. 1963. Culture and social structure in the Caribbean: some recent work in family and kinship studies. *Comparative Studies in Society and History* 6, pp. 24–46.

Smith, William. 1744. *A New Voyage to Guinea...describing the customs...and whatever...is memorable among the inhabitants...* London: J. Nowell.

Stevenson, H. W. & Stewart, E. C. 1958. A developmental study of racial awareness in young children. *Child Development* 29, pp. 399–409.

Stocking, G. W. 1968. *Race, Culture and Evolution: essays in the history of anthropology*. New York: Free Press of Glencoe.

Street, B. V. 1975. *The Savage in Literature: representations of 'primitive' society in English fiction 1858–1920*. London: Routledge & Kegan Paul.

Tajfel, H. & Dawson, J. H. (eds.). 1965. *Disappointed Guests: essays by African,*

References

Asian and West African students. London: Oxford University Press for the Institute of Race Relations.

Tenkorang, S. 1964. *British Slave Trading Activities on the Gold and Slave Coasts in the Eighteenth Century and their Effects on African Society*. M.A. dissertation, University of London.

Thompson, M. A. 1970. *A Study of Generation Differences in Immigrant Groups with Particular Reference to Sikhs*. M.Phil. dissertation, University of London.

Turner, C. 1967. Conjugal roles and social networks: a re-examination of an hypothesis. *Human Relations* 20, pp. 121–30.

Vaughan, G. M. 1963. Concept formation and the development of ethnic awareness. *Journal of Genetic Psychology* 103, pp. 93–103.

Vaughan, G. M. 1964. Ethnic awareness in relation to minority group membership. *Journal of Genetic Psychology* 103, pp. 119–30.

Wallman, S. 1978. The boundaries of 'race': processes of ethnicity in England. *Man* 13 (New Series), pp. 200–17.

Walvin, J. 1973. *Black and White: the Negro and English society 1555–1945*. London: Allen Lane.

Ward, E. 1938. *The Yoruba Husband–Wife Code*. Ph.D. dissertation. Anthropological Series, No. 6, Catholic University of America. Washington D.C.

Wells, A. 1970. Towards a non-pathological view of judgemental attitudes. *Race* 12, pp. 219–28.

West, R. 1970. *Back To Africa: a history of Sierra Leone and Liberia*. London: Jonathan Cape.

Willmott, P. & Young, M. 1960. *Family and Kin in a London Suburb*. London: Routledge & Kegan Paul.

Wirth, L. & Goldhamer, H. 1944. The hybrid and the problem of miscegenation. In *Characteristics of the American Negro*, ed. O. Klineberg, pp. 249–369. New York: Harper & Row.

Young, M. & Willmott, P. 1957. *Family and Kinship in East London*. London: Routledge & Kegan Paul.

Young, M. & Willmott, P. 1973. *The Symmetrical Family: a study of work and leisure in the London region*. London: Routledge & Kegan Paul.

Unpublished material

Inner London Education Authority (Lambeth Divisional Office).
    ILEA Division No. 9 (Lambeth): Immigrants in Lambeth schools, September 1970.

Office of Population Censuses and Surveys, Census Branch, Titchfield, Hampshire.
    Table DT 1553: Private household with head present, by age, birthplace outside UK and socio-economic group of head. 1971 census, 10% sample, Lambeth L.B.

Tate Central Library, London Borough of Lambeth.
    Office of Population Censuses and Surveys, Small Area Statistics. 100% population, Census 1971: population and housing tables. (Ward tabulations, London Borough of Lambeth.)
    Office of Population Censuses and Surveys, Small Area Statistics. 10% sample

References

census, 1971, economic activity tables. (Ward tabulations, London Borough of Lambeth.)

Office of Population Censuses and Surveys. 100% population, Census 1971: population and housing tables. (Enumeration district tabulations, London Borough of Lambeth.)

Index

Africans in England, *see* black settlement in the UK; West Africans

Bagley, Christopher, 22
Banton, Michael
  predicted increase in interracial unions, 7–8
  research in Stepney, 6–7
birthplace and ethnic origin, correlation of, 14–16
'black men's women', stereotype of
  in Brixton, 49, 50, 70, 75, 96
  response of interracial couples to, 96, 97, 119
  in UK-based West Indian press, 12
black partners, research set
  alienation from cultures of origin, 60–1, 82–3
  and 'assimilationist' attitudes, 61–2
  and attempts to dissociate themselves from the local black population, 61, 97–9, 100, 122, 127–8
  commitment to black Brixton world, 101
  conjugal expectations of, 82–3, 91–3
  contact with kin overseas, 103
  contact with kin in the UK, 103–5
  detachment from family and kin at time of meeting with partner, 60, 70, 103–4
  disrupted childhoods of, 59–60
  ethnic identity of, 51–2
  and a family history of interracial unions, 61
  migration to the UK, 51–4, 59
  reaction of family to interracial union, 70–2
  relations with kin of white partner, 74
  and scapegoating of other ethnic groups as a response to stigma, 97–9
  see also isolate families; social networks, research couples
black settlement in the UK
  after World War II, 6, 7
  and the American War of Independence, 4
  diminishing importance of in the nineteenth century, 4
  in the era of the slave trade, 3–4
  see also Brixton, 'Coloured Quarters', Lambeth, London Borough of, New Commonwealth and Pakistani population
Bott, Elizabeth
  on the character of conjugal role relationships, 81 n.1
  on social networks, 95
Brixton
  black population of, 34
  black residents' attitudes towards, 36–8
  black settlement in, 29–30
  changes since this study, viii, 23–4 n.1
  English population of, 30–1
  ethnic divisions in, 43–8
  history of, 24
  outsiders' attitudes towards, 35
  perception of ethnic differences in, 39–42
  position of mixed race children in, 134
  relationships across ethnic boundaries in, 48–50
  research couples' attitudes towards, 99–102
  as a residual area, 30
  social deprivation in, 28–9
  social geography of, 23
  white residents' attitudes towards, 35–6
  see also ethnic divisions; ethnic identities; Lambeth, London Borough of

Cayton, Horace, 95
children of mixed race
  position in Brixton, 134
  research on patterns of friendship choice among, 134
  see also children, research set
children, research set
  ambiguous position of, 138–9
  friendship choice, 143–4

children (*cont.*)
  predominantly English upbringing of,
    84–5, 137–8
  rejection of black ethnic identity,
    139–40, 141–3
Churches, 45
Collins, S.F., 1, 9
colour
  as diacritical sign of ethnic identity, 39
  as social stigma, 39
  stigma of neutralised by class position
    of the individual, 49–50
  see also race, European concepts of
'Coloured Quarters', 6–7
common-law unions
  in the Caribbean, 82 n.2
  financial insecurity and, 87
  long duration associated with absence
    of kin ties, 77
Community Projects, 46

Drake, St Clair, 95
drinking clubs, 48–9

ethnic divisions in Brixton
  and class divisions, 37, 49–50
  and guest–host relationships, 48
  and interracial sexual relationships,
    48–50
  and perceptions of ethnic difference,
    39–41
  reinforced by differences in appearance
    and culture, 41
  in schools, 43–4
  signalled by differences in appearance
    and culture, 41
  and the social ecology of the area,
    44–8
  in work situations, 43
  see also colour, ethnic identities in
    Brixton
ethnic hypergamy, 2–3, 21–2, 56
ethnic hypogamy, 21–2
  see also reciprocal compensatory
    pairings
ethnic identities in Brixton
  negotiated by individuals, 42–3
  situational selection of, 40, 42
  see also colour, ethnic divisions

General Household Survey, 14, 145
Goffman, Erving
  and the concept of 'spoiled identity',
    96
Golden, J., 95

Harkness, James, 35
Hill, Clifford, 9, 95

ILEA
  ILEA definition of the 'immigrant'
    child, 31 n.5
Inner Area Survey, 30, n.3, 34
interracial unions
  and assimilation in UK, 95
  in the 'Coloured Quarters', 6–7
  cultural differences and incidence of,
    19–21
  demographic variables affecting the
    incidence of, 7–8, 15–16, 19
  in England in the era of the slave
    trade, 4–5
  as an essential feature of British race
    relations, 7–8
  incidence in the contemporary UK, 15,
    16–19
  in post-World War II areas of black
    settlement, 8–9
  and problems of classification in UK
    official statistics, 145–6
  in the slave societies of the Americas,
    2–3
  and social isolation, 95
  on the West African coast in the era of
    the slave trade, 2
  see also interracial unions, black
    people's attitudes towards;
    interracial unions, English attitudes
    towards; research couples
interracial unions, black people's
    attitudes towards
  in Brixton, 70, 75, 76, 85
  in the Caribbean, 12
  among colonial students in the 1950s, 7
  in the 'Coloured Quarters', 7
  in Nigeria, 71–2
  in Rhodesia, 56
  as reflected in the press, 12–13
interracial unions, English attitudes
    towards
  and the British press, 10–12
  in Brixton, 76
  in the 'Coloured Quarters', 6
  in the area of the slave trade, 5
  as focus for anxieties about
    immigration, 9–10
  in post-World War II black
    settlements, 9
  and scientific racism, 5–6, 10, 12 n.4
  social surveys of, 9
  in World War II, 56
  see also miscegenation

isolate families
  Ademola case history, 129–30
  definition of, 117, 129
  and isolation from kin, 130–1
  and lack of fit between social resources
    and aspirations, 131–2
  and personal problems in making
    friends, 131
  and problems with children, 143

Lambeth Housing Occupancy Survey, 28,
  30
Lambeth, London Borough of,
  demographic structure of black
    population of, 34
  disadvantage among black population
    of, 34
  geography of, 23
  housing stress in, 25–8
  levels of unemployment among
    minority groups living in, 31
  migrant settlement in, 24–5, 31
  numbers and distribution of black
    population of, 31–4
  social and economic characteristics of
    population of, 28–9
  see also Brixton

marginality
  as a factor in the decision to enter into
    an interracial union, 59–61, 66–7
  as a result of the detachment of an
    individual from his/her ethnic
    community, 49–50
Merton, R.K.
  and the theory of 'reciprocal
    compensatory pairings', 22, 64, 68
Milner Holland Report, 25
miscegenation
  alleged harmful effects of, 5–6, 10, 11,
    12, 73
  see also interracial unions; race,
    European concepts of

New Commonwealth and Pakistani
    population (UK)
  definition of, 7, 15 n.4, 145–6
  demographic structure of, 7–8
  extent of interracial union within, 145
  size as at 1971, 145
  see also black settlement in the UK

patois
  use within the research set, 61
  use within West Indian population of
    Brixton, 42

Patterson, Sheila, 9, 11, 29, 95
  prediction of increase in interracial
    marriages in the UK, 8–9
polygamy
  as a disruptive factor in Yoruba
    domestic life, 61, 83
Powell, J. Enoch, 12 n.4, 35, 146
prostitutes
  accompanying original settlers to
    Sierra Leone, 5
  in Brixton, 9, 36, 49

race, European concepts of, 5–6
research couples
  associational contacts of, 112–13
  attitudes towards Brixton and
    surrounding areas, 99–102, 110
  disagreement over children's ethnic
    identity, 136
  disagreement over domestic
    organisation, 79, 85, 91
  disagreement in friendship choice,
    108–9
  domestic division of labour among,
    88–9
  emigration to black partner's country
    of origin, 93–4
  ethnic composition of social networks
    of, 116–17
  financial organisation, 85–6
  friendship choice, 107–8
  kin resources, 102–4
  leisure activities of, 89–93
  longstanding friendships of, 107–8
  parental preferences for children's
    ethnic identity, 134–6
  preferences in cuisine, 79, 83, 85
  preferences in domestic decor, 83
  reactions of wider community to, 75–6,
    96, 111
  reciprocal compensatory pairings and,
    64
  recruitment for this study, 151–4
  relations with neighbours, 109–11
  relations with workmates, 112–13
  role of kin in anchoring the research
    family in a social field, 105–7
  role of kin in supplying goods and
    services, 76–7, 104–5
  socio-economic characteristics, 51
  strategies for handling children's
    problems, 138–9
  strategies for handling the stigma
    attached to their position, 97–9
  termination of relationships among,
    93

research couples (*cont.*)
  'working misunderstandings',
    development of among, 87–8, 92–3
  see also black partners, research set;
    isolate families; social networks,
    research couples; white partners,
    research set
Rhodesia
  racial inequalities in, 55–6
  social segregation of white and
    Coloured in, 56
Rhodesian Coloured, definition of, 51 n.1
'Rude Boys', 37, 47

skinheads, 49
social networks, research couples
  black-oriented, 117–20
  ethnically composite, 128–9
  ethnic composition of, 116–17
  and 'fit' with aspirations of the couple,
    132–3
  interstitial, 125–8
  and 'Janus' households, 122–5
  segregation in, 108–9, 129
  and social resources, 113–15
  white-oriented, 120–2
  see also isolate families
street crime in Brixton, 35

West Africans
  distribution in Lambeth, 34
  occupational patterns in Lambeth, 34
West Indians
  conjugal roles, 82, 85
  hostility in Brixton towards West
    Africans, 40
  liaisons with white girls, 49
  occupational patterns in Lambeth, 34
  settlement in Lambeth, 29–30
  and youth clubs in Lambeth, 46–8
white partners, research set
  and attempts to dissociate black
    partner from his/her ethnic group,
    92, 121–2

conjugal expectations of, 79–81, 91–2
contact with black people before
  present union, 57–8
contact with kin, 104
ethnic stereotyping of partner's
  domestic failures, 88, 89, 90
prejudice against black people, 110–11
reactions of families to interracial
  union, 72–4
reactions of friends to interracial
  union, 75
reactions to stigmatisation of
  interracial union: and anxieties
  about self-presentation, 97; by
  dissociating black partner from
  his/her ethnic group, 74, 97–8, 111;
  and emphasis on respectable status
  of black partner, 62–4, 99–100; and
  scapegoating of other ethnic groups,
  62–4, 99–100
rebellion against family background
  and decision to enter into an
  interracial relationship, 66–8
'reciprocal compensatory pairings'
  and, 64
refusal to make adjustments to
  partner's culture of origin, 79, 84
socially disadvantaged status of, 64–6
see also isolate families; social
  networks, research couples
working wives
  effect upon domestic division of
    labour, 88–9
  effect upon financial organisation of
    the household, 85–6

Yoruba
  child-rearing practice, 84
  conjugal roles, 82, 85
  see also West Africans
youth clubs, 46–8, 49

Zimbabwe, *see* Rhodesia